1656 LOUIS HENRI SULLIVAN 1924
BY HIS BUILDINGS GREAT IN IN-
FLUENCE AND POWER; HIS DRAW-
INGS UNSURPASSED IN ORIGINAL-
ITY AND BEAUTY; HIS WRITINGS
RICH IN POETRY AND PROPHESY;
HIS TEACHINGS PERSUASIVE AND
ELOQUENT; HIS PHILOSOPHY
WHERE, IN "FORM FOLLOWS FUNC-
TION", HE SUMMED UP ALL
TRUTH IN ART. SULLIVAN HAS
EARNED HIS PLACE AS ONE OF
THE GREATEST ARCHITECT-
URAL FORCES IN AMERICA.
IN TESTIMONY OF THIS, HIS
PROFESSIONAL AND OTHER
FRIENDS HAVE BUILT THIS
MONUMENT.

THE AUTOBIOGRAPHY OF AN IDEA

By

LOUIS H. SULLIVAN

With a Foreword by

CLAUDE BRAGDON

*With a new Introduction by RALPH MARLOWE LINE
Associate Professor, Department of Architecture
University of Illinois*

*and thirty-five illustrations, selected and photographed
by Ralph Marlowe Line for this edition*

DOVER PUBLICATIONS, INC., NEW YORK

This Dover edition, first published in 1956, is an unabridged republication of the work originally published by the American Institute of Architects, Inc., in 1924. A new introduction and selection of illustrations have been prepared specially for this edition by Ralph Marlowe Line.

International Standard Book Number: 0-486-20281-X
Library of Congress Catalog Card Number: 57-2899

Manufactured in the United States of America
Dover Publications, Inc.
180 Varick Street
New York, N.Y. 10014

CONTENTS

LIST OF PLATES

LIST OF PLATES

INTRODUCTION

I T APPEARS most appropriate at this time to again bring to
the reading public this autobiography on the one-hundredth
anniversary of the author's birth.

"History," according to a quotation which I once scrawled
in an old textbook, "is time's negative. Looking at it, it is the
mirror of the past; looking through it, it is the lens to the
future."

Several have written of Louis Henri Sullivan, his architecture, his creation of organic ornament, his literature (both
prose and poetry), his philosophy, his prophecies and his teachings. Some writers, still entwined with Renaissance architecture
and art, were too close to the mirror to see Sullivan and his
work as well as we believe we can today. A few others like
Claude Bragdon, who wrote the foreword for the first edition
of this book in 1924, were able by thought and deed to remove
the academic film from the mirror. Bragdon saw Louis Henri
Sullivan as a man to be coupled with Whitman and Lincoln.
Thirty-two years ago, this evaluation of Sullivan may have
seemed an exaggeration borne of enthusiastic appreciation by a
few friends; today, it is not at all remote.

My introduction to Louis Henri Sullivan reflected this academic film which clouded the mirror. As a student of architecture a few years after Sullivan's death, I was taught that
Sullivan was a radical in the profession of architecture and
that his work was not to be followed. This was the view of
many who were still entrenched in the Renaissance as a source
of inspiration for. all architectural design. But the strong, clean
proportions of the designs of Sullivan and others who followed

him could not be denied, and architectural schools today have practically no Renaissance followers.

In ten years of studying and photographing all of Sullivan's known architectural works which are still standing (seventy-five—some of those photographed have since been demolished) I have been stirred deeply each time I have come upon one of his buildings even though it was in the shabbiest of neighborhoods or hemmed in by Main Street prosaism. The straightforwardness of design, which gives Sullivan's architecture an ageless quality, and his bold, organic ornament make his buildings most inspiring to observe.

Sullivan is the only individual who has developed a system of ornament that is altogether excellent in design; others have tried, but their designs did not live. The styles of ornament known as Classic, Romanesque, Gothic, and Renaissance are the result of generations of creation and development. The ornament of Sullivan is as fresh today as when it was created. His was an organic ornament—it grew out of his buildings and was a part of them, rather than being applied. So original were his designs, so bold their character, so unique, that they cannot be copied successfully.

It is interesting to note that many of Sullivan's buildings are still serving the purpose for which they were designed-a true tribute to his architectural ability, his foresight, and his philosophy that "form follows function."

This phrase, evolved by Sullivan "through long contemplation of living things," guided him in all his work. He was firm in his conviction "that no architectural dictum or tradition or superstition or habit should stand in the way . . . of making an architecture that fitted its functions—a realistic architecture based on well defined utilitarian needs." The significance of this statement is better realized today than in 1924 when it was quoted by Bragdon in his foreword.

As a member of the firm of Dankmar Adler and Company, and later of Adler and Sullivan, Louis Henri Sullivan fulfilled one hundred commissions before he designed the Transportation Building for the World's Columbian Exposition—the building from which modern architecture as a movement is generally conceded to have begun. Nestled in the maze of white buildings designed in the Classic and Renaissance styles, the colorful Transportation Building stood out because of its expressive form. For his design Sullivan was awarded three medals by the Union Centrale des Arts Décoratifs. From this seed in an era of Classic and Renaissance architecture, the modern movement grew slowly in small areas for four decades. It was not until the 1930's that the movement gathered momentum.

During the last thirty-one years of his life, Sullivan designed only twenty-four buildings, five of which were large commissions and eight, small banks. All of the bank buildings are considered jewels of modern design—proof that his creative power and sensitivity did not falter during the prolonged periods of inactivity between commissions.

Within the pages of this book, the story of his life told in the third person, Louis Henri Sullivan sets forth his hopes, accomplishments and philosophy in a flowing prose that is almost poetic.

As with guiding principles in most men's lives, Sullivan's philosophy reflected lasting impressions established during the formative years of his youth. His conception of ornament was influenced by his love of nature gained through summers spent roaming over a New England farm. His freedom in architectural design resulted from his understanding of "self discipline of self power" taught to him by Moses Woolson, his high school teacher. His need to have a reason for everything with "NO EXCEPTION" sprang from the realization that he possessed a mathematical imagination brought out by Monsieur Clopet, his tutor in Paris.

The story ends with his appraisal of the World's Columbian Exposition in 1893, which was characterized by almost complete devotion to Classic and Renaissance architecture:

"The damage wrought by the World's Fair will last for half a century from its date, if not longer. It has penetrated deep into the constitution of the American mind, effecting there lesions significant of dementia."

We are now far enough removed by time to know that his prophecy was true.

So great was Sullivan's concern with the fate of contemporary architecture in this country, that during the last thirty-one years of his life he devoted much time to establishing his architectural philosophy. Through the designs of his buildings, the few men trained in his office, and his writings, Sullivan presented with conviction his idea of functional architecture.

Students of architecture—and others—will find this book a lens to the future, as well as a mirror of the past. It should give to those who have discovered the full meaning of "self discipline of self power" both courage and inspiration.

RALPH MARLOWE LINE

University of Illinois, 1956

FOREWORD

ONLY because architecture is so largely an anonymous art does Louis Sullivan stand in need of an introduction, for he is eminent in his chosen profession.

As an author, as well as an architect, in his buildings and in his written words, his aim has been to declare certain truths, to publish certain principles, so vital, so fertile, so fundamental and necessitous that I mentally couple him with Whitman and Lincoln, however little he belongs in their category, or they in his.

He is like them at least in the untainted quality of his Americanism, having Lincoln's listening ear for the spiritual overtones amid the din of our democracy, and Whitman's lusty faith in the ultimate emergence into brotherhood and beauty of the people of "these states."

Beyond this, doubtless, the similarity ceases, but the point I wish to make is that Sullivan is somewhat different from us others, refusing to be glamored by our pleasant illusions—and by "us others," I mean architects academic, beaux-arty, mediæval, stylistically pure and purely stylish, now so busily engaged, with such gusto and mutual admiration, in setting the American scene.

Louis Sullivan has the distinction of having been, perhaps, the first squarely to face the expressional problem of the steel-framed skyscraper and to deal with it honestly and logically. Later solutions, in so far as they are good, have been along the lines that he, by precept and example, first laid down. This, to the layman, needs a little explaining. The academically educated architect of the generation which produced the skyscraper found something that refused to submit itself to the canons and categories with which his mind had been filled: he could neither fit it into his mental frame, nor could he expand that frame to fit it. So he produced architectural monstrosities.

Now along comes Louis Sullivan, fresh from Europe, but unglamored by the light of its magnificent yesterdays. He held the conviction that no architectural dictum, or tradition, or superstition, or habit, should stand in the way of realizing an honest architecture, based on well-defined needs and useful purposes: the function determining the form, the form expressing the function. To him the tallness of the skyscraper was not an embarrassment, but an inspiration—the force of altitude must be in it; it must be a proud and soaring thing, without a dissenting line from bottom to top. Accordingly, flushed with a fine creative frenzy, he flung upward his piers and disposed his windows as necessity, not tradition, demanded, making the masonry appear what it had in fact become—a shell, a casing merely, the steel skeleton being sensed, so to speak, like bones beneath their layer of flesh. Then, over it all, he wove a web of beautiful ornament—flowers and frost, delicate as lace and strong as steel.

His inexorable logic, resulting as it did in so many surprising simplifications and admirable economies, imposed itself upon the minds even of architects averse to his philosophy and indifferent towards his work, with the result that the more obvious merits of our upstanding colossi of the market are traceable, however deviously, to Louis Sullivan's influence.

The purely structural and economic aspect of a building is necessarily more or less of a mystery to the man in the street; but he has usually an interested eye for ornament. This accounts for the fact that Sullivan is known to the layman (insofar as he is known) as the creator of original and beautiful surface decoration. His Golden Doorway to the Transportation Building at the Columbian Exposition in Chicago, in 1893, charmed the unsophisticated eye of the native son more than the hackneyed ornamental motifs employed in the buildings surrounding the Court of Honor. It charmed also the eyes of certain highly sophisticated visiting foreigners. Alert, in a new country, for any Newness, they found that quality almost nowhere save in Sullivan's designs, to which they accorded unhesitating and enthusiastic praise.

That he should be thus known merely as an ornamentalist seems deeply ironical, because he himself seriously recommended that we abandon the use of ornament in architecture until we had mastered the essentials of straightforward design. This indicates that of all his gifts he holds the decorative one as least essential.

With no disparagement to his achievements as architect and designer I hold that Louis Sullivan makes his most powerful and lasting appeal as author and teacher; for though you will look in vain for any book of his in any library, he has nevertheless written and he has been read. Although his writings have appeared only in pamphlet form, and as contributions to journals of limited circulation and short life, they were of a kind to imprint themselves upon the mind of youth, "wax to receive and marble to retain." His *Kindergarten*

[7]

Chats, impatiently awaited, week by week, as they appeared in a trade journal long since vanished, hidden under draughting-boards until the exit of "the boss," and then eagerly read, destroyed for many young men —I was one of them—the world of ideas into which they had been educated, but only to create another and a better world of ideas in their stead.

The *Chats* proved to be a vigorous, bitter, bludgeoning assault upon the then existing architectural order (is it different now, I wonder?), but they pointed out a way to freedom to any sincere young architectural talent stifling in the tainted air of our industrialism or bogged in the academic morass. Large, loose, discursive, a blend of the sublime and the ridiculous, as though Ariel had collaborated with Caliban, *Kindergarten Chats* remains in my memory as one of the most provocative, amazing, amusing, astounding, inspiring things that I have ever read.

The *Autobiography of an Idea* I am not called upon to discuss, either critically or otherwise, this being an introduction, not of the book, but of the author, and of him not as a person, but as a personage. His personality will inevitably reveal itself to the reader as he progresses, far more truly than could I, who look through other and older windows, possibly rose-colored and scribbled over with memories, admirations, gratitudes. I am content to leave it thus, because I believe Louis Sullivan to be one able to endure the scrutiny made possible, made inevitable, by the autobiographical form—who might conceivably gain by it something which no appraisement of a friend and fellow craftsman could give.

CLAUDE BRAGDON.

CHAPTER I

The Child

ONCE upon a time there was a village in New England called South Reading. Here lived a little boy of five years. That is to say he nested with his grandparents on a miniature farm of twenty-four acres, a mile or so removed from the center of gravity and activity which was called Main Street. It was a main street of the day and generation, and so was the farm proper to its time and place.

Eagerly the grandparents had for some time urged that the child come to them for a while; and after a light shower of mother tears—the father indifferent —consent was given and the child was taken on his way into the wilderness lying ten miles north of the city of Boston. The farm had been but recently acquired, and the child appeared, shortly thereafter, as a greedy parasite, to absorb that affection, that abundant warmth of heart which only Grandma and Grandpa have the intuitive folly to bestow. In short they loved him, and kept him bodily clean.

To the neighbors, he was merely another brat-nuisance to run about and laugh and scream and fight and bawl with the others—all bent on joy and destruction. The peculiar kink in this little man's brain, however, was this: he had no desire to destroy—except always his momentary mortal enemies. His bent was the other way.

Now lest it appear that this child had come suddenly out of nothing into being at the age of five, we must needs authenticate him by sketching his prior tumultuous life. He was born of woman in the usual way at 22 South Bennett Street, Boston, Mass., U. S. A., on the third day of September, 1856. And, for the benefit of the exigent and meticulous, it may be added, on the authority of the young mother, that the event occurred on the second floor: day Tuesday, hour 10 P. M., weight 10 pounds. The mother, at that date, had arrived at the age of 21 years, while the father would be 38 come Christmas.

The long interval of passing years has made it clear that this pink monstrosity came into the world possessed of a picture-memory. He remembers, even now, certain cradle indiscretions; and from that same cradle he recalls a dim vision of a ghostly lady in somber black, and veiled, entering through the open door and speaking in a voice strangely unlike the mellow tones of his nearby mother. He remembers that one night in mid-winter, he was lifted from his warm cozy refuge, bundled up and taken to the third floor. Grandpa was already there, scraping the heavy frost from one of the small square window panes; finally, after the ecstasies of Mama and the awed tones of Grandpa, the child was lifted up and held close to the pane to see what?—a long brilliant, cloud-like streak, which, he dimly fancied, must be unusual; but as it seemed to have no connection with the important concerns of his existence, he was glad to leave it to itself, whatever it was, and return to the warm spot from which he had been taken. This streak in the sky was Donati's comet of 1858.

Before going further into the doings of this two-year-old, it may be well to give an outline of his mongrel origin.

As to his father, Patrick Sullivan, no need for discussion—he was Irish. As to the mother, Andrienne List Sullivan, she seemed French, but was not wholly so. She had the typical eyelids, expressive hazel eyes, an oval face, features mobile. She was a medium stature, trimly built, highly emotional, and given to ecstasies of speech. But *she also* had parents: her father, Henri List, was straight German of the Hanoverian type—6 feet tall, well proportioned, erect carriage, and topped by a domical head, full, clean-shaven face, thick lips, small gray eyes, beetling brows and bottle-nose. He was of intellectual mold, and cynically amused at men, women, children and all else. Her mother, a miniature woman of great sweetness and gentle poise, was Swiss-French, born in Geneva—where also her three children were born. But her long Florentine nose suggested, unmistakably, an Italian strain. Her maiden name was Anna Mattheus. Like a true *mère de famille,* she ruled the roost, as was the custom in French society of the Middle Class. Her mind was methodic, her affection all-embracing.

Henri List was reticent as to his past, but the family gossip had it that as a young man he was educated for the Catholic priesthood, rebelled at the job and ran away from home.

The intervening years between this hegira and his arrival in Geneva, Switzerland, are a blank. There seems to have been some lack of clearness as to his vocation in Geneva; was he a Professor of Greek in the University, or did he coach rich young English gentlemen through their university course? In any event he was highly educated, and he prospered. It was further gossiped that, having met Anna Mattheus—considerably older than he—who kept a store filled with a sumptuous stock of choice linens and laces, he courted her. It was sneeringly said he married her for her money. At any rate, they were well to do, and lived in a marble house with large grounds called *La Maison des Paquis*. Here three children were born to them, in order of arrival: Andrienne, Jennie and Jules. The narrator has in his possession a small oval card with perforated edge, on the plain field of which is drawn with colored pencils, a park-like view, with house half-hidden among the trees. On the back, in the handwriting of her mother, is the notation "Terrace de la Maison des Paquis faites par Andrienne en 1849" —(that is at the age of 14). According also to family gossip, there seems to be no doubt that Henri List was tainted with cupidity. He speculated and finally lent ear to the wiles of a Jew. He ventured his all. The enterprise strangely and suddenly lost its credit, and the house of List tottered and collapsed in irretrievable ruin. Anna List borrowed money of her relatives to take the family to America, to forget the past and start anew in a strange land. Little wonder that Grandfather was reticent. It required a span of years for the narrator to pick up little by little the thread of the story.

As to Patrick Sullivan; he had no secrets, but his memory did not extend much back of his 12th year. He said his father was a landscape painter, a widower, and he an only child. That together they used to visit the county fairs in Ireland. That at one of these fairs he lost his father in the crowd and never saw him again. Thus at the age of twelve he was thrown upon the world to make his way. With a curious little fiddle, he wandered barefoot about the country-side, to fiddle here and there for those who wished to dance; and of dancing there was plenty. Thus traveling he saw nearly all of Ireland. This wandering life must have covered a number of years. The period that emerges from the wander-period seems obscure in transition, but his attention must have focused on dancing as an art. As to the grim determination of his character, his pride and his ambition, there can be no doubt; but what chain of influences took him to London is not known. Arrived there, he placed himself under the tutelage of the best—most fashionable—masters, and in due time set up an academy of his own. Not content with this advance, which was successful, he must needs reach the heights of his art, and in Paris, the center of fashion, took instruction of the leading masters. In those days dancing was a social art of grace, of deportment, and of personal carriage. It had many branches of development, from the simple polka to highly figurative formations, in social functions, upward to its highest and most poetic reach in the romantic classical ballet. It was an art of elegance that has passed with the days of elegance. Artificial it largely was, yet humanizing, and beneficent. In such wise must the social value of the dance, of the dancing master, and the academy of a day long since past be visualized, to be understood in this day.

This young Irishman had another grand passion.

To him the art of dancing was a fine art of symmetry, of grace, of rhythm; but parallel to this ran a hunger for Nature's beauty. He must have been a pagan, this man, for in him Nature's beauty, particularly in its more grandiose moods, inspired an ecstasy, a sort of waking trance, a glorious mystic worship. In this romantic quest, he had, through a series of years, footed it over a considerable part of Switzerland.

It seems strange at first glance that these highly virile and sensitive powers should be embodied in one so unlovely in person. His medium size, his too-sloping shoulders, his excessive Irish face, his small repulsive eyes—the eyes of a pig—of nondescript color and no flash, sunk into his head under rough brows, all seemed unpromising enough in themselves until it is remembered that behind that same mask resided the grim will, the instinctive ambition that had brought him, alone and unaided, out of a childhood of poverty.

Naturally enough he had not found time to acquire an "education," as it was then called and is still called. He, however, wrote and spoke English in a polite way, and had acquired an excruciating French. Hence by the standards of his time in England he was no gentleman as that technical term went, but essentially a lackey, a flunkey or social parasite. Perhaps it was for this reason he revered book-learning and the learned. He knew no better.

It is probable that, about this time, the lure of America, goal of the adventurous spirit, the great hospitable, open-armed land of equality and opportunity, had been acting on his imagination. This is surmise. The fact, of which there is documentary evidence, is this: that on the 22nd day of July, 1847, he took passage at London for Boston in the good ship *Unicorn* of 550 tons register burthen. This, in the eleventh year of the reign of Victoria; Louis Philippe nearing his political end; with revolution ripening in Germany; and the United States kindly relieving Mexico of its too heavy burden. And this, also, while a small prosperous family in a small European city was awaiting, all unconscious, the call to join him in the same city of the same far away land; and that but eleven brief years lay between them all and the advent of a child to whose story we must now begin a return. For the finger of fate was tracing a line in the air that was to lead on and on until it reached a finger tracing a line now and here.

Patrick Sullivan reached Boston in 1847, set up an academy and was successful. He always was successful. His probity was such that he could always command desirable influence and respect. He was familiar with polite forms. Later on, probably in 1850, the Geneva family also reached Boston. Somehow they met. The young Irishman, keen through training in the hard school of experience and self discipline was always wide awake; and this is what happened; he met the young girl, Andrienne, in the conventional way, was attracted by her grace of manner, her interesting broken English, her skilled piano playing; paid his court to her, professed love for her; they became engaged, and on the 14th of August, 1852, they were married. What is more likely is this; that he heard her playing of Chopin, Beethoven, *et al.,* with approval, for he was fond of music; that he asked her to substitute dance music; that after the first few bars he was electrified—he had found a jewel without price. Her sense of rhythm, of sweep, of accent, of the dance-cadence with its reinforcements and languishments, the *tempo rubato*—was genius itself. He lost no time in marrying her as a business asset. She was lovable and he may have loved her. It is possible but hardly probable; for there is nothing in the record to show that he loved others, or that he loved himself. He was merely self-centered—not even cold. He was moderate of habit; drank a little wine, smoked an occasional cigar, and was an enthusiast regarding hygiene. The stage-setting augured well for the coming child. The stock was sound. All the tribe were black-haired. So he came to pay his visit in due time, as recorded, believed by his mother to be an angel from Heaven, so great, so illusioning is the Mother-passion. But, as regarded from the view-point of the chronicler, he was not an angel from heaven. At the age of two he had developed temper, strong will, and obstinacy. He became at times a veritable howling dervish. He bawled, he shrieked, he blubbered, sobbed, whined and whimpered. He seemed to be obsessed by fixed ideas. Once in a while, as time passed, there came periods of relative calm within the pervading tempest, and now and then he was not wholly unlovable. A rising sun seemed to be dawning within him. He became interested in his bath, given daily in a movable tub. Grandma would allow none but herself to perform this rite, and as she sponged him down, he would sing to her something about *Marlbrouck s'en va-t'en guerre,* or tell what this giant did, or that fairy. Life was beginning to break in upon him from outside. A continuous breaking in from the outside and breaking out from the inside was to shape his destiny.

He loved to look out of the window; to see people moving to and fro. But it was when first he saw the street-cleaners at work that there upsprung a life-fascination,—the sight, the drama of things being done. South Bennett Street ran from Washington Street to Harrison Avenue, a short block, but for him a large world. The street was paved with cobble stones; the sidewalks were of brick. He was there at the window when the work began. Came on the front rank; four men armed with huge watering cans painted red; these they swung in rhythm one-two, one-two. The thrill began, the child breathed hard. Then followed the second rank—four men with huge brooms made of switches; they also, two-fisted, swung one-two, one-two, shaping a windrow in the gutter. Then came the glory of it all, the romantic, the utterly thrilling and befitting climax—an enormous, a wonderful speckled gray Normandy horse, drawing a heavy tip cart, and followed as a retinue by two men, one sweeping the windrows into hillocks, the other with shovel and with mighty faith, moving these mountains into the great chariot. Thus appeared from Washington Street, thus passed in orderly action, thus disappeared into Harrison Avenue the Pageant of Labor, leaving the child, alone, thrilled with a sort of alarm of discovery, held by an utter infatuation. He had missed nothing; he had noted every detail. He had seen it whole and seen it steady. It is a close surmise that what actually passed in the child's mind, aside from the romance, was a budding sense of orderly power. Indeed, the rhythm of it all! And then, to the wondering child, there began the dawn of a wonder-world.

His mother often dandled him on her foot, holding his puny outstretched hands in hers, and in great glee and high spirits sang to him about *Le bon roi Dagobert, Le grand St. Elois,* and other heroes of the nursery. He felt these tales to be true, especially when the high points and low points of knee action were reached in a rushing climax. But one evening his mother took him for a visit; and on the return walk he tired and wailed. The mother raised him to her shoulder, and when the tears had dried he looked upward at the sky and beheld with delight the moon plowing its way through fleecy clouds. He called upon his mother to share in the joy. She too looked upward, yet told him that the moon was not plowing a path through the clouds, but that the clouds were driven by the wind across the face of the moon. This astounding statement he received as an affront to his common sense, and so stated. But the mother was adamant in her folly. He looked again skyward, to confirm himself. As by accident his eye fastened on the moon; the moon held steady and he was amazed to see the clouds go by. Then consciously he tried it on the clouds and the moon again plowed on. This process he reversed and reversed until he felt sure, and *then* it was he confided to his weary mother sagging under the intolerable burden of him, that he had made a *discovery!* He felt a sense of mastery and pride. He, HE, had discovered this thing. In a world rising larger, difficulties appeared, and this particular thing was not quite what it seemed at first to be. But he had *mastered* it. That his mother knew all about it, had told him all about it, instantly faded; the child sank into sleep. The mother, weary unto death, reached her destination; she entered with her sleeping son while the clouds and the moon in the stillness of early night went their serene way undisturbed by further mundane intervention.

Ever at the window pane, he liked to watch the snow, falling gently in large moist flakes and, in the little gusts, swirling and piling here and there, gathering curiously in odd nooks, and crannies, gathering on the window panes across the street, gathering on his own window panes, mantling the trees in a loving way, building far out in a roll from the top of a neighbor house—and not breaking off (why did it not break off?). And the stillness, the muffled stillness, the lovely stillness. He was not satisfied to glance, he must look long, very long and steadily, he must see things move, he must follow the story, he must himself live the drama of dark things slowly changing into white things. It was all so real to him as he gazed through the window pane, alone and very quiet. And then when morning came, the hasty rattle and scoop and sip of the shovels, cleaning the sidewalks, heaping the snow in mountains in the street. Again the song of work, the song of action.

About this time a strange thing happened. It is the mother's story repeated many times in after years. It seems one afternoon she was at the piano playing a nocturne with the fervor and melancholy sweetness that were her sometime mood. Lost in dreamland she played on and on, when of a sudden she seemed to hear a voice low-pitched like a sigh, a moan. She stopped, looked, listened; no one there. She seemed mistaken; then from under the very piano itself, came a true sob, a child sob and sigh. Why tell what happened? Her precious son in her arms pressed tight to her bosom; tears, tears, an ecstasy of tears, a turmoil of embraces, the flood gates open wide, a wonder, a joy, a happiness, an exultation, an exaltation supreme over all the world. The child did not understand. Why did he, unnoticed, enter the room; why secrete himself where he was found; why was he overcome and melted into lamentation? Had anyone else been playing, would he have thus responded? Had a new world begun to arise, this time a wonder-world within himself? Had there been awakened a new power within this child of three,—a power arising from the fountainhead of all tears?

FOLLY COVE

The family had decided to spend the summer on Cape Ann. They settled in a farm house of the very old fashioned kind, at a tiny spot called Folly Cove. The farm was a fairly large one and spread out to the rock-bound coast. It had its weather-beaten orchards, its meadows and its fields, its barn and outbuildings, its barnyard with a well and bright tin bucket worked with a pulley and chain. There were also the farmer, a typical extra-nasal Yankee; the faded, shriveled, worn-out wife; the usual dozen or more children, and a farm hand. Also in the meadow was a well without a curb. Presently the child wanders into this meadow, picking the sparkling flowers, feeling the lush grass, glorying in the open. Quite incidentally in his floral march he walked into the well. It was rather deep, and amid his shrieks he felt that his blue flannel skirt seemed to float about him. His father and mother were away fishing; the farmer busy at a distance. Came the hired man on the run; a quick descent, a quick ascent of the boulder wall of the well, the child was saved. In the arms of the man he was hurried to the farm house and turned over to the women-folk. The farm-man returned to his work. The children quickly gathered. The women-folk rapidly stripped the chilly child, rubbed him down with harsh towels, and stood him naked with back to the glow in the huge fireplace. The children, all older than he, looked on curiously, pointed, giggled. For the first time he was aware of a vague sensitiveness. He felt, uncomfortably, that there was something in the air besides atmosphere. He turned aside. A new world was gestating in the depths.

Upon the return of the parents all was in turmoil again. Appalled thanks, gratitude, relief, amazement, the precious, the precious, and again the precious!

The father, more sedate, bethought him it would be righteous should he hold early communion with the life-saver, the farm-man. They met. The father offered lucre in gratitude sincere enough. The offer was spurned. Would the farm-man, an American he-man, accept of gold for saving the life of an innocent child? He would not! Things looked bad. There was argument, persuasion, even supplication. Finally as by an inspiration he was asked if he would not accept something that was not money. The farm-man replied that if the father insisted and would not otherwise be calmed, he would with pleasure accept from him, as a casual gift, a plug of chewing tobacco. Thus was the value of a man-child ascertained.

In the course of his exploration, he came to the other well, the one in the barn yard with pulley, chain, and big bright tin bucket. He was curious, and began huge experiments. Somehow the bucket got loose from the hook, struck the water with a splash and began to fill. He leaned over the edge in alarm. What was to be done? The bucket began its swaying descent, glinting this way, darkening that way, became dusky and was gone. In its place arose from the well an accusation seeming to say "guilty," and there arose within and without the child a new world, the world of accountability.

He spent most of his time with his father; the bond of union was the love of the great out-of-doors. Too young to philosophize and search his soul to discover sin, he took all things for granted. It seemed natural to him that there should be flowers, grass, trees, cows, oxen, sunshine and rains, the great open sky, the solid earth underfoot, men, women, children, the great ocean and its rock-bound shore. All these he took at their face value—they all belonged to him. He would sit beside his father on a great boulder watching him fish with pole and line. He would remain patiently there, inspirited by the salt breeze, listening to the joyous song of the sea as the ground swells reared and dashed upon the rocks with a mighty shouting, and a roaring recall, to form and break and form again. It seemed to lull him. It was mighty. It belonged to him. It was *his* sea. It was *his* father fishing.

One day as he was sitting alone on the boulder his father swung into sight in a row boat, and pulled for the open sea. The child did not know about rowboats, he had not discovered them, he did not understand how they went. Suddenly father and boat disappeared, the child gave a shriek of alarm, then as suddenly man and boat re-appeared, to disappear again. The ground-swell running high, the breeze stiffening, the boat with the man grew smaller and smaller at each appearance; there was a flash each time. Smaller grew the boat until it became a speck, then it began to grow bigger and bigger. The child, dumbfounded, ran to meet his father, in wild excitement, at the landing. His father, very patient in such matters, explained it all as best he could, and the child listened eagerly, with some understanding. What was said must be true, because his father, who knew everything had said so. But what he knew, all of himself, and beyond the knowledge of others, was that the sea was a monster, a huge monster that would have swallowed up his father, like one of the giants he had told his grandmama about, if his father had not been such a big strong man. He felt this with terror and pride. Thus arose in prophecy the rim of another world, a world of strife and power, on the horizon verge of a greater sea.

For the remainder of the summer, nothing of special import occurred. The family returned to the city.

When all were settled, he was sent to the primary

school of that district. He reported to the family at the end of the first day that teacher had called him to the platform to lead the singing. What a dreary prison the primary school of that day must have been. His recollection of his stay there is but a gray blank. Not one bright spot to recall, not one stimulus to his imagination, not one happiness. These he found only at home. He learned his letters, he followed the routine, that is all. Nor were there any especially memorable events at home until the matter of the farm came up and was discussed interminably. He had been merely enlarging his geographical boundaries, and exhausting the material. The primary school had, for the moment, dulled his faculties, slackened his frank eagerness, ignored his abundant imagination, his native sympathy. Even the family influence could not wholly antidote this. The neighborhood was growing disreputable. Next came the farm.

PLATE 1. Charles H. Schwab residence (left), 1715 South Michigan Avenue, Chicago. 1883. Morris Selz residence (right), 1717 South Michigan Avenue. 1883.

CHAPTER II

"There was a child went forth every day."
W H I T M A N

THUS after traversing a long orbit inversely to the prehistoric of the family genealogy, and tracing, on the backward swing, the curve of a little one's experience in contact with the outer world and his individual impulsive responses thereto, we again take the train for South Reading.

Arriving at the station a man descends, asks directions, and follows the first dirt road to the left, leading over an almost treeless flat, and heading for a somewhat distant hill. Part way up the hill he notices a house on the right. Here lived a man named Whittemore, who having lost a leg, proceeded in due consideration of the remaining one, to invent, perfect and manufacture a new type of crutch, which has remained the standard to this day. The workshop stood some distance back of the house, just at the beginning of the pine woods that covered part of the hill. The road here takes a curve to the right, traverses the back of the hillside with a heavy growth of pines on the right ascension, and a neat valley to the left with scattering woods and meadow. The road then straightens, becomes of easy grade, and begins to emerge from the wilderness, so to speak. An orchard comes into view on the left, a field of herds-grass on the smoothly rounded hilltop at the right. Straight ahead, running at the right angles and terminating the road thus far traversed, was the main road from South Reading to

Stoneham. The land here was level for a moment or two. At the left-hand corner of the intersection stood a rather modern house, clap-boarded, painted white with green shutters, and in front of it on the Stoneham Road were two stately elms. Here lived the Tompsons. The person who made this trip had no sooner reached the intersection and made a mental note or two of the surroundings than he saw a middle-aged or elderly couple, quite near, slowly approaching from the left on the road running toward South Reading. They were leading between them a chubby child who was screaming at the top of his angry voice, crying savagely, declaring vindictively he would not go, he *would not* go to school. The traveler must have worn the tarnhelm of legend, for they saw him not. To our thinking he was a phantasm of years to come. The child was absurdly dressed. Under an immense straw hat, curving broadly upward at the brim and tied on with a ribbon, appeared his upturned face, red, bloated, distorted; angry eyes, terribly bright, running with tears in a stream; a mouth hideously twisted out of shape. Below this raging hell was a sort of white jacket and a big bow tie. Below this, *white pantalettes,* gathered in at the ankle and more or less flounced or frizzled. These pantalettes were the source of his fear, of his rage and his protest. He had already on account of them, he said, been regularly insulted by the neighbors' children who had formed a circle around him and danced, sneered, pointed the index of scorn, and made merry. Was that not enough? Must he now face a schoolful of tormentors? He would not go, he would *not* go! He bawled and screamed that

[26]

he would not *go!* The child was on the verge of hysterics; it seemed less agonizing to face death than ridicule. The elders consulted quietly, turned back, the child still between them, and disappeared at the entrance-way of a house a hundred yards or so beyond the Tompsons on the Stoneham Road. Next day, the child appeared in conventional garb. His name was Louis, or, as his Grandmother pronounced it, Louie. It was a joyous day for him, a sad day for her. For in her heart she knew that with the laying away of the pantalettes there was laid away a child—a child gone forever—a child soon to be but a sweet memory—a child soon to metamorphose into a tousle-headed, freckled, more or less toothless, unclean selfish urchin in jeans; and that he would continue to grow bigger, stronger, rougher, and gradually grow away from her —ever more masculine, ever more selfish. But this apprehension, this heart's foreboding was not to come wholly true, for she held his love—she held it to the end. The child was not an *enfant terrible;* he was, rather, an independent, isolated compound of fury, curiosity and tenderness. Subtle indeed were the currents flowing and mingling within him, embryonic passions arising and shaping, ambitions vaguely stirring; while his sharp eyes saw everything. Spring was on the wane. The birds were full-throated in glorification of the number of bugs and worms eaten, or the intensive discussion of domestic affairs. High up in one of the Tompson elms—the one to the east—hung the purse-like nest of the self-same golden orioles that came there year by year, while from a nearby meadow floated the tinkle of a solitary bob-o-link winging its way rejoicing. The day was beauteous; full sunshine flooded and enfolded all. The child, after much thought—of its kind—suddenly announced he was ready. His curiosity had been insidiously at work. He would see the school; he would meet new children; he had become eager; he would be a big boy in the world's opinion. So, on this same cheerful morning, hand in hand with Grandma, who alone habitually assumed responsibilities, he began the pilgrimage of learning that hath no end. They took the dusty road that led eastward, directly toward the north end of the village. They leisurely mounted a gentle grade until the crest was reached. At this exact point, just behind the stone wall to the right of the road—marvel of marvels —stood a gigantic, solitary ash tree. On account of a certain chipmunk, various flowers, pebbles, and other things, the child had not noticed it during the approach. But of a sudden, there it stood, grand, overwhelming, with its immense trunk, its broad branches nearly sweeping the grass, its towering dome of dense dark green; opposite it, across the road was a farm house; back of it an open pasture. From the vantage of the road spread out a view of things below. The grandmother was for going on. The child stood transfixed, appalled. A strange far-away storm, as of distant thundering, was arising within his wonderself. He had seen many trees, yes; but this tree—*this tree!* He trembled strangely, he wished to cry; with gentle scolding he was dragged away. From this point the road was bare and shaggy. Half way down, to the left, and set well back, was found not the little red schoolhouse of romance, but a rather large white one, clap-boarded, green blinds, gabled, a bell, a well with force-pump, trampled playground, and so on. He was duly presented to the teacher. Her face and form, alas, like many another face and form, have passed into memory's oblivion. All details settled, he was to come the next morning, which he did, after successfully passing the magnet tree, while saluting it affectionately in a calmer mood. Day after day he passed the tree. It became *his* tree—his Great Friend.

He was to spend many days at this barren hillside school. He became acquainted with the boys and girls there, for it was coeducational. What these children did during the recess hour would scandalize the wholly good. But to the casual sinner, scrutinizing the depths of his own past, reason might be found and a certain tolerance engendered whereby these vagaries of small animals, if not exactly condoned, might at least be minimized as the native output or by-product of inquisitiveness and emulation. The child was as yet too young to fight. But according to the rules and regulations of the gang his time was but deferred, for each new boy must establish his fistic status.

The school-room was large and bare with two wooden posts supporting the roof. The teacher sat at her desk on a raised platform at the wall opposite the entrance. The children sat at rows of desks (a row per grade) at right angles to the rear wall; in front of them an open space for recitation by class; blackboard on the wall and so forth. There were five grades in the single room. Teacher sat at her desk, ruler in hand to rap with or admonish. All the children studied their lessons aloud, or mumbled them. The room vibrated with a ceaseless hum, within which individual voices could be heard. Everything was free and easy; discipline rare. There was however a certain order of procedure. Came time for a class to recite. They flocked to the wall and stood in a row; neither foot nor head at first. Questions and answers concerning the lesson of the day. Teacher's questions specific; pupils' answers must be definite, categorical. Teacher was mild, patient; the answers were sometimes intelligent, more often hesitant, bashful, dull, or hopelessly stupid. Each answer was followed by a monotonous "go to the foot," "go to the head;" and all the time the hum went on, the unceasing murmur, a thin piping voice here, a deeper one there, a rasping out yonder, as they pored over their primers, first readers, geographies, arithmetics; while now and again Teacher's voice rose high, questioning the class on the rack, the children answering as best they could. This babel merged or deliquesced into a monotone; there seemed to be a diapason, resonant, thick, the conjoined utterance of many small souls trying to learn, entering the path of knowledge that would prove short for most of them. The children were all barefoot and rather carelessly clad; notably so in the matter of omissions. One thing is certain and the rest is lies: This school was of, for, and by the people.

The child was given his proper place in the lowest grade, or class, or whatever it was called. He took hold rather blithely. He seemed to feel the importance of his entry into this new world, so different from home. Little by little he seemed to feel that he belonged there; but he never succeeded in feeling that the school belonged to him except as to its externals. Somehow he did not fit into the curriculum or the procedure. He was of a pronounced, independent nature. He quickly became listless as to his own lessons. He seemed to be nothing but a pair of eyes and ears not intended for books, but for the world little and big about him. In this immediate sense he was almost devoid of self-consciousness. His normal place was at the foot of his class. But one day he awakened to the fact that unawares he had become interested, not in books, but in procedure; said procedure consisting in the oral examinations and recitations of the grades above his own, as they, in accordance with the arrangement of the school-room, stood directly in front of him, drawn up in line, undergoing the routine torture. He began to notice their irregular mass-effect and their separate persons. He followed their fortunes in going to the foot and going to the head. He transferred himself to them. He noticed, too, which girls were the prettiest and which boys were the gawkiest. He learned the names of all. He became solicitous of their personal fortunes, in their struggle for knowledge or their attempts to escape it. For him, it became a sort of drama, a sort of stage performance, and he began to note with growing interest what they said and what teacher said, which answers were correct, which were failures. Over and over he saw and heard this until he came to know the groundwork of what all the grades above him were struggling with. But as to his own lessons—Alas! Yet he followed the upper grades so intently that he became critical: What was this about the four men who built so many perches of stone wall in three days, and two other men who were to build some wall in six days? What did it amount to anyway? The real question was *where* was the wall to be built? For *whom* was it to be built? What was his name? What were the names of the men who were building the wall, (for it was becoming a real wall)? Were they Irish or Scotch? Where did they get the stone to build the wall? Did they get it from the rough quarry across the road from the schoolhouse? Did they gather up boulders from the fields? Was not this matter of four men and two men irrelevant? The information was too sparse, too unconvincing. He could not *place* the wall, and what good was any wall he could not see? And thus he went on, unaffected by the abstract, concerned only with the concrete, the actual, the human.

One evening when all were at home, a letter arrived addressed to Grandpa. He opened the envelope and read the letter aloud. It was from Teacher, and set forth with deep regret and concern that his grandson was a dull boy, that he was inattentive, would not study his lessons, was always at the foot of his class, but he was a nice boy. Could not Mr. List bring influence to bear to induce Louis to reform his ways? Would not a kindly word from him, concerning the need of education, have a moral effect? She had used all her powers of persuasion, and so forth and so on. At the end of the reading Grandpa dropped the letter on the floor, burst into volcanic laughter, roaring until the lid of the heater rattled, rocking forward and backward on his chair, clapping himself on the knee, in a series of subsiding outbursts, ending in a long drawn spasmodic chuckle, expressive of his cynical sense of humor, his infinite contempt for those who had eyes and yet saw not. To call his sharp-eyed grandson a dullard! Why, he said, one might as well call Sirius a flap-jack, and other joking words to that effect, for he was fond of teasing his grandson, whom he had so long watched out of the corner of his eye. But Grandma, more conservative, took the matter seriously. With her grandson standing at her knees, a bit abashed, a bit afraid, after giving her six propitiatory kisses, his arms about her neck and cheek to cheek, she found it, oh, so hard, to scold him. Instead she told him gently how necessary it was to acquire an education; how necessary to that end that little boys, particularly her own grandson, for the family's pride, should attend industriously to lessons. Could he not do better, would he not do better? He said he could and would; and all was peace.

Next day, at school, he pitched in, and the next day and the next; shutting out all else. Oh, it was so easy to head this class; so easy for one who knew what the upper grades knew, or thought they knew for a moment or perhaps a day. They knew not that it was all, save a bare remnant, fated to fade away forever. Tired of heading the class, which was so easy, he occasionally, and indeed with increasing frequency fell to zero, because of a lapse, because, perhaps, of a twitching squirrel in a tree nearby the window, or a beautiful white cloud curiously changing shape as it slowly drifted through a beautiful blue sky. And what did it all amount to? What signified it to be at the head of a row of dull-wits? He was becoming arrogant. For Grandma's sake, he kept on, after a fashion. He was becoming bored.

Summer was waning. The third of September was at hand. Six candles in the cake announced an anniversary. He was overjoyed. He was actually six.

The winter of 1862-3 passed along with its usual train of winter sports and hardships. Louis joined heartily according to his height and weight in all the sports. Of hardships he knew nothing. What fun it was to be drawn on a sled over the snow by his Uncle Julius. To be drawn on the same sled over the dark sheer ice of the pond by Uncle on newly sharpened skates. What thrill of courage it required not to cry out as he shuddered at the darkness below, and wondered whether the pace were not too swift. But Uncle, some fifteen years older than he, was to him a big man; and what could not a big man do? So he had faith in Uncle, if not entire confidence, as they flew here and there among the gay crowd of skaters. How they went way to the end of the pond and then swung back past the ice houses where men were beginning to work! And later on how thrilled and stilled he was by the thunderous boom and tear of an ice crack ripping its way from shore to shore! And many such booms he heard on similar trips in zero weather. And then the men at work cutting ice! How exciting it was to watch men at work. They used large hand saws to cut ice into square blocks and there was one strange saw drawn by a horse. Then men with poles shoved and dragged the ice-blocks through the clear water to the bottom of the runway, and then it was hauled up the runway by a horse that walked away with a rope that ran through a pulley and then back to the ice cake. The ice seemed very thick and clear.

And then came splendid snow-storms, decorating the trees, forming great drifts through which he struggled in exultation, every now and then stumbling and falling with his face in the snow. How he rolled over and over in glee in the snow of a white world, a beautiful world even when the gray skies lowered. And why not? Had he not warm woolen mittens knitted by Grandma, and hood and stockings by the same faithful hands, and "artics"? Was he not all bundled up?

And the sleigh rides. Oh, the sleigh rides in the cutter with the horse looming so high, and the row of bells around the horse's collar, jangling and tinkling in jerky time. And he so warm under the buffalo robe. And they met so many other sleighs in the village when they went to the post-office or the grocery store, and he noticed so many men walking about clad in buffalo coats. And he made snowballs and did all the minor incidentals. It was his first experience within the pulchritude of a winter in the open. His mother came frequently to see him and caress him. He could hardly understand why she loved him so; he had so many other personal interests and distractions. But he hailed her comings and deplored her departures.

While his name was Louis, he had other names—interesting ones, too. He had not been christened or baptized. The question had called for a family council. The father, a nominal Free-mason, not sure whether he was a Catholic or an Orangeman or anything in particular, expressed no serious interest; he would leave it to the rest. Grandpa, as usual, vented his view in scornful laughter. Grandma, a Mennonite, was opposed to baptism. But Mother in her excited way was rampant. What! Would she permit any man to say aloud over the body of her pure and precious infant that he was born in sin and ask for sponsors? Never! That settled it and they named him Louis Henri Sullivan. It has been declared and denied that the name was given in order to heap honors upon Napoleon III. Be that as it may. The name Henri, obviously, was to deify Grandpa. The Sullivan could not be helped. It was scorned by all but its owner. They detested the Irish, whose peaceful penetration of Boston had made certain sections thereof turn green. Even his wife could not stand for it, much less for Patrick. So sometimes she gallicized the name; which wasn't so bad, when she used it in the third person, nominative, singular. Then she had an inspiration, an illumination one might say, and invented the word *Tulive,* whatever that may have meant, as a general cover-name, and thus secured a happy, life-long escape. But later on, say about the age of twelve, the scion asked his father about this name Sullivan, which seemed to coincide with shanty-Irish. So his father told him this tale: Long ago in Ireland, in the good fighting days, there were four tribes or clans of the O'Sullivans: The O'Sullivan-Moors, the O'Sullivan Macs, and two others. That *We* were descended from the O'Sullivan-Moors, and that all four tribes were descended from a Spanish marauder, who ravished the west Irish coast and settled there. His name it appears was O'Soulyevoyne or something like that, which, translated, meant, The Prince with One Eye. Now, however great was the glory of this pirate chief, his descendant, Louis Henri Sullivan O'Sullivan-Moore-O'Soulyevoyne, had this specific advantage over him of the high-seas. The prince had but one eye that must have seen much; the youngster of six had two eyes that saw everything, without desire to plunder.

These became part of that child who went forth every day, and who now goes, and will always go forth every day.

And these become part of him or her that peruses them here.—WHITMAN.

CHAPTER III

And Then Came Spring!

THE beauty of winter was fading as the thaws began their work, patches of bare ground appearing, patches of deep snow remaining in the gullies, remnants of drifts. Each day the scene became more desolate; mud and slush everywhere. But the child was not downhearted. Any kind of weather suited him, or rather he suited himself to any kind of weather, for he was adaptable by nature—which meant in this case abundant glowing health.

The hounds of spring *may* have been on winter's traces; he knew nothing about that. His immediate interests lay in the rivulets which emerged at the lower end of the gully drifts. He wished to know just where these rivulets started. So he shoveled off the snow and broke off the underlying decaying ice until the desired point of information was reached. Then he would go immediately to another drift, and operate on that to see if the result tallied with the first. This work completely absorbed him. It gave him new and exciting sensations. Then, too, he would tramp over the sodden stubble of the fields, and plow along the muddy roads. He would hunt about eagerly to find by actual test which places were the soggiest, and just where the mud was deepest and stickiest. Then came rains upon rains. The snow vanished. Earth, fields, trees: All was bare. The child took this for granted.

He did not know, he did not suspect, because of the city life he had led, that out of this commonplace bare earth—indeed now hidden within it—was to arise a spectacle of entrancing beauty. The rains became showers, occasionally sparkling in the sunshine. The winds became mild breezes. There settled over all a calm, a peace, an atmospheric sense that caressed and encouraged. And thus came spring. The grass appeared as a delicate deepening influence of green. Did not the child soon find the earliest pussy-willows, the first crocuses in the garden? Did he not note the delicate filigree appearing as a mist on tree and shrub, and the tiny wild plants peeping through the damp leaves of autumn in his favorite woods? Did he not really see things moving? Was not the filigree becoming denser and more colorful? Was not the grass actually growing, and the tiny plants rising higher? Was not the garden becoming a stirring thing like the rest? The outburst of bloom upon peach tree, cherry and plum, evoked an equal outburst of ecstasy and acclaim, an equal joy of living. Was not something moving, were not all things moving as in a parade, a pageant? Was not the sunshine warm and glowing? Had not the splendor come upon him as upon one unprepared? He heard the murmur of honey-bees, saw them burrowing into flowers, fussily seeking something and then away; and the deep droning of the bumble-bee, the chirping of many insects, the croaking of crows, as in a flock so black, they flew heavily by, and the varied songs of many birds; riotously shaping, all, on one great tune with bees, insects, flowers and trees. Were not things moving? Was not something moving with great power? Was there to be no end to the sweet, clamorous joy of all living things, himself the center of all? Could he stand it any longer? Then of a sudden the apple orchards sang aloud! What made them thus burst forth? Was it that same power, silent amidst the clamor? Was it a something serene, sweet, loving, caressing, that seemed to awaken, to persuade, to urge; yea, to lure on to frenzy, to utmost exaltation, himself and the world about him, the new, the marvelous world of springtime in the open—a world that became a part of this child that went forth every day, a world befitting him and destined to abide with him through all his days? Oh, how glorious were the orchards in full bloom! What mountains of blossoms! What wide-flung spread of enravishing splendor! The child became overstrung. Yet his heart found relief from suffocation in his running about, his loud shouts of glorification and of awe, his innumerable running-returns to the house to say breathlessly, "Come Grandmama! Come see! Come see!" He wished to share his joy with all. These wonder-orchards were *his,* the fields, the woods, the birds were his; the sky, the sun, the clouds were his; they were his friends, and to this beauteous world he gave himself. For how could he know, that far, far from this scene of love, of pride and joy, men were slaughtering each other every day in tens, in hundreds and in thousands? True, at the appointed hour, he had run about the house shouting "Fort Donelson's taken! Fort Donelson's taken!" and equally true he had made monitors out of a bit of lath and the bung of a flour barrel, and with greater difficulties a *Merrimac.* He had sailed them in a wash-tub filled with water. Further, he had listened to some talk about the war between the

North and the South. He heard some talk about "Rebels" and "Yanks." Yet it was all vague, and distant beyond his hills. It was all indistinct. He knew nothing about war—he does now.

Spring passed slowly on, things were surely moving. The petals had fallen, and tiny round things appeared in their places. Trees were coming to full foliage, their branches swaying, leaves fluttering in the breeze. Plowing, harrowing and seeding were over. He had been given a tiny patch in the main garden to be all his own, and with toy tools he worked the soil and planted flower seeds. He became impatient when certain nasturtium seeds failed to show above the surface, so he dug them up with his fingers, only to be astonished that they had really put forth roots. He pressed them back into the earth. To his sorrow that was the end of them. For a first attempt however he did **pretty** well.

He learned little by little. He was now abundantly freckled, and in a measure toothless. His heavy thatch of black hair seemed to have known no brush. His hands were soiled, his clothes were dirty. Hatless, barefooted, his short pants rolled above his knees, and unkempt with activity, he was effectively masked as a son of the soil. To the passerby, he was a stout, stocky, miniature ruffian, let loose upon a helpless world. The more discerning noted two fine eyes, clear and bright. He saw all things just as they were. The time had not arrived for him to penetrate the surface. Exceedingly emotional—though unaware of it—the responses of his heart, the momentary fleeting trances, the sudden dreaming within a dream, perturbed him.

[41]

He wished to know about these; he wished to know what it was that enthralled him time after time. And in this he failed also; he could not interpret—few can. For that which perturbed him lay far deeper than his thoughts—a living mystic presence within the self-same open that was his. *Per contra,* he was generally regarded as a practical little fellow who liked to work. Casually speaking the family was "without the pale." The father had some nondescript notions, without form, and void. He was attracted by the artistic, especially by the painter's art. He was well posted as to the names and works of contemporaries, and was a fairly good judge of landscape and still-life; also he admired a fine orchestra. He had tried church after church seeking what he wanted. What he wanted was not priest or preacher, but a thinker and orator. At last he found, in Theodore Parker, the satisfaction of his quest. Going alone, he attended regularly. From this it may be inferred that he leaned toward Unitarianism. Nothing of the sort—he leaned toward oratory. If Unitarianism went with it, well and good. It was of no moment. He praised Parker highly.

Mother had a fixed idea that existence was continuous in a series of expanding becomings, life after life, in a spiral ascending and ever ascending until perfection should be reached in a bodiless state of bliss. This ethereal belief, opened to view the beauty and purity of her heart. Moreover, she read with avidity Renan's *Vie de Jesu.*

Grandpa looked upon religion as a curious and amusing human weakness—as conclusive evidence of universal stupidity. Grandma alone was devout. Quietly she believed in her God; in the compassion of His Son, in the wondrous love He bore—a love freely given to the outcast—a love so great, so tender, so merciful, that for its sake he yielded up in agony His earthly being, the supreme sacrifice, to the end that all men might be blessed thereby; that, as His mortality passed, His supernal love might be revealed to men throughout all time; that His divine being ascended through the firmament to join the Father in Glory on the throne of Heaven. These things she firmly believed. They were the atmosphere of her inner life, the incentive of her daily deeds. She believed in doctrine—and it may be in dogma. She held the scriptures of the Hebrews to be sacrosanct—as verily inspired of God. She did not seek to proselyte. She was satisfied to abide in her faith, undisturbed and undisturbing. Perhaps this is why her grandson loved her so. Innocent of creed, of doctrine and dogma, he loved her because she was good, he loved her because she was true, he loved her because to his adoring eyes she was beautiful. Such was Grandmama.

Otherwise Grandmama was the responsible head of a family consisting of herself, her husband, her son and her grandson. She was methodical, orderly, knew the true meaning of thrift, entered every item promptly in the account books, struck the monthly balance, had a fine mind for figures, and withal she was prudently generous. Her main business was to give private lessons in French to certain brahmins and their off-spring in that curious city called Boston. In her leisure moments, she knitted, knitted, knitted; gloves, mittens, scarves, socks, stockings, shawls; she knitted in silk, in wool, in cotton; she knitted with wooden needles and with steel needles; sometimes she used two needles, sometimes three. Frequently in night's still hours, she read in her Bible. Her precise hour of retiring was always 1 A. M. She had her coffee served in bed, and arose precisely at 10 A. M. Grandpa's hours were reverse. At or about 8 o'clock in the evening he would lay down his long-stemmed clay pipe, yawn, chirrup a bit, drag himself from his comfortable chair, kiss everyone goodnight and make his exit. His grandson, following soon after, passed the open door at the head of the stairs. He always looked in, and always saw grandpa stretched full length in bed, reading by the light of a student lamp some book on astronomy. The child did not intrude. He knew full well that however much Grandpa ridiculed so many things, he never poked fun at the solar system. In this domain, and the star-laden firmament, he lived his real life. This was his grand passion. All else was trivial. The vastness awed him; the brilliance inspired him; he kept close track of the movements of the planets. He read endlessly about the moon and the vast, fiery sun, and the earth's spiral path.

But it was in Autumn, when the full train of the Pleiades, the Hyades, Orion and Canis Major had cleared the horizon and stood forth in all their conjoined majestically-moving glory, that Grandpa went forth in the early hours of night to make vigils with the stars, to venerate, to adore this panoply of constellations, to be wholly lost within the splendor of the sky. Here was the man—all else was husk. What communion he held within the stillness of night, within his own stillest hour, no man shall know. Now and then he would, bit by bit, endeavor to impart a little of his knowledge. But he knew well enough his grandson was not of age. Still, the boy learned to recognize and name several of the constellations as well as some of the larger stars and planets. One evening they were walking together along the garden path. The crescent moon was smiling just above the tree-tops to the westward. They had been silent, thus far, when Grandpa of a sudden asked, "Louis, have you ever seen the penumbra of the moon?" When the meaning of penumbra had been asked and answered, when the child had grasped the idea that it was the rest of the moon next to the crescent, he said, "Yes, Grandpa, I see it."

"What is it like?"

"It is curved at the edge and flat the rest of the way. It is pale blue, like a fog. It is beautiful."

"Ah!" exclaimed Grandpa, "how I envy your young eyes! I have never seen it. I have tried with opera glasses, but still could not see it. It must be wonderful—and I shall never see it. Ah, my dear boy, little do you know what treasures your sharp eyes may bring to you. You see things that I cannot see and shall never see. When you are older you will know what I mean."

The child was startled. He did not know his Grandpa was near-sighted. True, he had noticed that when Grandpa read in bed, he held the book very close to his eyes. He had noticed that some people wore spectacles, that his Grandma wore spectacles in the evening. But Grandpa didn't wear spectacles at all. Why then could he not see the penumbra of the moon? It was all strange, very strange to him; it was anything but strange to Grandpa—it was a sorrow. To that eager mind, burdened with reluctant eyes, it was a calamity that he could not see and would never see the penumbra of the moon.

Grandma on the other hand was not imaginative. In place of this divine power she had well-defined, solidly settled ideas concerning decorum, breeding, formal and informal social intercourse, and a certain consciousness that Mrs. Grundy resided as definitely in South Reading as elsewhere. Upon her arrival there, one of her first activities was to seek out a church, attendance upon which would at one and the same time insure to her unquestioned respectability, and, as nearly as possible, coincide with her individual views of doctrine. Indeed Grandmama was conservative of the social order of her day. She seemed oblivious to hypocrisy and cant. She was devoid of them. In this instance, she differed diametrically with her daughter Andrienne, who railed bitterly at that cloak of respectability which to her view camouflaged the sins of the world. Candor and sincerity were her ideals of character and conduct. There was but limited choice in the village and Grandmama soon fixed upon the Baptist Church as her selection. She began regular attendance. The child had now reached the age at which she deemed it proper that he, also, should attend divine service. Thus another new world was to arise above the limited horizon of his experience.

Among the treasures of barn and pasture, there was a certain and only horse named Billy. He was an object at the time technically known as a "family horse—safe for any lady to drive." Billy was a sallow plug, who, as a finality, had resigned himself to a life of servitude, but not of service. Within the barn was housed what was mentioned familiarly as the "carryall." It was a family carriage, having an enclosed body. It was a neat solid affair, well built, well finished and upholstered, and with good lines. It was of the essence of respectability, even as Billy was of the lower classes. Billy's harness was all that could be desired, and on Sundays Billy was groomed to the extent of his limited adaptability to the exactions of high life. Billy, harness, and carryall, made a rather interesting combination, even though Billy, as fate would have it, was as a fly in an ointment. The combination, however, is explainable. Grandma was timid, or at least apprehensive, and very cautious. She wished to be sole guardian of her physical safety, to the extent, even, that she permitted no one but herself to drive. Her husband was too nearsighted and absent-minded, her son too reckless, her grandson, too young. Hence her determination to take matters into her own hands. The idea of a glossy, dignified, high-stepper to match the aristocratic carryall could therefore not be entertained by her. It involved risk, possibly disaster. So Billy was selected as a compromise between the desired tone and the much more desired security. That is, as a deletion of a certain, or uncertain percentage of village respectability, for South Reading was of ancient settlement.

Grandma would not countenance a checkrein for Billy; she maintained that it was cruel. The normal center of Billy's head, in consequence, was nearer the earth he feebly loved than the heaven Grandma hoped to reach with Billy's material aid. There was a whip, in its socket, to be sure, but Grandma would not strike a dumb beast. When Grandma wished to start, or, on frequent occasions, to accelerate Billy's pace—if such it might be called—she waved the lines with both hands and chirped encouragement—never becoming aggressive—and satisfied that she had a horse "safe for any lady to drive." But just here appearances became deceptive; for Billy, soon after his transfer in exchange for legal tender, revealed a defect in character. He was given to unlooked-for fits of insanity. From a turbid dodder, he would suddenly break into a runaway. This was alarming; yet there seemed a method in the madness. Like a clock, with mainspring breaking, and the works rattling fiercely toward a silence soon reached, even so were Billy's runaways. Their distance-limit seldom exceeded one hundred yards. So, after prudent observation of his antics, and with due allowance for the fact that he did not run away every time, Billy was reinstated as a family horse, safe for any lady to drive, provided she were familiar with his mannerisms. Such was now the case.

Of a Sunday morning, fair to look upon, in early summer, all prepared and ready, Billy and carryall connected into a material totality, the family set forth, following the dusty road to the village, without mishap. Upon arrival at the church, a white-painted wooden structure in imitation of stone, pretentious, and ugly,—as if indoctrinated with sin,—so much talked about within—Billy was hitched to the general railing and the family entered, after Louis had sufficiently patted Billy's nose. Climbing a wide flight of stairs to the second floor, all entered a large, dim, barren room, and reached the family pew. Louis immediately felt a pang of disappointment. There was nothing here to recall an echo of the spring song he had shared in the open. He thought there should be. Looking about at the congregation, he was astonished at the array of solemn faces: Why solemn? And the whispering silence: Why whispering? What was to follow? What was to happen? He enquired, and was hushed. He awaited. The service began; he followed it eagerly to the end, noting every detail.

He greatly admired the way the minister shouted, waved his arms terrifically, pounded the big Bible magnificently, and then, with voice scarcely exceeding a whisper, pointed at the congregation in dire warning of what would surely befall them if they did not do so and so or believe such and such. He roared of Hell so horribly that the boy shivered and quaked. Of Heaven he spoke with hysterical sweetness—a mush of syrupy words. He had painted the same word-pictures year after year; worked himself to the same high pitches and depths. His listeners, now thrilled, relaxed, expanded, held these sermons, these prayers, these hymns as precious; for the man looming in the pulpit was of their world. He gave pith, point and skilled direction to those collective aspirations and fears, which otherwise would have lacked symmetry and power. The sermons invariably ended with a tirade against the Papists. This epilogue appealed to all as a most satisfying finale. After the closing words of benediction the congregation remained for a while outside the church, gathered in groups, the men swapping lies and horses, the women-folk exchanging idiosyncrasies. All declared their satisfaction with the sermon. This was the routine. Then they went home.

To the child, however, as a first violent experience, the total effect was one of confusion, perturbation, and perplexity. One particular point puzzled him most: Why did the minister, when he prayed, clasp his hands closely together and so continue to hold them? Why did he close his eyes? Why did he bow his head and at times turn sightless face upward toward the ceiling? Why did he speak in whining tones? Why was he now so familiar with God, and then so groveling? Why did he not shout his prayers as he had shouted and roared through his sermon? Why did he not stand erect with flashing eyes, wave his arms, clinch his fists and pound the big Bible, and walk first this way and then that way, and otherwise conduct himself like a man? He seemed afraid of something. What could it be? What was there to be afraid of? And then this matter of the Papists. Why so bitter, why so violent, why so cruel as to wish these people, who-ever they were, to be burned throughout all eternity in the flames of awful hell? And the minister had said he was sure they would be. The boy asked at home what Papists were. Grandma said they were Catholics. Grandpa said they were imbeciles. Then he asked what were Catholics, and Grandma said, simply, they were not Protestants. And what were Protestants? And Grandma said, as simply, but with a touch of detail, that they were not Catholics, to which Grandpa added that they, also, were imbeciles. But at the end of the next sermon the minister explained it all. He declared in his wrath that they, the Papists, were pagans, heathen, infidels, idolators, worshippers of saints, low beasts, vile savages, ignorant, depraved, the very scum and slime of earth whom God in his mercy had segregated from the elect, in this world, in order that he might damn them totally to Hell in the next.

The minister made it quite clear that no Papist could by any chance enter the Kingdom of Heaven, and equally clear that a good, strict Baptist could and surely would. As to other denominations, he felt dubious, indeed plainly doubtful, almost certain. Still, he said, grace was infinite, and the wisdom of the Father beyond the grasp of mortal man. On the other hand, he acknowledged himself a sinner, and frequently proclaimed, as with a sort of pride, that his entire congregation, individually and collectively, were miserable sinners; and they agreed. He told them, moreover, the wages of sin was death. He told them also, with unction, of the bloody source whence came the wages of purity in redemption. The child appealed to Grandpa, who said the minister was an idiot full of wind and nonsense. The child suffered. Nothing in this new world agreed with his own world. It was all upside down, all distorted, cruel and sugary. It was not like his beautiful springtime, it was not even like his beautiful winter. There was no laughter, no joy as he knew these things. He appealed to Grandma, but his questions were too persistently direct, too embarrassing to her placidity. She explained perfunctorily; he got no satisfaction there.

He began to think perhaps Grandpa was right. After more sermons, and prayers, and denunciations, he began to feel distinctly that his world, his life, which he had frankly felt to be one, was being torn in two. Instinctively he revolted. He would *not* have the beauty of life torn from him and destroyed. These things he did not say; he felt them powerfully. A tragedy was approaching. He was about to lose what he loved, what he held precious in life; he was about to lose his own life as he knew or felt life. He rebelled. He lost confidence in the minister. He no longer believed what was said. More than that he soon disbelieved everything that was said. He was regaining his freedom. The services increasingly irritated him; he asked to be transferred to the Sunday School. He would at least see children there. The Old Testament amused and pleased him with its interesting stories. He could almost live them over. But when it came to the crucifixion he rebelled again in spirit, this time so ardently that it was thought prudent at home to release him from Sunday School and Church alike. His rumination now was to the effect that fortune might perhaps also separate him from the schoolhouse, standing white and bare on the hillside.

PLATE 2. Residences built for Mrs. N. Halsted, 1826-34 Lincoln Park West, Chicago. 1884.

PLATE 3. Benjamin Lindauer residence, 3312 Wabash Avenue, Chicago. 1885.

CHAPTER IV

A Vacation

LOUIS became moody. Day by day the hillside school and all its doings irked him ruthlessly. In wood, field and meadow, his friends the birds were free. Why should he remain within these walls imprisoned and sad? He was a child of sudden resolves. On a morning early he went to the pantry. As he glanced over the shelves, his thoughts wandered to the pink and white smiling baker who delivered "Parker House rolls" every so often, and, with a cheery word left thirteen for a dozen. "A baker's dozen" he would say every time he drove up to the kitchen door; and then in a busy way inquire: "How's all the folks? Guess I don't need ask if this boy's a sample." Then he would make a quick step into his light wagon and away with a rattling start. The boy in the quiet pantry unbuttoned his blouse, as his thoughts went on: Not so at the school; Teacher was not always kind. Twice with a rattan she had whipped the palm of his right hand while he placed his free arm across his eyes and bent his head and cried. It did not hurt much, but Teacher said it hurt her more than it did him. She told all the class so. She said she must make an example by having him stand on the platform and she said she did it to "learn him to mind and pay attention"; that it was her moral duty to do so; that she could not fail in her moral duty even though it pained her; that she punished not in anger but in grief; and then she cried, her forehead bowed between her hands, as she sat at her desk on the raised platform. He recalled that she had cried this way every time she had whipped a child, and she didn't whip very often either; so he bore her no ill will; yet he wondered why he should be whipped at school when he was never whipped or punished at all, at home; and again came floating the thought of the dainty baker-man; nimble, pink-faced, blue twinkling eyes and jolly chuckle. Thus musing but intent he filled his blouse with rolls and doughnuts and cookies —and buttoned up. Also, he had, hidden in his bosom, a small tin cup, for he knew where he was going. He was preparing to answer the call of a wooded ravine through which wandered a noisy rivulet. He had seen it but once, while on a walk with Grandpa, but he marked it then as the favored spot in his imaginary world. Once found and marked for friendship, it often had called to him in his school—a distant call— he could not come. This morning it called to him irrevocably and nearby.

Without a word to any one he set forth, following the Stoneham Road westward until he reached the gate of a right of way leading northward. He climbed the padlocked gate, and, following the road, soon passed a long hillock to the left crowned with tall hardwood trees, then down grade, then upgrade to a crest where the road ended. He climbed the gate and in new freedom, lightly traversing the down slope, reached the depths of the promised land. One bright particular spot was his goal. It lay in the narrow bottom of the ravine just where the gurgling water passed hurriedly among field stones under tall arching oaks. Here was the exact spot for a dam. He got immediately to work. He gathered the largest field stones he could handle, and small ones too. He had seen Scotchmen and Irishmen build farm walls and knew what to do. He was not strong enough to use a stone hammer if he had had one. So he got along without. He found a rusty remnant of a hoe, without a handle; with this he dug up some stiff earth. So with field stones, mud, twigs and grass he built his dam. It was a mighty work.

He was lost to all else. The impounded waters were rising fast behind the wall, and leaking through here and there. He must work faster. Besides, the wall must lengthen as it grew higher, and it leaked more at the bottom. He had to plug up holes. At last child power and water power became unequal. Now was at hand the grand climax—the meaning of all this toil. A miniature lake had formed, the moment had arrived. With all his strength he tore out the upper center of the wall, stepped back quickly and screamed with delight, as the torrent started, and, with one great roar, tore through in huge flood, leaving his dam a wreck. What joy! He laughed and screamed. Was he proud? Had he not built the dam? Was he in high spirits? Had he not built this dam *all by himself?* Had he not planned in advance just what happened? Had he not worked as hard as he had seen big men work? Wasn't he a strong boy for his age? Could anything at school or at home compare with this? Exhausted with work and delight he lay stretched on his back, in the short grass, looking far up at the spreading branches, glimpsing bits of blue between the leaves, noting how these self-same leaves rustled softly, and twinkled in the sunshine. This rested him. Then hunger sharply called. He had câched his Parker House rolls and doughnuts and cookies, and his tin cup, on a big boulder in the shade. The "hired girl," Julia, had taught him to milk. Dipper in hand he went afield to hunt up a cow. All cows were his friends. Soon he had the dipper filled with warm fragrant milk—his delight. Then came the repast near the site of his triumph. Then he loafed and invited his soul as was written by a big man about the time this proud hydraulic engineer was born. But he did not observe "a spear of summer grass"; he dreamed. Vague day dreams they were,—an arising sense, an emotion, a conviction; that united him in spirit with his idols,—with his big strong men who did wonderful things such as digging ditches, building walls, cutting down great trees, cutting with axes, and splitting with maul and wedge for cord wood, driving a span of great work-horses. He adored these men. He felt deeply drawn to them, and close to them. He had seen all these things done. When would he be big and strong too? Could he wait? Must he wait? And thus he dreamed for hours. The shadows began to deepen and lengthen; so, satisfied, with a splendid day of work and pondering, he reached home in time for supper. Grandma said the usual grace; all heads were bowed as she appealed to her Lord of love to give strength and encouragement and to bestow his blessing upon this small family in their daily lives and tasks and trials and to give abundantly of His divine strength unto all that loved and obeyed Him. But

[56]

the child's thoughts were concrete and practical; parallel to the prayer but more locally concentrated. His Grandmama, in her appeal, spoke the beautiful old French with its liquid double-ell. Her voice soft and heartfelt meant peace on earth. He understood a little of it; he knew that the words *Que Dieu nous bénit* which sounded to him like one word: Kudgernoobaynee, meant: May God bless us. He had no objection to God as a higher member of the family; it was only the minister's God, the God of Hell that he disliked and avoided. Nevertheless he wished the ceremony might be shorter—it would do just as well —for while Grandmama prayed, his mouth watered. He would have accepted prayer as a necessary evil were it not for the reconciling thought that God seemed to be Grandmama's big strong friend; and what Grandmama loved he knew he ought to love too; even as he loved his own idols—his mighty men.

The prayer done, a silver bell tinkled by Grandmama and Julia appeared, a glowing Irish vision, bearing high stacks of her wonderful griddle-cakes, a pitcher of real syrup, and a—but why parade or parody a dreamer's gluttony rising thus thrice daily like a Jinni of old within his nascent dream of power? After supper he visited his small garden in the large garden. It was more sizable than last year. Satisfying himself that the four o'clocks, nasturtiums, geraniums, mignonettes, and the rest of the family were doing well, he trotted down the granite steps to the dirt road in front where he might practice at throwing stones—a sport strictly taboo in the fields, but permissible in the sterile pastures. Between his house and the Tyler farm-house opposite, was quite an open space, containing, at a level considerably lower than the road, a small spring-fed pond. In this pond were colonized bullfrogs, mud-turtles, minnows and leeches; bulrushes grew at each end. Stray cattle browsed about at times. This pond was one of his possessions. It didn't make any difference if it were called *Tyler's Pond*, it was his own just the same. Stone-throwing finished, he went to look things over and satisfy himself that everything was all right and as it should be. As he approached, the host of frogs were beginning their evening chant to the invisible King of all frogs; he waded in a bit; the clamor increased; then the bass volume became overtoned by the awakening sounds of tree toad, Katydid and cricket, while fireflies softly shone here and there. These were his familiars. Then he found a glow-worm in the damp grass. As he held it in his hand he noticed with surprise that the surface of the pond was crimson: This was new to him. He waded a little ahead and was pleased to see the ripples turn silver and crimson as they moved away from him. He was pleased and somewhat perplexed. Somehow he looked straight ahead from where he stood in the water, and there right in the woods on Tompson's knoll, he saw the setting sun, the trees silhouetting against it, and the lower sky aglow. He had seen many sunsets, but there was something peculiar about this sunset—he would speak to Grandpa. The sun sank from sight; the western sky softened into gray, twilight deepened into gloaming as the child stood knee deep in the warm shallow water, lost in reverie so faint, so far, so near, so absorbing, so vibrant that the once noisy chorus seemed a tranquil accompaniment to a melody that was of earth and sun in duo with his dream. He awoke! He must speak to Grandpa about the sun.

Grandpa was willing, but careful. He well knew that a child's mind was a tender thing. He was keenly observing, but said little. He quietly, even eagerly observed his grandson, as one might watch a precious plant growing of its own volition in a sheltered garden, but far was it from him to let the child suspect such a thing. He had often laughed at the child's outrageous frankness. It infinitely amused him; but when it came to *knowledge,* he was cautious—dropping information by crumbs. But this time, when his grandson in eager child-words dramatized the sunset and climaxed all by a sudden antithesis, saying he had never seen the sunrise! How did the sun rise? Where did it rise? How did it rise? Would Grandpa tell him? Would Grandpa please tell him? Then Grandpa wide-eyed knew a mystic golden bell had struck the hour. He told the boy at once that the rising sun could not be seen from the house because Cowdrey's hill shut off the view; that the sun truly arose far beyond this hill. That to see the sun rise one must go to the crest of the hill, whence one could see to the horizon. He used the word horizon boldly, as one throws down a card, and then with strategy of simple words, and easy similes he produced a sort of image for the child; difficult to do in a hilly country, and for the mind of one who had never viewed the open sea. Then he explained that the lay of the land westward of the house was not so hilly as that to the east, therefore one could view the sunset to fairly good advantage.

In his discourse, he was careful not to mention the revolution of the earth. He knew well enough the child was living in a world of the senses. "But Grandpa, is the sunrise as beautiful as the sunset?" "Far more so, my child; it is of an epic grandeur; sunset is lyric, it is an elegy." These words escaped Grandpa in a momentary enthusiasm. He felt foolish, as he saw a small bright face turn blank. However, he patched up the "lyric" and the "elegy" fairly well, but "epic" was difficult. Had he but known of his grandson's big strong men,—how simple. Then Grandpa went on: "But you must know that in summer the sun rises very early, earlier than I; and I scarcely believe my young astronomer will get out of his comfortable bed long before daylight, just to see the sun rise out of *his* bed," and Grandpa chuckled. "Yes, I will, Grandpa, yes, I will"—and he slipped from his Grandfather's knee to arouse the somnolent cat, and shape his plans for tomorrow.

Restless through the night, he arose at twilight, made ready quickly, and passed up the road leading to the great ash tree whose companionship he ever sought on high occasions. Here, under the wondrous tree— and with Cowdrey's farmhouse resting silently across the way—here in stillness of oncoming dawn punctured here and there by a bird's early chirp, and chanticleer's high herald call heard near and far, raucous, faint, and ever fainter far away; the few remaining stars serene within the dome of pale passing night, he stood, gazing wistfully over the valley toward a far away range of dark blue drowsy hills, as the pallid eastern sky, soon tremulous with a pink suffusion, gave way before a glow deepening into radiant crimson, like a vanguard of fire—as the top of the sun emerging from behind the hills, its slow-revealing disc reaching full form, ascended, fiery, imperious and passionate, to confront him. Chilled and spellbound, he in turn became impassioned with splendor and awe, with wonder and he knew not what, as the great red orb, floating clear of the hilltops overwhelmed him, flooded the land; and in white dazzling splendor awakened the world to its work, to its hopes, to its sorrows, and to its dreams. Surely the child, sole witness beneath his great ash tree, his wonder-guardian and firm friend sharing with him in its stately way as indeed did all the land and sky and living things of the open—the militant splendor of sunrise—the breaking of night's dam—the torrent and foam of far-spreading day—surely this child that went forth every day became part of sunrise even as this sunrise became forevermore part of him. The resounding power of the voice of the Lord of the sky and earth found in him a jubilant answer—an awakening world within, now aroused from its twilight dream, its lyric setting sun, its elegy of the gloaming. The great world was alive to action. Men resumed the toil of countless ages; the child, illumined, lost in an epic vision, came slowly to a consciousness of his own small self, and the normal doings of his own small day.

He made a long detour through the solemn pine woods near Whittemore's, crossed the road there, descended into the small valley, followed it to and

THE AUTOBIOGRAPHY OF AN IDEA

through a lumpy bog where skunk-cabbages grew and their synonyms wandered, scaled a low wall, followed a rivulet that traced from the considerable spring in the hollow of his own pasture, sat there watching a small frog, fell asleep, woke up, followed the hollow to the pasture's high ground, turned into the walled road leading to the barn, stopped at the pump in the kitchen yard—and was late to breakfast. Grandpa looked at him quizzically, but said nothing—he knew what the imp had been up to—he had heard him leave the house and had hastily donned gown and slippers, to watch his grandson disappear up the road to sunrise land. Julia was furious in rich brogue concerning punctuality, and the child, usually so naïvely communicative, said not a word to anyone about his adventure —it seemed to have happened for himself alone. Grandpa, amused, amazed and disturbed by this freak of his grandson, feared precocity—in much the manner that academically trained men are apt to fear manifestations of instinct.

The only thing that reassured him was the fact that his grandson, between spells, was as ridiculously practical. As a matter of fact Louis was living almost wholly in the world of instinct. Whatever there was of intellect consisted in keen accuracy of observation, and lively interest in all constructive affairs. Without reflection he admired work. To see men at work, and himself to work, especially if he could participate, was his childish joy. With never a serious illness, most carefully reared as to his diet and early hours, he was sound. Though he was his grandparents' pet, disparity in age, occupation and thought left him much to himself and he did mostly as he pleased. What marked him apart and comforted his elders was an entire absence in him of destructive tendency. Therefore they allowed him the utmost freedom to go and come and do. This morning, breakfast out of the way, and Julia also, he went at once to his garden. His quick eye detected a fallen nasturtium; with his finger he dug up the offending cut-worm. How could a cut-worm do so shocking a thing? Had he not reared all these cherished beauties from the very seed? Had he not watched them growing, day by day, from infancy to blossom-time—putting forth tender leaf after leaf, and unfolding their tiny buds into lovely flowers? Had he not watered them and weeded? How often had he wondered at what made them grow. How often, on hands and knees—close up—had he peered and gazed long, hungrily, minutely at them one by one, absorbed in their translucent intimacy; indeed worshipped them in friendship until he seemed to *feel* them grow; that they were of his world and yet not of his world; that they seemed to live their own lives apart from his life. But he never said a word of this to Grandpa or to Grandma—*They might not understand* —and Grandpa might laugh.

After further careful inspection, he left his garden friends for the day; and equipped as before, made his way to the ravine with its sturdy rivulet and the wreckage of a dam. But this he judged was not dam-building day. He had not seen the full spread of his domain. He must explore. So saying, he followed the rivulet eastward out of the heavily wooded ravine, into a broad field of meadow grass where the small

clear stream now flowed—in tranquillity winding its
way. As he lifted his eyes from its course, there,
solitary in the meadow, stood the most beautiful tree
of all. He knew it at once for an elm; but such tall
slender grace he had never seen. Its broad slim fronds
spreading so high and descending in lovely curves entranced him. He compared it with the two Tompson
elms. They were tall and spreading but stiff and
sturdy. Now he knew why he had never adopted them:
—they were *pruned* from the ground way up to the
big strong branches, while this lovely sister of the
meadow, beneath her branching plume, put forth from
her slender trunk delicate frothy branchlets reaching
almost to the meadow grass. Her beauty was incom-
parable.

Then he thought of his great ash tree. How different it was—so grand, so brooding, so watchful on
the crest of the hill; and at times, he firmly believed
so paternal—so big-brotherly. But the lovely elm was
his infatuation—he had adopted her at first sight, and
still gazed at her with a sweetness of soul he had
never known. He became infiltrated, suffused, inspired
with the fateful sense of beauty. He melted for an
instant into a nameless dream, wherein he saw he was
sufficient unto herself, that like his garden plants
she lived a life of her own, apart from his life. Yet
they both lived in the same big world—they both, for
the moment, stood in the same green field. Was there
nothing in common? Did she not know he was there?

Then he awoke!—he came to his senses, and turned
to the practical business of hunting wild strawberries
in the meadow grass. His dream had flitted by like

a bird of passage. He looked upon her sanely now. She was still uniquely beautiful, he thought, in free admiration. So he had two trees now—all his own, and powerfully prized. It was all agreed. Then he moved further north to a dense mass of rather tall pines. He pushed in some distance, saw a crow's nest overhead, climbed painfully up to it, had barely looked in when came a horrible cawing; angry crows came suddenly from everywhere, bent on his destruction. Amid a fierce clamor, he descended to safety and then and there fixed those gloomy pines as the eastern boundary of his domain. He explored until he found in another field, on slightly higher ground, the deep clear wellspring from which the rivulet flowed. Thence he followed its windings, wading as he went. Grasshoppers in alarm hopped foolishly into the stream and floated along; now and then a small frog jumped the other way for safety. There were a few strawberries peeping from the grass along the banks; the channel was cutting deeper into the meadow and held more water; as he rounded a long curve he became aware of a great presence near him; it was his elm; he craned his neck to look at the branches way up in the sky, but his interest was centered in his new friend the rivulet; he had not room for both just now. The little stream began to ripple and sing sweetly to the child all alone in the meadow in the full sunshine—all alone; with plenty of company. Then the rivulet began to hurry and gurgle. Louis scaled the fence quickly to see the water descend all at once in a beautiful cascade of about his own height. After this, noisily foaming, it poured among the boulders to the lower level where he had built the dam, and, as he knew, moved on to the marsh.

He had reached his sanctuary in the shady grove, and sat a while on the lower or northern bank, to watch the squirrels. It seemed so funny to see a gray squirrel run head first down a tall tree, sit up straight in the grass, frisk his tail, wag his head, scamper to the next tree, run up and out to the end of a branch and jump from that to a branch of the next tree. He laughed gleefully at these antics. Meanwhile came from the undergrowth the note of the brown thrush, and from above various twitterings, chirpings, and distant floating meadow songs. It was now time to establish the northern boundary. The north bank of the ravine sloped rather gently upward, and as it emerged from the grove it rounded and flattened into a lumpy pasture, with many boulders large and small, and plants of mullein scattered over its surface. He must include this pasture because here was the milk supply, and besides, the pasture was green. All along the north border of it stood a dense growth of young pines which he found impenetrable and repellant, so he fixed his northern boundary resolutely there. As to the southern boundary he was in some doubt. It should, properly, be located a little way south of the crest of the ravine where the grove ended. He mounted the height and stood at the edges of a sterile stony sunburned pasture—no trees, no cows; nothing but mulleins. This would not do. Yet he yearningly gazed beyond it to the long Tompson hillock crowned with beautiful lofty hard wood trees running parallel to the ravine. He wished this grove to be his, but could not accept the miserable pasture. He thought hard,—and solved his problem this way: He would fix the south boundary at the crest of the ravine, and would annex the Tompson Grove as an outpost. The boundary of the meadow he had already fixed, much farther south than the ravine, at a cross fence near the spring, where the meadow ended and a cultivated field began. He contemplated for a while, and saw that all thus far was good.

Now for the marsh at which he had cast covetous eyes as he, yesterday, peered under the lower branches of his grove as through a portal. His expectations were far exceeded by the revelation. It was a lovely marsh, shaped like an oval, enshrined by the diminishing trees of his grove and a margin of heavy shrubbery all around. In the near background beyond the far end of the marsh were scattering swamp pines and cedars standing very straight and tapering to a point; they were welcome to him as they stood on guard behind the dense thicket. But the marsh itself—how beautiful— covered with water half-knee deep, filled with groups of tall bulrushes, of reeds, of blue flag, and slender grasses; and bright flowers here and there along the wavering edge. What joy to wade and wade, lengthwise and crosswise, pulling up a flag now and again and stripping it to reach the edible core; following the margin to seek out hidden flowers. It was too much; too much at one time for one small boy. And then, in mingled affection and gratitude he established as western boundary a vague semicircle of deep green holding in its heart a marsh—his marsh without price. Slowly he returned to the dam-site to think it all over.

Now was the work done. The boundaries of his domain established. The domain his very own. **His**
breast swelled with pride. It was all his. No other
boy should ever enter those lovely precincts. No other
boy could understand. Besides, he loved solitude as
he loved activity, and the open.

Thus an entire month sped by as he reigned supreme.
Not a soul came to disturb him: Rabbits, squirrels,
birds and snakes were company enough. When he
wished to play with other boys he went to them and
joined in their games. While his heart was fixed in
one spot, he made many tours of exploration; he called
on many farmers and shoemakers. He even went so
far one day as to enter the stove foundry beside the
tracks, near the depot. He went frankly to a work-
man, watched him a while and told the man he liked
to see him work. The moulder, much amused, said he
would show him how it was all done. Louis spent
the entire afternoon there; the moulder carefully explained to him every large and minute procedure. The
child was amazed; a new world had opened to him
—the world of handicraft, the vestibule of the great
world of art that he one day was to enter and explore. He went away holding this moulderman in
special honor, although he was not very big nor very
strong. He even visited the rattan works but did
not like the dust and noise. He saw nothing but a
long slender cane coming out of a machine.

One day he saw a man in a wagon. The wagon
was going without a horse. Also he visited a shoemaker named Boardman who lived near his home and
whom he knew well; a swarthy little man, with black

beard, black beady eyes, who both worked and chewed tobacco furiously. There he learned every detail of making pegged and sewed shoes; he saw them *built* from beginning to end. He would spend hours with this shoemaker who made shoes every day, while the farmers made shoes only in winter. The man liked to have him around; and once in a while he would suspend work, and, to amuse the child, would extinguish the life of a fly on the opposite wall with an unerring squirt of tobacco juice. Louis danced with joy. What a wonderful man to spit like that. He tried to spit that way himself—failing ignominiously. The man told him he must spit hard between his teeth; and Louis did spit hard between his teeth; without avail. Then the Boardman man would catch flies with his hand and eat them, or pretend to eat them. Louis believed he really ate them. Then the shoemaker would return to his furious work, and Louis in admiration would wander on. The neighbors said this man Boardman was a lowdown sport who staid sober and worked hard only to get money to bet on the races—whatever that meant. But thus far Louis had made no social distinctions. It did delight him, though, at a certain season, to see Boardman, all dressed up and flashy, jump into his surrey behind a nervous high-stepping steed, start away with a prancing rush and disappear down the Stoneham Road lost in a trailing cloud of dust. For a long time after this event Boardman would not be seen thereabouts.

Also he would visit Farmer Hopkins to watch him break a fallow field with his monstrous team of oxen, swaying and heaving heavily against the yoke, with low-bending heads and foaming mouths, as the man, with one booted foot in the furrow, guided the plowshare as it turned up the beautiful black soil of the bottom land, while the man said, "gee-haw"; "haw"; "haw-gee." Many such trips he made, always starting from his secret domain. Evenings he would tease Julia to tell him Irish fairy tales. How lovely, how beautiful they were, with fairies, elves, gnomes and a great company, weaving spells of enchantment in the moonlight. He lived them all. Julia was a robust Irish peasant who remained with the family for nine long years. Fiery was her hair; brilliant her white perfect teeth of which same she was very proud. And had she a temper? Sure! She had a temper that came and went like a storm. She was not long since come to America. Many evenings her Irish women friends called and they talked Irish together. He had never heard anything so sweet, so fluid, except the rivulet. He could listen by the hour; and Julia taught him a few words.

All was running smoothly. It had not in the least occurred to him that all this time he had been a truant. No one had said anything for a whole month; or asked any questions.

Then came the crash! Teacher had written. Little was said at home. He was simply sent back to school. Here he languished in misery. But help soon came as suddenly as the crash. His father had opened a summer school in Newburyport. Grandma had written to Mama; Mama had told it to Father; Father decided that the grandparents were too soft; they had let his child grow up like a weed; they had pampered him

PLATE 4. Auditorium Building, Chicago. 1887-89. View from the east.

PLATE 5. Auditorium Building Tower. View from the southwest.

outrageously; it was high time his son was brought to him, that he might establish in him a sense of respect, order, discipline, obedience. So Mama took the train to South Reading. She spent a few days there visiting her parents. She looked at her son with a sadness he could not understand, but she found it not in her heart to chide. The day of their departure arrived. With many a sob he had said good-bye to all. They were driven to the depot. Mother and son boarded the train for Newburyport. The engine puffed—the train sped on its way. Came to an end the day-dreaming of a child.

CHAPTER V

Newburyport

THE train now well under way for Newburyport, our poet, he of the dream-life, crawled forth from his cave of gloom and began to take notice. Soon he was all notice and no gloom. His prior and only trip in a railway train was now over two years back in ancient history, which signified oblivion. Hence all was now new and novel. He began at once, at the very beginning of the beginning, that intolerable, interminable series of questions which all children ask and no mother can for long stand the strain of answering. He did his mother the wholly unsolicited and unwelcome honor of assuming as a finality that she knew the names of every farmer along the route, that she knew why the trees went by so fast, why the telegraph wires rose and fell and rose again; that she was personally acquainted with the conductor and the brakeman. At the forty-seventh question, Mother, who was only twenty-eight and not very strong, became drowsy with fatigue just as her son was becoming rigidly interested. Mother was not the only one asleep; everybody was asleep; and he noticed that they were all greasy with sweat and dust and grotesquely relaxed. He was intent on knowing the brakeman's name. For that purpose he moved up the aisle, managed to open the door, was on the platform and would have been pitched to Kingdom Come as the ramshackle train rounded a sharp curve, had not a white-faced brakeman grabbed him, thrust him back into the car and, with a string of New England profanities, wanted to know why in thunder he was out on the platform. The child replied that he had come to ask him his name; to which the brakeman replied: "Wall, I swow, you be a cute un; you'll be President some day." So the child immediately transferred his questionnaire from oblivious Mama to his wide awake new friend whom he found good natured, and much amused, and whose name as far as this recorder knows, may have been Matthew, Luke, David or Moses—all favorites in that day; but there were also many Johns, Jameses, Marks, Samuels, Ezechiases—but no Solomons. He put the brakeman through an exhaustive examination and cross-examination concerning this, that and the other, after he had induced him to detail his family connections and home life, and to give assurance that he was not a Papist, and had not hated his teacher.

Then began the technical inquisition: Why did the wires move up and down all the time? What were the wires for? Why did the poles whizz by? What did "telegraph" mean? What made that funny noise all the time, click-a-lick-click-click, click-a-lick click-click-click? And so on and so on. He was amazed at what the brakeman knew. It was *wonderful* how much he knew. Then came a toot for the next station; the brakeman swung open the door, let out a yell that startled the child, reminding him of the Baptist minister in South Reading, and began to twist the hand-brake with all his strength. The child saw all this through the open door. How wonderful that one man could be so strong as to stop a car that had been going so fast? Wasn't it splendid to see a man in action? He adopted "Luke" immediately. At the station Luke helped him down the steps, and he began verifying certain statements. For Luke had only *told* him; he wanted to *see*. So he examined the link and coupling pins, the flange on the wheels, the iron rails which he found badly frayed from wear, the open joints, the fish plates, the spikes, the ties, and was crawling under the car to examine the trucks when a strange man yanked him out and asked him if he was crazy. The bell rang; the brakeman hoisted him aboard before he had had time to go forward and ask the engineer his name, and the fireman his name, and how much wood it took, and what made the choo-choo. True the brakeman had told him all about it, but that wasn't seeing; and besides he wished to know the engineer and the fireman personally, for they must be great men—it must be a wonderful man who could keep the engine on the track and steer it around all those curves as the brakeman said he did. And the brakeman said the fireman expected to be an engineer some day, but that he himself didn't expect to brake no cars all his life—it was just hell in winter; and he went on to tell of his ambition, said he'd be damned if he'd work for anybody much longer; he'd save up some money and was going to have other men work for *him*, and he'd make more money out of *them*. He'd drive 'em, he said; he'd learn 'em what a day's work meant when they worked for him, he would; and so on, excitedly. The child took no interest in this and wandered back to his mother, who, having observed him in safe hands, had not troubled. He started to tell her all about his new friend, what

a great man he was, that he wore three woolen under-
shirts in winter, and knew the name of every station,
and all about links and pins, and engines and telegraph and everything, until Mama wearily turned
toward him and gasped: "Louis! Louis!! *Mon dieu,*
you are a pest!" Louis thought it strange that his
Mamma was not interested in what interested him,
yet failed to reflect that the brakeman's get-rich romance had bored him. So on went the train swaying,
rattling, banging, clanking, sinking suddenly, rising
suddenly, screeching infernally around the curves,
amidst smoke and dust and an overpowering roar.
Soon there were two bedraggled ones sweatily sleeping
side by side, and from the roar unfolded for one of
them a dream of much mixed up brakemen, wheels,
engineers, telegraphs, wood, links, pins, firemen, trucks
—but no conductor; the conductor had not interested
him, for he had a big belly, a heavy gold watch chain
across it, gray chin whiskers, wore spectacles and did
nothing but walk up and down, punch tickets and
stick bits of cards in people's hats. Faintly the brake-
wheel creaked; and a distant voice seemed to call the
name of a station—NEWBURYPORT! !

* * *

The town, in, by, and of itself, made no first impression on him, other than one of quiet commonplace.
It was not very different from the village of South
Reading, only it was larger and had more streets and
houses.

The family had taken quarters in an old-looking
building called a hotel—a word new to the child. The
hotel fronted on a square in which were trees, and

on the other side of the square but not opposite the hotel was the town hall, and in front of the town hall was the town pump—of which, more later. Thus the family "boarded" at the hotel. The dining room was a large dreary cave containing one long table at which the boarders sat facing each other. From the middle one could not see the end of the rows of vacant sallow faces. The family had places in the middle— Louis sitting next to Mamma. He was hungry— always hungry. It was their first joint struggle against dyspepsia. Not much was said for a while; then Louis, in confidential tones, suitable to a pasture, uttered this sage judgment: "Mamma; this gravy isn't like Grandmamma's gravy; this is only just a little flour and water!" Mamma made big eyes and grasped his arm, a titter went along the opposite row, napkins to faces, whispers exchanged, some rude persons laughed, and some one said "Hurrah!" Lucky Grandpa wasn't there—the ceiling would have fallen. Everybody was stunned at the child's bravado, but assent was beaming. Perhaps, even, they yearned for some of Grandmamma's gravy; why not? if they but knew! The child looked at the opposite row of faces in astonishment. What was it all about? If the gravy was only a little flour and water, why not say so? Besides, he was only talking to Mamma anyway. And moreover, he did not see anything to laugh at, at all. It was a serious matter, this flour and water.

Mamma said she would tell him something after a while when they were alone. And she did. According to her view, children, in public, should be seen but not heard; they should speak only when spoken to; they should be well mannered, circumspect; they

should especially be respectful toward their elders; they
must never put themselves forward, or try to be smart
or show off, or otherwise attract attention to themselves; must remain in the background; speak in subdued tones and say: "yes, sir," "no, sir," "yes, ma'am,"
"no, ma'am," and she thus went on setting forth a complete code of ethics and etiquette for children in general
and for her child in especial particularity, for she trusted
he would not become, so she said, a young ruffian like
other people's children that were devoid of table manners in particular, and used the language of the streets.
This was Mamma's theory. In practice she vacillated,
oscillated, vibrated, ricochetted, made figures of eight
and spirals in her temperamental emotionalism and
mother love, meanwhile clutching at the straw of her
theory. And this was not all. Secretly she kept a
note book. In this she entered carefully and minutely
all the wonderful sayings of her son as observed by
herself, or as transmitted in long letters from Grandmamma. True to form, she immediately entered the
gravy item, wrote a long letter to Grandmamma about
it, confessed she nearly strangled in suppressing her
delight; and how the other people present were con-
vulsed, as a loud voice, within the dining room's wilderness, proclaimed the unholy truth that this was not
like Grandmamma's gravy—it was only just a little
flour and water. Officially the child was squelched;
and officially Mamma kept an eye to weatherward.
But in her secret book she gave way to self flattery.

Not so with Father. There was no sentiment, no
nonsense about him. He would not rave for thirty
minutes over a single blossom; a brief moment of
appreciation sufficed; during which he would express

regret at the absence in him of the sense of smell. This was the regular formula—unless it came to "Scenery." What he had fixed firmly in mind was a practical program fitted to a child that had grown up like a weed—a program of physical training, combined with presumptive education and sure discipline. This program he set in motion by pulling his son out of bed at five in the morning, standing him upright, hurrying him into his clothes and leading him by the hand straight to the town pump. Here Sullivan Senior pumped vigorously until certain the water was of lowest temperature; then he gave unto the child to drink. The child, as commanded, drank the full cup, shuddered, and complained of the chill. Well, if he was chilly, he must run,—to establish circulation—again a new word. There was no help for it. After a sharp quarter mile, the son of Patrick Sullivan was convinced that "circulation" was now established, and said so. They settled to a brisk walk. At the end of two miles they came upon a narrow arm of the sea, which spread into a beautiful sequestered pool, at the point reached, with water deep, and clear green, and banks quite high. Strip! was the order. Strip it was. No sooner done than the high priest dexterously seized the neophyte, and, bracing himself, with a back-forward swing cast the youngster far out, saw him splash and disappear; then he dived, came up beside a wildly splashing sputtering unit, trod water, put the child in order, and with hand spread under his son's breast began to teach him the simple beginnings of scientific swimming. "Must not stay too long in the water," he said. "Would Sonny like a ride astride Papa's shoulders to a landing?" Sonny would and did.

[78]

He gloried as he felt beneath him the powerful heave and sink and heave of a fine swimmer, as he grasped his father's hair, and saw the bank approach.

On land he took note of his father's hairy chest, his satiny white skin and quick flexible muscles over which the sunshine danced with each movement. He had never seen a man completely stripped, and was pleased and vastly proud to have such a father, especially when the father, an object lesson in view, made exhibition dives and swam this way and that way in lithe mastery. And he asked his father to promise him he would teach him how to do these things, that he too might become a great swimmer. For he had a new ideal now, an ideal upsprung in a morning's hour—a vision of a company of naked mighty men, with power to do splendid things with their bodies.

The return journey passed quickly and excitedly. Would Papa take him again to the pool? Yes, Papa would take him every morning to the pool. And would he have to swallow any more salt water? Not unless he opened his mouth at the wrong time. And why was the water salt, and why did it tingle the skin so queerly? Because it was sea water. And would Papa show him the sea? Yes, Papa would show him the sea, and ships under sail; and Papa would some day take him to the shipyards where ships were built. Ah, what prospects of delight! How big the world was growing, how fast the world was spreading. Had not Papa promised him?

The dingy hotel loomed ahead; a mighty craving arose. To the child, the bowl of cold oatmeal was super-manna. Father's dietary law was strict; simple foods, no coffee, no tea, no pastry, a little meat; and strictly taboo was white flour bread, for the millers had even then begun their work; lots of milk, some brown sugar, plenty of greens and fruit, potatoes only when baked, or boiled in their jackets and so eaten; no greasy things; and at times a tiny sip of claret as a bonus. His time-law for young people was: Taps at eight o'clock, reveille five o'clock. He put his son through a fine and highly varied course of calisthenics to make him supple and resilient. He took him daily to the pump and the pool, made of him for his age a competent diver and swimmer, made him vault fences, throw stones at a mark; taught him to walk properly —head up, chin in, chest out; to stride easily from the hip, loose in the shoulders. And the child worked with gusto; it became play; for the father did all these things with him jointly—they even ran races together, and threw stones at marks, in competition. Surely it was intensive training; but Father was wise in these respects: He knew that where there was hard work, there must also be leisure and relaxation, and time for carefree play. Father was forty-five then, and wondrous wise for his day and generation. To be sure his profession gave him the time to spare.

So, the family frequently went a-picnicking to the lovely banks of the Merrimac River, and elsewhere to shady groves and beauty spots.

This Sunday, it was the first trip to the Merrimac— a clear, calm summer day, not too warm.

They found, at the bend of the river, a bit of greensward, sufficiently shaded, yet leaving an open view of the woods across the water.

The great stream flowed by tranquilly: its dark brown mirror solemnly picturing woods and sky.

The child had never seen a river. Was it not wonderful, this river so wide, so dark, so silent, so swift in its flow? How could such things be? Why had he not known?

Here and there a small fish jumped, leaving a pretty circle of ripples where it fell; and then arose into the air an enormous sturgeon, to fall heavily back, making a great hole whence came a rush of circles expanding magically to the shores, causing sky and trees to totter and twist; then all would be calm again and silent, as the great stream flowed on and on careless of trifles; on and on, so Papa said, until its waters should mingle with the sea's; on and on, day and night, winter and summer, year after year, before we were born, when we are gone, so Papa said, its waters had flowed and would evermore flow to the sea.

Papa and Mamma had begun to draw pictures of the opposite shore, and were absorbed in the doing.

The child watched sturgeon after sturgeon leap and fall; they seemed to shoot out of the water's surface. He had never seen such big strong fishes; he had seen nothing larger than minnows and sunfish in South Reading. But here on this river everything was large.

So thinking he wandered downstream along the water's edge, musing about South Reading, recalling his rivulet, his dam, his marsh. How small they seemed. And then there arose his tall, slender elm, his great ash tree to comfort him. Mechanically he ascended a hill, entered a heavy grove, musing, as he went, upon the great river Merrimac; lost in the thought that the world about him was growing so large that it seemed out of proportion to him—too great for his little size, too bewildering for his untutored mind. Meanwhile something large, something dark was approaching unperceived; something ominous, something sinister that silently aroused him to a sense of its presence. He became aware; he peered through the foliage. What was it? He could not quite see; he could not make out; except that it was huge, long and dark. He thought of turning back, for he was but a little boy, alone in the woods bordering a dark-running river whose power had stilled him, and the lonely grove that stilled him; he was high strung with awe; he could glimpse the river; he was moving forward, unthinkingly, even while he thought of turning back. The dark thing came ever nearer, nearer in the stillness, became broader, looming, and then it changed itself into full view—an enormous terrifying mass that overhung the broad river from bank to bank.

The child's anxious heart hurt him. What could this monster mean? He tried to call for Papa, but found no voice. He wished to cry out but could not. He saw great iron chains hanging in the air. How could iron chains hang in the air? He thought of Julia's fairy tales and what the giants did. Might there be a fairy in the woods nearby? And then he saw a long flat thing under the chains; and this thing too seemed to float in the air; and then he saw two great stone towers taller than the trees. Could these be the giants? And then of a sudden, mystery of mysteries, he saw a troll, not much bigger than a man, come out of the fairy forest, driving a fairy team.

The troll went right across on the flat thing that floated in the air, and vanished. This must be the land of enchantment that Julia told about. A wicked wizard has done this thing. A giant will come soon to eat up a little boy. And the trees murmured: "Yes; a wicked wizard has done this thing—a giant will come to eat up a little boy—good-bye, little boy"—and the river said: "Good-bye little boy"—and the great iron chains said: "Good-bye little boy." The child shrieked: "Papa! Papa! Papa!" Instanter Papa appeared—ah, the good fairy had waved her wand in the enchanted wood! Papa had become concerned at the child's long absence, and was angry that his son should have gone away without asking permission. He had intended to spank the child; but one look at that upturned face, at those eyes glazed with approaching madness halted him in alarm. "What's the matter, Sonny? Did something frighten you?" "Oh, Papa, Papa, see the big iron chains hanging in the air, see the two giants turned to stone, see the flat thing floating in the air. A troll just came over it with horses and wagon. I am to be eaten up by a giant. The troll with the magic wagon is coming to get me now. I am to be eaten by a giant, Papa; the trees have just said good-bye, little boy; the river has said good-bye, little boy; Oh, Papa, did the good fairy send you to save me?" Papa, thoroughly alarmed, impulsively said: "Yes, dear"; then, soothingly: "Sonny, you must not listen any more in memory to Julia's Irish tales. They are not true, now. There are not any giants or goblins, or trolls or elves or even fairies any more anywhere. They lived only in people's fancy long ago, when Ireland was young. It is only the *tales* that are told today—for the Irish have ever loved romance. Their heads are filled with queer notions. They imagine things that are not so. Papa lived in Ireland once; he knows what is true. Now we will go to the bridge and see it all." "And what is a bridge, Papa?" "That is what you are to see. Don't be afraid. It won't hurt you." So they went to the nearby bridge.

As they crossed to the Amesbury side the Father felt the nervous clutch of his child's hand about his forefinger. His own mind began to clear; now the child's mind must be cleared. So he explained that the roadway of the bridge was just like any other road, only it was held up over the river by the big iron chains; that the big iron chains did not float in the air but were held up by the stone towers over the top of which they passed and were anchored firmly into the ground at each end beyond the towers; that the road-bed was hung to the chains so it would not fall into the river. That the bridge was so strong that many people and loaded teams could pass over it at the same time; and as he said this, happily some teams and people came and went. Father was clever in making simple explanations of things he knew something about. This expertness came of his long training in teaching little tots to dance. His skill and patience in this respect were fine art. So, gradually, he brought his son out of nightmare-land into the daylight of reality. For shameful fear, he substituted in his son's heart confidence and courage. Thus was the child-mind freed again to wonder what men could do; to adjust itself to the greater world into which it had been suddenly catapulted from South Reading's tiny world. Within that little spot of earth he had never seen a river, never a bridge, for neither river nor bridge were there to be seen. On their way to rejoin Mamma, the child turned backward to gaze in awe and love upon the great suspension bridge. There, again, it hung in air —beautiful in power. The sweep of the chains so lovely, the roadway barely touching the banks. And to think it was made by men! How great must men be, how wonderful; how powerful, that they could make such a bridge; and again he worshipped the worker.

Mamma had become alarmed; but Father, on the approach, gave her a hush-sign. Evening was on the wing; dew was in the air; dark Merrimac still flowed, sturgeons still leaped high, a cricket chirped its first, cheerful note. They returned to the dismal house of flour and water.

This child was soon abed; the father sank into deep thought: This would never do; the boy must be protected against himself; he was overexciteable; he must not be let go into the woods alone, nor near any mystic thing. His blood must be cooled—more water; no meat; his mind must be directed to everyday things; he would take him into the active world, to the ship-yards, to see ships a-building; he would take him to Plum Island, to get the salt sea air, to see the real ocean, with its ships coming and going under full sail; he would explain all these practical things to him and keep his mind wholesome; he must be educated to realities, disciplined, shown life as it is. And Father, thus ruminating, turned in.

Now they are at the shipyards, father and son. Four or five ships are in progress on the ways; others are being rigged in the slips. One is a skeleton, another almost ready to launch. There is much hubbub; men going here and there. The strident song of the caulking iron saws the air; odor of tar everywhere; fine view of the harbor, craft of all kinds moving this way and that—some at anchor. Here in the shipyard were crowds of men working, doing many things, all moving at the same time—all urging toward a great end. The child was in a seventh heaven; here were his beloved strong men, the workers—his idols. What a great world it was into which he had been thrust— the great river, the wonderful bridge, the harbor, the full rigged ships so gallantly moving. And what new words too—circulation, calisthenics, catenary, dietary, suspension bridge and others, that seemed very long, very strange indeed. Was he also entering a world of words? Were there many more such words?

Eagerly he watched a man working with an adze. The man was lying on his back and chipping overhead. Then the man turned on his side and chipped sidewise; then he chipped between his feet and in front of his feet. Was it not wonderful? He had never seen an adze, nor a man at work with an adze. Here, the man took off heavy chips and there only thin shavings; was it not wonderful? He wished to talk to the man, but the man was too busy; perhaps the man wished to keep his feet to walk home with. And all the other men were too busy to talk to him; they did not seem to know he was there, except one man near a kettle of hot tar who told him to get out of the way. And there were men boring holes in great planks; other men steaming planks, other men carrying planks, other men bending the planks against the ribs of the ship, other men driving in with sledge hammers great iron bolts to keep the planks in place, and these men, he guessed, had no time to talk to him. He wondered why the ships were all set stern-end toward the water. He wondered how "they" were going to get them into the water. And there were men who drove oakum —a new word—into the joints between the planks. They did it with a thin wedge and a funny looking mallet, and made a sound that beat upon his ear drums. He could get near enough to some of these men to talk to them, but they were too busy to hear him; and he saw men painting another ship which was all ready to be pushed into the water. And there was such a rush and crowd of things that were new to him that he was joyfully dazed—very happy, very serious.

He had his first view of the power of concerted action; but he did not look at it that way. To him it seemed the work of individual men working separately, or of small groups of men helping each other —a great crowd of men each doing his own work in his own way. To be sure, he saw men walking about who spoke to the workmen, and the workmen always had to listen to these men. In the great confusion he had not sensed order, and therefore did not ask Papa about it. Yet he saw the ships grow, and saw the workmen make them grow.

He walked all over the place with Papa, ever inquisitive, peering here and there. The hum of work was everywhere. He keenly sensed its greatness. What could men not do if they could do this, and if they could make a great bridge—suspended in the air over the Merrimac. He poured forth his questions and Papa answered them pretty well, but a bit pedantically where he was not posted. He used too many big words. He concealed with them what he did not know.

A few days later father and son saw the launching of a ship, and the child had another spasm of wonder, for the ship seemed to him to launch itself; he did not see any men pushing it, and Father recited something about "she seems to feel the thrill of life along her keel," which he said was poetry because it all rhymed, so the child learned at once what poetry was —it was a *new word*. And again came the regular questionnaire, and again Father did his best, using however, so many strange long words that the child became drugged and drowsy with them and said he wanted to go home; so they both, father and son, went home.

And soon the child began to tease to be taken to Plum Island, to see the ocean his father had talked about. Strangely enough there wasn't any ocean at South Reading, any more than there was a great river and a wonderful bridge there; any more than there was a great shipyard and a great harbor. At South Reading there was only a railroad and two ponds—a big pond and a little pond and some hills. So the son, accompanied by the father, went to Plum Island, for he had said, "This is to be mine, isn't it, Papa?" And the father had relaxed at the idea.

There they stood, in a stiff salt breeze, on the sharply sloping rounded beach; some drifting clouds in a pale sky, some ships in the offing. True, he had seen the ocean at Cape Ann, seen it in furious, terrifying, storming moods; seen it as huge glossy ground swells, as glancing, dancing wavelets in the sunshine; but that was long, long ago when he was three; he had wholly

forgotten what happened when he was three—and
four—and five. He had forgotten even that he had
fallen into a well there. He had, like the workmen
in the shipyard, been too busy—all these years, these
months, these days.

Even South Reading was fading before the glory of
the new-risen day; this engulfing splendor of Newburyport, as they stood there, on the hard wet sand, two
figures solitary, a mere speck, a minute accent on the
monotonous miles of beach and pounding surf. The
child looked far seaward, without emotion, save a sense
of dull platitude, of endless nothingness, of meaning-
less extension. The sea was merely rough, without
mood, dull in color, spotted here and there by a cloud's
shadow. It left him indifferent, all except the green
and white combing surf which was in merry mood.
He wished to wade in but Father said positively no,
the beach was too steep, the undertow too strong.
Undertow? Undertow?—another word—more explanations. He built sand forts which the rising tide
made short work of; he ran up and down the beach,
waded in the dry sand, found some wild cranberry
bushes. He ran back to Papa who was wrapped in
thought, standing with folded arms, facing the sea.
Far to the east, far over the waters lay Ireland, he
said to his son. The son looked for Ireland; it was
not to be seen; but he cried out of a sudden: "Papa,
some of those ships are sinking! One is all gone but
the top of the masts; one is just beginning to sink!"
Father, who wished to educate his son, now found
his work cut out for him. How explain the curvature
of the sea? How explain the horizon? How prove
that the ships were not sinking? He went at it bravely,

patiently, doggedly, step by step; he even made diagrams on his drawing pad. Little by little the child grasped the idea; he brightened with intelligence. His Father had opened for him then and there a new, an utterly unsuspected world—the world of pure knowledge—vaster than the sea, vaster than the sky. And for the child, the portal to that limitless world was an illusion—a sinking ship.

Now it was time to return to Boston. The school must open soon. In the bustle of preparation the day he was *seven* passed unnoticed even by himself. Newburyport departed—Boston came.

PLATE 6. Walker Warehouse, 200-214 South Market
Street, Chicago. 1888-89. Demolished in 1953.
View from the southeast.

PLATE 7. Walker Warehouse (see Plate 6). Impost on east facade.

PLATE 8. Walker Warehouse (see Plate 6). Detail from an impost on the north facade.

PLATE 9. Martin Ryerson Tomb, Graceland Cemetery, Chicago. 1889. Constructed of highly-polished blue-black Quincy granite.

CHAPTER VI

Boston

AS ONE in tranquillity gazes into the crystal depths
called Memory, in search of sights and sounds
and colors long since physically passed out from
what is otherwise called memory; when one is intent,
not upon recalling but upon re-entering, he finds a
double motion setting in. While out of the gray sur-
face-obscurity of supposed oblivion, there emerges to
his view, as through a thinning haze, a broad vision
assuming the color and movement of a life once lived,
of a world once seen and felt to be real, so likewise,
the intensive soul moves eagerly forward descending
through intervening atmospheric depths toward this
oncoming solid reality of time and place, a reality growing clearer, more colorful, more vibrant, more alluring,
more convincing—filling the eye, the ear with sound
and color and movement, with broad expanses, with
minute details, with villages and cities, farms and
work shops, men and women densely gathered or
widely scattered, and children, little children always
and everywhere. So moving, the two great illusions,
the two dreams of the single dreamer, accelerating,
rush onward, and vanish both into a single life which
is but a dream;—the dream of the past enfolding and
possessing the dreamer of today; the dreamer of today
enveloping, entering and possessing the dream-reality
of the past; all within the inscrutable stillness of a
power unknown, within which we float, with our all,
and believe ourselves real. We believe in our reality
in our strenuous hours, in our practical doings, in our
declamatory moments, and even in our hours of silence.

In sleep there come images before us, floating by, irretrievable, or steadfastly convincing; and these we speak
of casually as dreams.   We are willing even to extend
the idea of dream to man's ambition.   We say such
or such a man had or has dreams of empire, of dominion, of achievement, of fulfilment of this or that sort.
And occasionally we acknowledge, upon information,
that such dream had taken full possession not of a man
we read about, or see in the plenitude of his power,
but that the dream arose within a child, in broad daylight—as night-dreams do in their way—and aroused
in him a passionate desire.

We do not associate the idea of dream with our
strenuous hours of thought and deed in the selfsame
broad daylight.   Nor do we see the stars at noon—
but they are there.   So is a dream there, within every
human, ever—day and night unceasingly.

We impeach the dream idea, calling certain men
"Dreamers."   We do this in derision—much as the
pot might call the kettle black.   We do not suspect
that we could not put one foot forth before the other
were we not dreaming; so artificial and sophisticated
are we in our practical moments.   And it is even so
as we forget that each of us was once a child; even
as we banish the thought, as crude, that out of that
very child we have grown inevitably to be what we
are; that the thoughts, the feelings, the emotions, the
reactions, the waking dreams of that child have gov-
erned and determined us, willy-nilly, through the course
of our lives and careers with compelling power—that
what the child accepted we accept; that what the child
rejected we reject.

Thus from the abysm of Memory's stillness, that child comes into being within Life's dream, within the dream of eternal time and space; and in him we behold what we were and still are. Environment may influence but it cannot alter. For it is the child in multiple and in multiple series that creates the flowing environment of thought and deed that shall continuously mature in its due time. It is the moving child-in-multiple of long ago that created for us the basic environment within which we now live. Thus in a memory-mirror may we re-discover ourselves. Expecting to find therein a true reflection of ourselves as we believe we are, the image dissolves as the features of a long forgotten child confront us. Deny him, we dare not.

Turning about from self-contemplation we find children everywhere. We see the tidal wave of children moving on and on, we partly under their dominion, they partly under ours. But theirs is the new, ours the old; and, as ancients, we move on, unchanged from the children that we were—leaving our thoughts and deeds as a beaten trail behind us.

With this image in view the narrator has laid extended stress upon an authentic study of child life. Maturing years have made it but too clear that only on such foundation, resting deep within the vast-moving and timeless heritage of Instinct and Intellect, might a valid superstructure be reared into the light of our day. Men in their fatuity believe that they cause replicas of themselves to be born of woman; that they create children like themselves for themselves. They are picturesquely unaware, in mass, that they are but instrumental, normally, in bringing forth full grown men and women whom they may never see, but who, it must be so, are in essence of being with them at birth, specifically differing from them. Hence the unceasing flood of child personalities, accepting or rejecting influences in an environment they had no share in making. Historically, and in mass, victims of Fate rather than Masters of Destiny. For Destiny and Fate alike have birth in what is accepted or rejected by the child.

*   *   *

With this digression as a commentary we may now resume in its natural course the story of a growing child well known to us, and proceed to extend that series of rejections and acceptances—beginning in his infancy—into an ever enlarging world of fact and fiction until we may perchance obtain a glimpse of what they really were, and of their significance in determining his onward drift—a drift that as yet has developed no self-defined momentum.

Shortly after their return to Boston from Newburyport, the father, for reasons of his own, whatever they were, decided to move his family to Halifax, Nova Scotia. They were away six months.

*   *   *

A small boy stood on the dock at Eastport, Maine, holding in his hand a huge greengage plum. The same small boy suffered and saw the agonies of those who cross the Bay of Fundy. He saw and lived in a hotel in Halifax, where an Academy was opened. Later he endured in patience the terrible discipline of his father, who in below zero weather walked him for miles along the bleak "Northwest Arm," to return with white cheeks and nose, only to be told to wash his face in snow—the father doing the like. He saw his gods blasting a deep trench for water pipe through the solid slate ledge, and again he marvelled at what men could do. He saw the great citadel crowning the heights, and from it, he viewed the harbor. Then came calamity. Mamma was taken down with diphtheria; and he saw the great and grand Newfoundland dog, that had welcomed them effusively on their arrival and had adopted them at once, lying day after day, night after night, faithfully guarding her chamber door. Mamma recovered; but her illness was prophetic of change.

In the spring they returned to Boston, and Louis was sent to live with his grandparents in South Reading, as before, with the proviso that he was to return to his parents in the fall. He became at once deeply immersed in the miniature activities of the farm, taking the initiative wherever he could, doing small things with large enthusiasm. He did not consider such things work, but joy. He was physically active and mentally active too. He was always excited in his work and always constructive. As Grandpa also worked, they became great pals, and planned and worked together. His natural surroundings became less mystical to him. He held them in affection, but no longer in dreamy wonder. The delicate bloom of early childhood was passing, while the vigor and aggressiveness of budding boyhood were rising as branches from the same deep root. His love of the open remained constant and intense. He was developing pride, ambition, and a sense of growing power over material things. The desire some day to exercise such power to the full became in him a definitive dream, within which, unnoticed, was resident the glow of a deeper power—a power that had suffused a swiftly-moving, vocal springtime, which he had seen and heard and lived in this same spot.

Grandpa did not bother about the child's education, for, being wise, he knew the child was daily self-acquiring an education exactly suited to his temperament and years. But Grandmamma believed otherwise. She thought her grandson needed polish, and that he should now begin a systematic study of the French language. Louis was willing enough and started in gaily. He liked the sound, and the words in italics looked pretty; all went well for a while. As he got in deeper he began to be oppressed by the inanities of the grammar-book, and the imbecilities of a sort of first reader in which a wax-work father takes his wax children on daily promenades, explaining to them as they go, in terms of unctuous morality, the works of the Creator, and drawing therefrom, as from a spool, an endless thread of pious banalities. Louis rebelled. He declared he was an AMERICAN BOY!—that none of his playmates spoke French—why should *he?* Grandmamma, in habitual indulgence, discontinued polishing. She could not enter the child-mind. To her, her grandson was an object of boundless love— and little more; and yet this little more was an impassable gulf, lying as a chasm between old age gently petrifying in the thoughts of her own childhood, and a vigorous young animal with thoughts and an impetuous will of his own. And he in turn held his grandmamma to be the sweetest of mortals—and little more.

Thus summer passed on broad pinions sweeping, and Louis saw it moving thus. He *saw* such things. Beneath all the overlay the child was a mystic; inarticulate, wondering, believing. These fleeting revelations of Life came and went as interludes within the chosen practicalities of his realistic and material activity. He had rather help build a stone wall than listen to a poem—all except the fairy tales that Julia told—for here was Romance—and romance he could not withstand.

One morning;—it happened to be September 3rd of that year,—Louis Henri Sullivan arose early and sallied forth in pomp and pride. On the Stoneham road he met a farmer friend:

Hello! Do you know I am eight years old today?

No, wall, wall, that's fine. Heow old did yeh say yeh be?

I am Eight! Don't you think I'm a big boy now? Do you want to feel my muscle?

My sakes—but yeh aire strong!

Yes I am. I can lift a stone almost as big as my grandfather can; but of course he's older.

How old did yeh say yeh be?

I say I am eight years old today and I want you to know it. Do you want to pound my chest?

Can't say's I do.

You may pound my chest as hard as you like and I won't say a word. Have you noticed my new boots? It's my first pair. My grandma gave them to me for my birthday.

No I hadn't saw them.

Well, look at them now. See; they're copper-toed
and have red tops. Don't you think they're fine?
Yaas; how old did yeh say yeh be? I think yeh
got a mighty fine granny t'give yeh them boots.

And the Ancient doddered down the road dustily
regurgitating the thoughts of his childhood now become decayed and senile; while bounding boyhood clat-
tered on, from house to house, from field to field, wherever might be found man, woman, or child to whom
he might sing his own saga in vainglory. For was he
not right? Was he not Eight? Was he not hero-
ically aware that that day he was crossing the invisible
line between childhood and boyhood? Were not the
gaudy boots his plain certificate of valor and of deeds
done and to be done? Were they not for him symbols of that manhood toward which he so ardently
yearned that his pride might come to the full? He
said it was so. In this joyous mood was his saga sung,
as of one with a growing faith.

Then came, as it were, a bugle call from the south.
He answered the call in person. Boston City swallowed him up.

The effect was immediately disastrous. As one
might move a flourishing plant from the open to a dark
cellar, and imprison it there, so the miasma of the big
city poisoned a small boy acutely sensitive to his surroundings. He mildewed; and the leaves and buds of
ambition fell from him. In those about him, already
city-poisoned, even in his own kin, he found no solace,
and ceased openly to lament. Against the big city
his heart swelled in impatient, impotent rebellion. Its
many streets, its crooked streets, its filthy streets, lined

with stupid houses crowded together shoulder to shoulder like selfish hogs upon these trough-like lanes, irritated him, suffocated him; the crowds of people, and wagons, hurrying here and there so aimlessly—as it appeared to him —confused and overwhelmed him, arousing amazement, nausea and dismay. As he thought of the color, the open beauty of his beloved South Reading, and the great grand doings of Newburyport, where men did things; where there was obvious, purposeful action; an exhibit of sublime power; the city of Boston seemed a thing already in decay. He was so saddened, so bewildered, so grieved, that his sorrow, his bitter disappointment, could find no adequate utterance and relief. Hence he kept it all within himself, and became drugged to the point of lassitude and despair. The prospect of a whole winter to be spent within these confines, shut out from the open world that had been growing so large and splendid for him, filled him at times with a sudden frantic desire to escape. Had not his father at once taken up again the rigorous training of cold baths and outdoor exercise, had he not taken him on long walks to Roxbury, to Dorchester, even to Brookline, where the boy might see a bit of green and an opening-up of things, the boy would surely have carried out his resolution to run away. To run where? Anywhere to liberty and freedom!

He had partly revived from the first shock, when his ruthless father placed him in the Brimmer School on Common Street. Louis found it vile; unspeakably gloomy; a filthy prison for children. He learned nothing. There was no one to teach him, and what he saw there shall not be recorded here. So passed the winter; Louis looking, ever aimlessly, yearning, for *a teacher*. As a rose springs upward from the muck and puts forth gracious blooming, even so out of the muck of this school a re-action sprang up, a fervent hungered yearning within, for a kindred spirit to arise that might illumine him and in whom he might rejoice; a spirit utterly human that would break down the dam made within him by sanctioned suppressions and routine, that there might pour out of him the gathered cesspool, and the waters of his life again flow on. Of such a nature was the hunger of a well-fed child.

As the Boston winter of '64 was groaning on its way to the tomb of all winters, Mamma was again stricken with diphtheria; and again she recovered. The city winter passed, a city springtime passed. With vacation at hand, Louis returned to his grandparents, resumed his activities now enlarged in scope, and in the fall returned to the City, his wounds somewhat healed. He was immediately placed in the newly organized Rice School—temporarily housed in another gloomy structure, but not so foul—at that time situated on the west side of Washington Street and a short distance south of Dover Street. Here he learned nothing at first except in-so-far as there was a sort of mechanical infiltration going on. But, at a nearby book store, "Beadle's Dime Novels" appeared in a whirlwind of popularity. Louis Sullivan pounced upon them. He devoured the raw melodramas and cried for more. Here at last was Romance! Here again were great men doing great deeds. Here was action in the open. He could live these scenes. He could visualize these acts even within the deadly philistine air of Washington Street and its Rice School where he was

supposed to know that 2:4:: 4:8. He did not especially care for the standardized lady in the case who
was always ravishingly beautiful and always eighteen;
and to the villain he was sometimes lenient, but the
hero, that magnificent man-god whose ear had just
been grazed by the arrow of a huge red savage—him
he took to his bosom. He got a thrill out of every
page, which was more than he ever got out of the
school. He was to remain at this school for several
years, during which time he slowly became citified. His
activities naturally spread over an ever widening field;
and these years were filled with multifarious details
large and small. His geographical ventures extended
from South Reading as a center to Stoneham, Woburn,
North Reading, Saugus and Ipswich; and from Boston as a center to Rockport, Gloucester, Marblehead,
Salem, Lynn and Nahant; and southward into Jamaica
Plain. Between Boston and South Reading were dotted, as villages or hamlets, Somerville, Malden, Mel-
rose, Greenville and South Reading Junction. West
of the Junction was a small affair called Crystal Lake,
with bare and sterile surroundings, including an ice-
house on its northern shore. The big pond to the north
of South Reading—then a village of possibly two
thousand souls—was officially known as Lake Quannapowitt. From the western shore of this lake projected
a promontory, and within this promontory was a cemetery.

During these years, Louis Sullivan, always inquisitive and foolhardily curious, had ferreted out every
street, alley and blind court, and dock and wharf from
end to end and crosswise within the limits of Boston,
and had made partial explorations of Charlestown,

Chelsea, and South Boston. Thus there gradually arose within his consciousness a clearing sense of what a city meant objectively as a solid conglomerate of diverse and more or less intricate activities. He began indeed to sense the city as a power—unknown to him before— a power new-risen above his horizon; a power that extended the range and amplified the content of his own child-dream of power as he had seen it manifested in the open within the splendid rhythm of the march of the seasons. Nevertheless, he saw, in his boy-way, and felt it strongly, a great mysterious contrast between the two. In the open all was free, expansive and luminous. In the city all was contraction, density, limitation, and a cruel concentration. He felt that between himself and the city, as such, lay a harsh antagonism that seemed forever insoluble; as though men had made the city when they were mad; and that as it grew under their hands it had mastered and confined them. Yet men, women and children seemed to move about freely enough at certain hours. These waves of doubt and apprehension came and passed at intervals, but each wave left its precipitate, in solution as it were, in the boy's quizzical mind. He became less and less unfriendly toward the school, as sporadic knowledge crept out of his books and took on a certain segregated appearance of validity, having slight connection, however, with his own world. He ceased to be wholly rebellious, and took his small doses of formal routine education much as he might take a medicine supposedly for his good. Thus far his father had been his only successful teacher.

The boy had acquired and was continuing to acquire the education he possessed partly through a series of

shocks—frequently humiliating—which inverted his illusions into realities; partly through his own keen powers of observation, and perhaps something in the way
of intuition; but mainly and fundamentally through
his high sensitiveness to externals which, always with
him, took on character, definition and, as it were, a
personality. He was now ripe for another shock.

One day his father took him on a walk to South
Boston, and made him run up a high hill on the top
of which was a reservoir. This altitude reached, a
great view spread before them. The boy at once became exalted with awe at the living presence and
expanding power of Mother Earth. Never—since the
long forgotten days of Halifax—had he reached such
a peak of observation. His father's love for "scenery"
had taken them there. As the boy gazed in thrilling
wonder, his father called attention, one after another,
to special points of beauty in the land and water-
scape, finally coming around to the Blue Hills, which
indeed were blue and enchanting against the far horizon and its haze. After explaining the nature of the
haze, father called attention to two outstanding peaks,
near together but differing in size, and asked his son
a point-blank question: Which of the two hills is the
larger? His son walked straight into the trap, saying
that of course the larger one was the larger—why
did Papa ask? Then the trap fell—knocking Louis
senseless—for Papa said, (beyond a doubt maliciously
he said it) that *the smaller was the larger*. When
Louis came to, he protested vehemently; but Papa said
he had been there and knew. Then, relenting, believing he had carried his practical joke far enough, he
told his son, seriously, that the effect, the appearance,

the illusion was, in fact, due to what he called PER-SPECTIVE; and the nature of this particular perspective, and perspective in general, he explained with notable skill, simplicity, and with many objective instances. But Louis instead of receiving this information with acclaim and joy, as a new world opening before him, was deeply saddened and perturbed. His father, sincerely believing he was educating his own, came near to destroying him. He was no psychologist, he had indeed but little human sympathy or insight—hence he had no suspicion of what was going on beneath the surface of his own son. For had not that son built up a cherished world all his own, a world made up of dreams, of practicalities, of deep faith, of unalloyed acceptance of externals, only now to find that world trembling and tottering on its foundations, threatening to collapse upon him, or to vanish before this new and awful revelation from the unseen. This ghostly apparition which his father called "perspective" terrorized him. What his father said about it did not help. For behind the perspective that the father saw was a perspective that the child saw—invisible to the father. It was MYSTERY—a mystery that lay behind appearances, and within appearances, and in front of appearances, a mystery which if penetrated might explain and clarify all, as his father had explained and clarified a little. Did this mystery reside also in his lovely slender elm tree? Was his great friend the ash tree involved in mystery? Was the sunrise that had glorified him and the earth around him part of this mysterious perspective that lay behind appearances, that lay behind even the clear apparition his father called perspective? Must he lose his faith in what

seemed real? Was Boston itself and all within it but
a mask and a lie? Was there within it and behind it
a perspective, a mystery which if understood might
reveal and clarify it, making it intelligible? Could
this mystery be penetrated? He was determined it
should be, soon or late—and that he would do it. Thus
had a father's playful joke set up in a child a raging
fermentation. Such high-pitched emotion could not
last. Such vision was bound to fade. Such fear must
pass. And so it happened. The turmoil, the chaos
lasted but as the span of a day-dream. But within that
dream, within that turmoil, there awakened a deeper
dream that has not passed. Thus Louis Sullivan accepted and rejected; rejected and accepted.

He returned to the school and the streets which
were much the same thing to him. At recess he
promptly announced that he could lick any boy of his
size. Whereupon "his size" knocked him in the eye,
and the two "sizes" went at it, according to regulations which consisted in beginning fairly and ending
foully—two boys rolling over and over in the middle
of the street, in the center of an eager, urging, admir-
ing circle of excited ruffians of varied sizes, who cried
at the proper time: "He's had enough; let him up."
Sometimes Louis's prophecies were verified. Sometimes they proved unfortunate. But it was all the same,
all in the game; and there was established in the school
a "Who's Who" that never reached print. Moreover
there was established a Hierarchy in which each "who"
was definitely ranked according to the who's he could
lick, and the who's and sizes who could lick him. And
while all this was going on, Louis picked up, in addi-
tion to a bit of geography and arithmetic, every form

of profanity, every bit of slang, and every particle of verbal garbage he could assimilate. In other words he was one of the gang and a tough. But his honor required that he refrain from licking the good boys just because they were good—which could not be said of some.

He was progressing so well at school, his mother thought—for his teacher so certified for reasons unknown—perhaps to conceal the truth—that she believed it time he learn to play the piano. Louis thought otherwise. Mamma was stern, Louis yielded. Mamma promised it should be half an hour only, every day. She placed her watch in good faith on the piano shelf —fatal error—and the series began. It was not that Louis disliked music; quite the contrary. Had not his parents but recently taken him to Boston Music Hall, there to hear a great Oratorio rendered by the Handel and Haydn Society? Had he not been overwhelmed by the rich volume and splendor of choral harmonies —again a new and revealing world? Had he not thrilled to the call: "Lift up your heads, O ye gates; and be ye lift up, ye everlasting doors; and the King of Glory shall come in."

Was he not always teasing his mother to play for him any one of a group of brilliant five-fingered exercises arranged as stately composition? No; Louis loved his Mamma but hated the piano when annexed to himself. So the series moved on to disaster. The five-finger work bored him, the dinky tunes enraged him; he watched the watch, he kicked the piano, he struck false notes, he became utterly unruly; and at the agonizing end of one especially bad half-hour, Mamma burst into hysterical tears; and Louis, seeing the damage he had done, threw his arms about her neck and cried his heart out with her. Thus the series ended, by mutual understanding and Mamma's forgiveness—as Mamma's tears still flowed from bitterly swollen eyes, as she gazed blindly in unspeakable sorrow at her repentant but incorrigible son. But—let it be said in a whisper—Mamma should have known that Louis's hands were not made for the piano. Louis did not know it; yet there lay all the trouble.

Then the father thought he would teach his son drawing. His son thought otherwise. His son detested drawing. The prospect of copying a lithographic plate setting forth a mangle, a step-ladder, a table, a mop and a pail, was not alluring. Louis demurred. Father thought a thrashing would help along some. He started in. A she-wolf glared. He quailed—End of still-born drawing lesson. No series.

Meanwhile the name of the village of South Reading was, by popular vote, changed to Wakefield. Cyrus Wakefield, rattan magnate, thought it good business to offer a new town hall in exchange for his name. The townspeople thought so too. The deed was done; both deeds were done; and, as if on a magic carpet the farm that Louis had lived on floated from South Reading into Wakefield—meanwhile remaining stationary as of yore. This occurred in the summer of 1868 when Louis was in his twelfth year.

Meanwhile, also, in 1868, a new school building was in course of construction on new made land in the Back Bay district. It was to be up to date in all respects, and was to be called The Rice Grammar School Building.

In the winter of this year, Mamma, for the fifth

time, was stricken with diphtheria and her life despaired of. She pulled through on a perilous margin. Father, now thoroughly frightened, finally got it through his head that the east winds meant death. So in the summer of 1869 he moved his family to Chicago—leaving Louis behind, to live with his grandparents, and continue his education. Louis sobbed on his Mother's shoulder, but was much relieved to say to his father: Good-bye! Now he was free!

PLATE 10. Carrie Eliza Getty Tomb, Graceland Cemetery, Chicago. 1890. Constructed of large blocks of gray Bedford limestone.

PLATE 11. Getty Tomb (see Plate 10). Door, showing
pierced bronze outer gates.

PLATE 12. Getty Tomb (see Plate 10). Side lunette.

PLATE 13. Charlotte Dickson Wainwright Tomb, Bellefontaine Cemetery, St. Louis, Mo. 1892. Constructed of gray limestone.

CHAPTER VII

Boston

The New Rice Grammar School

ONE day, in Boston, a boy of nine was walking northward on the east side of Washington Street. Just then "Yankee Doodle" came along whistling his tune to a brisk step, a pair of boots slung over one shoulder of his faded blue jeans; and, under a stovepipe hat, much battered in the strife of years, this agile elderly man wore a grey chin beard after the manner of Uncle Sam. And thus went Yankee Doodle tirelessly up and down Washington Street, always on the east side of it, day after day, year after year. In a legendary sense he was a cobbler. The boy watched his kindly face approaching, and for the hundredth time admired in despair the clear sharp whistle which he had tried in vain to emulate; and, as Yankee passed on southward the boy turned east into South Bennett Street following the south sidewalk. About midway to Harrison Avenue a paper bag struck the sidewalk in front of him, burst, and hard candies scattered over the pavement. The boy, startled, looked around, and then up. In a second story window, straight across the way, appeared two fat bare arms, an immense bosom, a heavy, broad, red face, topped with straight black hair. A fat finger beckoned to him; a fat mouth said something to him; and at the doorway of the house was the number 22—the house he had been born in; but the silver nameplate marked P. Sullivan in black script was no longer there.

He had been led to the spot, which he had not seen

for years, by a revived memory of a sweet child named Alice Look, who lived next door when the two of them were three together. He had wished to see once more the sacred dwelling wherein she had lived and the walled yard in which she had mothered him and called him Papa in their play.

Much troubled, he walked on to Harrison Avenue, where Bennett Street ends its one block of length. There he noticed that the stately trees were bare of leaves and sickly to the sight, while on the twigs and among the branches and even on the trunks were hundreds of caterpillar nests which made the trees look old, poor and forsaken. While he was counting the nests on a single tree, caterpillars now and then would come slowly downward from the heights. Some of them would remain for a time in mid-air, suspended invisibly, before completing their descent, perchance upon a passerby. The boy was examining one of these caterpillars undulating upon his coat sleeve, when his quick ear detected the sound of snare-drums. Crowds began to gather on the sidewalks. Slowly the drums beat out their increasing sadness, pulsing to a labored measure of weariness and finality, as a faint bluish mass appeared vaguely in the north. The sidewalk crowds became dense—men, women and children stood very still. Onward, into distinctness and solidity, came the mass of faded blue undulating to the pathos of the drums. The drum corps passed—and in the growing silence came on and passed ranks of wearied men in faded blue, arms at right shoulder, faces weather-beaten, a tired slow tread, measured as a time-beat on the pavement, the one-two of many souls. And to these men, as they marched, clung women shabbily clothed,

[110]

with shawls drawn over their heads, moving on in a way tragically sad and glad, while to the skirts of many of these women clung dirty children. Thus moved in regular mass and in silence a regiment of veterans, their women, their children, passing onward between two tense rows of onlooking men, women and children, triple deep, many of them in tears. So vivid was this spectacle, so heartrending, so new this aching drama of return, that the boy, leaning against a caterpillared tree, overflowed with compassion. When he had ceased weeping upon his coat sleeve, Harrison Avenue was vacant; but not so the boy—he in fullness of sympathy was ill with the thought of what all this might mean. What was the mystery that lay behind these men in faded blue? He found no sufficing answer. The men had been mustered out, he had been told; that was all.

He chafed until he got permission to go to South Reading for a week end; ostensibly to visit the grandparents, surreptitiously to visit Julia, to whom alone he could bare his heart. He knew in advance what Grandpa would say; he knew in advance what Grandma would say; he wished eagerly to learn what Julia might say. So after earnest greetings with Grandpa and Grandma he slipped quietly to the kitchen. Julia was not there. He moved to the barn; Julia was not there. Then, in dime-novel fashion he made a detour through the "old" orchard, dodging from tree to tree in Indian fashion, examining the grass, crawling slowly on all fours, bent on surprise, signalling to an imagined companion in the rear, cautiously advancing until he caught a glimpse of a broad back, topped with massy hair on fire. He approached at a flat crawl and, from behind the next tree, saw Julia sitting on a milking stool peeling potatoes. Now came the villain's mad rush. Julia was seized savagely—with an arm around her neck, her head pulled back, her face kissed all over, her hair roughly tousled, her shoulder pushed hard, her stool kicked from under her as Louis, in a warwhoop of joy, hailed her as Ireland's hope, Queen of the orchard, and was greatly pleased.

Not so Erin's daughter. Sitting broadly on the grass, shaking a clenched fist, she screamed: "Ye rat, ye vile spalpeen. To think o' the likes o' ye takin' me unawares; and ye've upset the spuds and me pan of fresh water. May the divil fly away with ye. Get y'self out o' here before I smash ye with the stool"; and Julia's language became violent in a torrent of brogue, as, madly erect, she swung the stool and let fly while Louis danced about her singing an impudent Irish song he had learned from her. Then Julia sat largely down again in the grass, gasping for breath, while Louis went for the distant stool. Grandpa passed that way, remarking simply: "Ah, I *hear* you and Julia are visiting today." Louis walked up to Julia and said, in a manner: "Julia Head, I now present you with this stool. It is far less beautiful than yourself, but in its humble way, it is as useful as your own valued activities, inasmuch as it, on many an occasion, has served as your main stay while you were drawing from our gentle kine the day's accumulations. Will you accept this emblem of industry in the same simplicity of spirit with which it is offered you?" Julia, tired of ranting, laughed. "Sure," she said, " 'tis well ye know that had ye come at me dacently, it's a hearty welcome I'd a given ye." And she resumed operations, still sitting, the pan of spuds resting upon her enormous thighs. And Louis sat down meekly beside her, his small hand barely touching the expanse of freckled arm. He said he was sorry, and went on to pacify her. He used Gaelic words she had taught him, words romantically tender and sweet. Julia softened. With both hands she turned his face toward her; looked at him roguishly:

"Now what the divil is it ye want?"

"Julia, tell me a fairy story, won't you? Just a little one, won't you, Julia?"

"Divil a fairy tale there'll be told this day! Tell me about Boston. I've a brother working there. I want ye to find how he's getting on. His name's Eugene Head. He's younger than meself, he's only here wan year. He's tendin' bar in a saloon on Tremont Street near King's Chapel. I've heard he's steady and don't drink; and I've heard, too, that he knocks down quite a bit. Naw! I don't mean that he knocks down people. I shouldn't be talking such things t'ye anyway. It's sorry I am I said a word. But Boston is a hell ye know."

Then Louis opened the subject nearest his heart. He told her all about the soldiers in faded blue, and the wives and children hanging to them. What did it all mean? Why was it so sad; why did he have to cry?

"Well, Louis dear, ye know war's a sad business; those men ye saw had just been mustered out of the army; they were good fighting men, but all tired out. From the shawls the women wore and the dirty childer, I know the whole crowd was Irish and poor; and as everyone knows, the Irish won the war. Think of it! Holy Virgin!—the Irish fighting for the naygers! What will it be next time?"

"But, Julia, what was it all for? What was back of it all?"

"I'll not be telling ye what was back of it all, tho' well I know. I'll waste no breath on one who has no moind. Besides you're too young and ye have no education. Ye wouldn't understand. Why the divil don't ye stick hard to yer books, and learn? What in the name of all the saints d'ye think your father is spending his good money on ye furr? Filling yer belly with food, giving ye a good, clane bed to sleep in, putting nice clothes on ye, buying ye books, except that he wants ye to have an education? The Irish are proud of education, and yer father's a proud man, and he wants to be proud of his son. In God's name why don't ye do yure share? Ye remember the tale, I told ye of the man who looked too long at the moon? It's a tender heart indade, ye had likewise to be lookin' at thim dirty childer hangin' to the mithers' skirts! It's a big heart ye had and a fine education ye have that ye didn't think at wanst whin ye saw thim that ye haven't a care in the world, that ye've niver known rale hunger, niver a rale sorrow, niver a heart-break, niver despair; niver heard the wolf bark at the doore as yer blood went cold! And yerself, Louis, wid yere big heart and small head couldn't see with yer own eyes and without any books at all, that thim very childer was part of what as ye say lies behind it all? God! me heart aches in the tellin; for the min ye saw come back wuz not all the min that wint out; but I'm through. I'll tell ye no more of what lies behind it all; but I'll tell ye some more about education, for I want to knock a bit of sinse into yure empty skull. Yere all sintiment, Louis, and no mercy. You've kissed the Blarney Stone right well, and ye kicked the milking stool from under me.

"Now the story I'm to tell ye I got from one of me girl friends whose brother said he knew the man by reputayshun, and that he came from County Kerry where the Lakes of Killarney a're I've told ye so mooch about, and I suppose ye've forgotten it all; and faith, I have me doubts, with yere scatter brains if ye can say fer a truth wither Ireland's this side o' the water or the other. Now its not meself as'll make a short story long nor a long story short, so I'll tell it in the words I heard it.

"This man from Kerry was in some way connected with the army, as most of the Irish were, for they're natural fighting min from the oldest times. And wan day as he was out a-walking fer his health, and faring to and fro, he came upon a blanket lying on the ground; and at once he picked it up and with great loud laughter he sed, sed he: Sure I've found me blanket with me name upon it: U fer Patrick and S for McCarty; sure edication's a foine thing, as me faather before me wud say."

"Oh, Julia, I don't believe that's true. That's just another Irish yarn."

"Will, maybe it isn't true and maybe it's just a yarn; but I belave it's true and I want to till ye this; the man from Kerry had a rale edication. Ye may think I'm a-jokin' now, but when ye get older and have more sinse ye'll be noticin' that that's the way everywan rades; and the higher educated they are, the more they rade just as Pat McCarty did, and add some fancy flourishes of their own. Now run along and carry in the wood, and do the chures. Me two feets is sore wid me weight. And take along the pans and the stool as ye go. I suppose it's the whole batch of yees I'll have to be feedin'; and I've a blister on me small toe, and me back is broke with handlin' the wash tubs; an' it's little patience I have with ye, furr ye don't seem to learn in school or out, and yit, be the powers, ye ask some mighty quare questions for a lad, so I suppose there's something in the back of yer head that makes yer father support ye when ye ought to be wurkin'."

And thus Julia grumbled on to the kitchen door and Louis did the chores. But his heart was not in them. Julia had told the story mockingly. She seemed to leave in it somewhere a sting he could feel but could not understand; and he mused as to what might perhaps be behind Julia, Irish to the core. She had set him vibrating at the suggestion of an unseen power and he became rigid in his resolve to penetrate the mystery that seemed to lie back of the tale she told.

*   *   *

Later on, say about the age of twelve, this same boy, to his own surprise, became aware that he had become interested in buildings; and over one building in particular he began to rave, as he detached it from the rest and placed it in his wonder-world. It stood at the northeast corner of Tremont and Boylston Streets. It was a Masonic Temple built of hewn granite, light gray in tone and joyous of aspect.

Boston, as a conglomerate of buildings, had depressed Louis Sullivan continuously since he became engulfed in it. These structures uttered to him as in chorus a stifling negation, a vast No!—to his yea-cry for the light-hearted. In their varied utterance, they were to him unanimous in that they denied the flowers of the field. Some were austere, some gave forth an offensive effluvium of respectability, some fronted the crowded street as though they had always been there and the streets had come later; some seemed to thank God that they were not as other buildings, while others sighed: I am aweary, aweary. Most of them were old and some very new; and individually they impressed Louis, in their special ways, as of an uncanny particularity. He seemed to feel them as physiognomies, as presences, sometimes even as personalities; thus the State House with its golden dome seemed to him a thin, mean, stingy old woman; while Park Street Church seemed to tower as a loyal guardian above its ancient graveyard, and as friendly monitor of the crowds below. And one day as they looked at Faneuil Hall, Grandpa said of it: "The Wild Ass of the City stamps above its head but cannot break its sleep." This sounded thrilling and imaginary to Louis, like a wild thing out of Julia's land of enchantment; but Grandpa said he got it out of a book and that its meaning was too deep for the boy—that he was talking to himself.

Thus buildings had come to speak to Louis Sullivan in their many jargons. Some said vile things, some said prudent things, some said pompous things, but none said noble things. His history book told him that certain buildings were to be revered, but the buildings themselves did not tell him so, for he saw them with a fresh eye, an ignorant eye, an eye unprepared for sophistries, and a mind empty of dishonesty. Nevertheless, a vague sense of doleful community among buildings slowly suffused him. They began to appear within his consciousness as a separate world in their way; a world of separated things seemed, in unison, to pass on to him a message from an unseen power. Thus immersed, he returned again and again to his wonder-building, the single one that welcomed him, the solitary one that gave out a perfume of romance, that radiated joy, that seemed fresh and full of laughter. How it gleamed and glistened in the afternoon sunlight. How beautiful were its arches, how dainty its pinnacles; how graceful the tourelle on the corner, rising as if by itself, higher and higher, like a lily stem, to burst at last into a wondrous cluster of flowering pinnacles and a lovely, pointed finial. Thus Louis raved. It has been often said that love is blind! If Louis chose to liken this new idol of his heart unto a certain graceful elm tree, the pulchritudinous virgin of an earlier day, surely that was his affair, not ours; for he who says that love is blind may be himself the blind—and love clairvoyant.

*   *   *

One day, on Commonwealth Avenue, as Louis was strolling, he saw a large man of dignified bearing, with beard, top hat, frock coat, come out of a nearby building, enter his carriage and signal the coachman to drive on. The dignity was unmistakable, all men of station in Boston were dignified; sometimes insistently so, but Louis wished to know who and what was behind the dignity. So he asked one of the workmen, who said:

"Why he's the archeetec of this building."

"Yes? and what is an archeetec, the owner?"

"Naw; he's the man what drawed the plans for this building."

"What! What's that you say: drawed the plans for this building?"

"Sure. He lays out the rooms on paper, then makes a picture of the front, and we do the work under our own boss, but the archeetec's the boss of everybody."

Louis was amazed. So this was the way: The workmen stood behind their boss, their boss stood behind the archeetec—but the building stood in front of them all. He asked the man if there had been an "archeetec" for the Masonic Temple, and the man said: "Sure, there's an archeetec for every building." Louis was incredulous, but if it were true it was glorious news. How great, how wonderful a man must have been the "archeetec" of his beloved temple! So he asked the man how the architect made the outside of the temple and the man said: "Why, he made it out of his head; and he had books besides." The "books besides" repelled Louis: anybody could do that; but the "made it out of his head" fascinated him.

How could a man make so beautiful a building out of his head? What a great man he must be; what a wonderful man. Then and there Louis made up his mind to become an architect and make beautiful buildings "out of his head." He confined this resolve to the man. But the man said:

"I don't know about that. You got to know a lot first. You got to have an education. Of course us mechanics has our books too. That's the way we lay out stairs, rails and things like that. But you got to have more brains, more experience, more education and more books, especially more books, to be an archeetec. Can yer father keep yer at school long enough?"

"Yes; he says he'll keep me at school until I'm twenty-one if I wish."

"Well, that being so, yer may stand a chance of coming out ahead, but I honestly don't think yer have the right kind of brains. That far-away look in yer eyes makes me think yer won't be practical, and y' *got* to be practical. I'm a foreman and that's as far as I'll get, and I've done work under a good many archeetecs; and some of them that's practical ain't much else. And some of them that's fairly practical has so much education from books that they gets awful fussy, and are hard to get on with." The latter part of this monologue interested Louis rather faintly, for he'd made up his mind. He thanked the foreman who said in parting: "Well, I dunno—mebbe."

* * *

Shortly before his father left Boston for Chicago, Louis confided to him his heart's desire. The father seemed pleased, greatly pleased, that his son's ambition was centering on something definite. He "allowed," as they used to say in New England, that Architecture was a great art, the mother of all the arts, and its practice a noble profession, adding a word or two about Michael Angelo. Then he offered a counter proposal that made Louis gasp. It was none other than this: That Louis was fond of the farm and the open, that he had shown himself a natural farmer with ready mastery of detail of common farming. Why not go further. After proper preparation he would send Louis to an agricultural college, he said, and thus Louis would be equipped as a *scientific farmer*. Louis was dazzled. The word *scientific* was electrical. Before him arose the woods, the fields, the cattle, the crops, the great grand open world as a narcotic phantom of delight. The father was eloquent concerning

[120]

blooded stock, plant cross-fertilization, the chemistry of soils and fertilizers, underdrainage, and so forth; Louis wavered. He sat long in silence, on his father's knee, lost to the world. Then he said: "NO: *I have made up my mind.*"

And thus it was agreed that Louis should remain in Boston to complete his General Education; after that to a Technical School; and, some day—Abroad.

* * *

During the years preceding his decision, Louis, in practice, was essentially scatter-brained. His many and varied activities and preoccupations, physical, mental, emotional, his keen power of observation, his insatiable hunger for knowledge at first hand, his temperamental responses to externals, his fleeting mystic trances, his utterly childlike flashes of intuition, his welcoming of new worlds, opening upon him one after another, his perception that they must grow larger and larger, his imagination, unknown to him as such; all these things, impenetrable to him in their vast significance within the gigantic and diverse world of men and things and thoughts and acts, a world as yet sealed tight to him; all these things seemed to exist within him formless, aimless, a disconnected miscellany rich in impulse but devoid of order, of form, of intention.

Yet this was not precisely the fact. It was an ostensible fact, objectively, a non-fact, subjectively; for a presiding order, a primal impulse, was governing and shaping him through his own marvel at manifestations of power, his constant wonder at what men could do; at men's power to do what they willed to do; and deeper than this moved a power he had heard in the

Song of Spring, and which awakened within the glory of the sunrise.

All this was vague enough, to be sure, but his memory was becoming tenacious and retroactive. Little given to introspection, as such, he was in daily conduct and appearance much like any boy, though perhaps he had a more stubborn will than is usual. His aversion from schools and books had been normal enough, becaused they failed in appeal. Nevertheless he began to swing around to an idea that there might be something useful to him in books, regardless of teachers; and this idea was vivified when he was transferred to the new Rice Grammar School building, the lightness and brightness and cleanliness of which put him at once in exceeding good humor.

True to form he reacted to these cheerful externals, and at once became filled with a new eagerness. A cloud seemed to pass away from his brain, a certain inhibition seemed to relax its hold upon him. As by the waving of a magic wand, he made a sudden swerve in his course, and became an earnest, almost fanatical student of books, in the light and joy of the new schoolhouse. Teachers were secondary; and in habit he became almost a recluse. For the idea had clarified that in books might be found a concentration, an increase in power; that books might be—and he later said they were—storehouses of what men had done, an explanation of their power to do, and that the specific knowledge stored within them might be used as tools of the mind, as men used tools of the hand. Louis saw consequences with extreme rapidity and daring once the first light of an initial idea broke upon him. His enthusiasms were pramagtic. He lost no time, once he saw an objective. His grammar-book in particular fascinated him. Here for the first time in all his schooling a light began to shine within a book and illumine his brain. Here opened up to him, ever more startling, ever more inspiriting, the structure of the language he spoke; its whys and wherefores. Here opened, ever enlarging, a world of things said, and to be said. The rigid rules became plastic as he progressed, then they became fluent; grammar passed into romance; a dead book became a living thing. He could not go fast enough. When would he reach the end?

And as the end approached nearer and nearer, there came forth from the book as a living presence, as a giant from the world of enchantment, with shining visage, man's power of speech. Louis saw it all, but it left him feeble. He had taken grammar at one dose. As usual his imagination had far outsped any possibility of reasonable accomplishment. For Louis, as usual, *saw too much at one time.* He saw, at a glance, ends that would require a lifetime of disciplined endeavor to reach. And so, in a measure, it was with his other studies, though not so ardently. There was little romance to be found in his arithmetic. It was in the main material and philistine. Yet he saw use in it. He accepted it as a daily task and plodded. It was not his fault but his misfortune that it was handed to him dry. Geography he took to kindly. He could visualize it as a diagram and it extended, on paper, his boundaries far and wide. Topographically and racially he could not see into it, even though he was informed, for instance, that the Japanese and Chinese were half-civilized. He asked what civilized meant and was told that *we* were civilized. There were various other things in the geography that were not clear; he found difficulty in making images of what he saw in the book. In his history book he was lied to shamefully, but he did not know it. Anyway, he had to take some things on faith. The history book did not interest him greatly because the people described did not seem human like the people he knew, and the story was mostly about wars. He got the idea that patriotism always meant fighting, and that the other side was always in the wrong.

As to compositions, the pupils had to write one every so often, on a given topic. The first subject for Louis was "The Battle of Hastings." He went at this dolefully, sought refuge in the encyclopedia, and in wabbly English produced a two-page essay weakly-hesitant and valueless; a mere task. He was marked low. The next subject was "A Winter Holiday in Boston." Louis filled the air with snowflakes, merry bells, laughter, movement and cross movement, amusing episodes and accidents, all joyous, all lively. In simple boyish English, he made a hearty story of it, a word-picture; yes, the suggestion even of a prose poem, for it had structure. Within it was a dominant idea of winter that conveyed a sensation of color, of form. Louis was happy. He had hard work to confine himself to four pages. He was marked high. He was commended before the class. But the topics seldom fired him; as a rule they were academic, arid, artificial, having no relation to his life experiences, concerning which he might have said something worth while had he been given the chance. Another feature of the curriculum that went against the grain with Louis was the course in declamation, or "speaking pieces." For Louis had a streak of bashfulness in his make-up, which, though invisible in his former street fights, came painfully into view when he must face the class and "speak out loud." The ensuing torture of self-consciousness made him angry and rebellious. Besides, he had his opinions concerning various "pieces" and was not in the least backward in venturing them. He ridiculed the "Village Blacksmith" unmercifully.

His pet aversion was "Old Ironsides," and it befell one day that he was to speak this very piece. As he approached the platform, he saw red; the class was invisible, no bashfulness now; teacher even, scarcely visible. His mind was made up; he mounted the platform, faced about; and in instant desperate acrimony, he shrieked: *Ay, tear her tattered ensign down!!!!!!* The class roared; teacher stopped him at once; sent him to his seat. She left the room. Louis boiled in his seat. In the hubbub he heard: "Now yer going to get it." "Serves yer right." "Yer made a fool of teacher." "Serves yer right." "Fatty'll fix yer." The teacher, Miss Blank, returning, stilled the storm, and said calmly: "Louis Sullivan, you are wanted in Mr. Wheelock's office." Mr. Wheelock, head master—called "Fatty" for short—was round, of middle height, kindly, with something of the cherub in his face. He wore a blond beard, had rather high color, merry blue eyes, a full forehead, sparsely covered with hair. He appeared not over thirty-five, had served in the army, and was judicial, considerate and human in his dealings.

As Louis entered he saw, not this Mr. Wheelock, but a Mr. Wheelock, gray of face, sinister of eye, holding in his left hand a long rattan. "Miss Blank tells me you have grossly insulted her before the class. What have you to say for yourself?"

Louis was fearless and aggressive by nature. He had crossed his Rubicon. He made a manly apology, wholly sincere as regarded Miss Blank. This cleared the ground but not the issue. He saw the rattan, and with steady eye and nerve he quickly wove about it his plan of action. The rod should never touch him; it was to be a battle of wits. He boldly made his opening with the statement that he regarded the poem as bunkum. Mr. Wheelock sneered. He then went on to take the poem to pieces, line by line, stanza by stanza. Mr. Wheelock looked puzzled; he eyed Louis quizzically. He edged about in his chair. Louis went on, more and more drastically. Mr. Wheelock's eyes began to twinkle, calm returned to his face, he dropped the rod. He laughed heartily: "Where in the world did you dig that up?" Then Louis let go, he waxed eloquent, he spread out his views—so long suppressed; he pleaded for the open, for honesty of thought for the lifting of a veil that hid things, for freedom of thought, for the right of interpretation, for freedom of utterance. He passionately unbosomed his longings. The head master, now sitting chin in hand, looked steadily at Louis, with grave, sad face. As Louis ceased, the master remained silent for a moment, then pulled himself together, relaxed, chuckled, and patting Louis on the shoulder said: "That was a pretty fine stump-speech, young man. When you got through with Holmes, you left his poem as tattered as his ensign. As for the rest: Irish accounts for that. I'm glad we had it out though. I might have thrashed you in anger. Go back to your class now, and hereafter be considerate of a woman's feelings." Louis returned to his room; before all the class he made full amends. Then, in his seat, he set to with a book. His plunge into grammar had not been in vain.

Thus Louis worked on and on, all by himself, as it were, digging into the solid vein of knowledge as a solitary miner digs; washing the alluvial sands of knowledge as a miner sifts—a young prospector grub-staked by an absentee provider now settled on the shores of a vast Lake far in the West.

Living again with his grandparents Louis felt at home once more. He had respites from the city bareness and baldness. He studied in the evenings, in the sitting room, unmindful of the family doings. He lost interest in playmates; waved aside all little girls as nuisances and inferior creatures—they became non-existent. He rose early, at all seasons and in all weathers, before the family were awake, walked the mile to the depot, took the train to Boston, walked a mile to breakfast and another mile to school. Many a night he was awakened by the rattling sash, and listened to the sharp wind moaning, groaning, shrieking, whistling through the crevices with many a siren rise and fall, from the depths of sorrow to the heights of madness, from double forte to piannissimo as this weird orchestra of the countryside lulled him again to sleep. And many a morning, in pitch darkness, he lit his little lamp, broke the skin of ice at the pitcher's top, washed in arctic waters, donned his clothing, neatly folded over a chair as Grandmamma had taught him—his stockings even, carefully turned in for orderliness, then left the house still in darkness and silence, to break his way, it may be, through fresh-fallen snow, knee-deep on the level, and as yet without a trail, his woolen cap drawn down, his woolen mittens well on, his books bound with a leather strap, held snug under the arm of his pea-jacket as the dim light at the depot shone nearer, and a distant double-toot announced the oncoming train, and the blinding headlight that shortly roared into view as he stood, waiting, on the platform.

Yet this was not heroism, but routine. It was an accepted part of the day's doings, accepted without a murmur of other thought in days long since gone by.

Thus Louis worked, in gluttonous introspection, as one with a fixed idea, an unalterable purpose, whose goal lay beyond the rim of his horizon, and beyond the narrow confines of the casual and sterile thought of the day. Hence Louis was bound to be graduated with honors, as he was, the following June of 1870. There and then he received in pride, as a scholar, his first and last diploma. Never thereafter did he regard life with the gravity, the seriousness and the futility of a cloistered monk. That summer, he spent part of vacation time on the farm, and part of it within the primeval forest of Brown's Track in the northern part of the State of New York. On his return to Boston in September, he passed the examinations, and at the age of fourteen entered the English High School, in Bedford Street—there to expand.

PLATE 14. Three residences built for Victor Falkenau, 3420-24 Wabash Avenue, Chicago. 1890.

PLATE 15. Dooly Block, 109 West 2nd Street South, Salt Lake City, Utah. 1890-91. Constructed of red sandstone.

CHAPTER VIII

Louis Goeth on a Journey

EARLY in the summer of '70, Henri List felt an impelling desire to visit his second daughter, Jennie, whom he had not seen in a number of years. In 1862, she was married to a certain Walter Whittlesey, a contracting railway engineer, and they lived on 300-acre farm at Lyons Falls, N. Y. On the 29th day of February, 1864, she added to the world's population a daughter, in due time named Anna, under Presbyterian auspices. Mrs. Whittlesey at the time we are considering, was 34 years of age— one year younger than her sister, Andrienne, greatly beloved mother of Louis Sullivan. When Henri List's desire had ripened into a resolve and was so announced, there was "the devil to pay," as was said at times in those days. Louis became frantic. He must go too. He, also, had not seen his *Tante Jennie* in many years. He must see where she lived and how she lived. He must see his dear little cousin Anna, and Uncle Walter too. He must see the farm, and the river and the great waterfall.

"Grandpa, I have never seen a waterfall, only in pictures, and in pictures they don't move and they don't roar; I want to live with a *real* waterfall; and I want to see the Berkshire Hills; and the Hudson; you know, Grandpa, pictures don't give you any real idea; why Grandpa, a picture of a tree isn't anything at all when you see a real tree, like our great Ash at Cowdry's; and to think, Grandpa, I've never been farther away than Newburyport; take me with you, Grandpa. I want to see something big; everything in Boston and Wakefield has grown so small; we are so shut in; my geography says there are big things as you go west, that outdoors gets bigger and bigger; I want to go Grandpa; now is the time; I may never have another chance."

Grandpa, at first was angry and obdurate. He thought only of what a pest, of what a continuous nuisance his growing grandson would be, and the thought became a nightmare; for Henri List, conforming to custom, was growing older, was acquiring nerves; his easy-going humor showed occasional thin spots of temper. He roared at the "dear little Cousin Anna" business, but the possible significance of the pleadings concerning a "shut-in life" and "big things as you go west" dawned upon him, grew stronger, and he came finally to believe that what he had heard was not altogether boyish nonsense but a rising cry for expansion, a defining hunger for larger vision, bigger things; that his grandson, as it were, was outgrowing his cocoon. Upon second and third thoughts he agreed; whereupon the few remaining sane ones also agreed that Louis needed kennel, collar and chain.

The day came. They departed *via* the Boston and Albany Railway in the evening. Sleepless, restive, Louis awaited, as best he might, the coming of the Berkshire Hills into his growing world. He knew he would see them near dawn. The *hour* came; he entered the foothills and began winding among them, as with labored breath the engines, like heavy draft horses, began a steady pull, the train dragging reluctantly into steadiness as succeeding hills grew taller— with Louis eagerly watching. The true thrill of action began with the uprearing of imposing masses as Louis clung to the solid train now purring in the solitudes in ever-lengthening swings—deep valleys below—until, amid mists and pale moon gleaming, arose the mighty Berkshires, their summits faint and far, their immensities solemn, calm, seeming eternal in the ghostly fog in the mild shimmer, clad in forests, uttering great words, runic words revealing and withholding their secret to a young soul moving as a solitary visitant, even as a wraith among them, the engines crying: "We will!" the mountains replying: "We will!" to an expanding soul listening within its own mists, its own shimmering dream, to the power without and within, amid the same echoes within and without, bereft of words to reply, a bare hush of being, as though through mists of mind and shimmer of hope, SUBLIMITY, in revelation, had come to *one* wholly unprepared, had come to *one* as a knock on the door, had come to *one* who had known mountains only in books. And Louis again, in wonder, felt the power of man. The thought struck deep, that what was bearing him along was solely the power of man; the living power to wish, to will, to do. That man, in his power, with broad stride, had entered the regioned sanctity of these towering hills and like a giant of Elfinland had held them in the hollow of his hand. He had made a path, laid the rails, builded the engines that others might pass. Many saw engines and rails, and pathway, and *one* saw what lay behind them. In the murky mist and shimmer of moon and dawn, a veil was lifted in the solitude of the Berkshires. Louis slept, his nerves becalmed, amid the whistle's sonorous warnings, the silence of the engine, the long, shrill song of the brakes, with mingling echoes, as the train, with steady pace, wound slowly downward toward the Hudson, leaving the Berkshires to their silence and their solitude—and Louis slept on, under the wand of the power of man.

They reached Albany in broad daylight. The Hudson, to Louis's dismay, did not impress him as greatly as he had hoped and believed it would. Its course was straight instead of broadly curving, and the clutter of buildings along its western flank seemed to belittle it. It appeared to him as a wide waterway, not unpleasant of its kind. It seemed to lack what Louis had come to believe the character of a river. The bridge crossing it, with its numberless short spans and lack of bigness, beauty and romance he gazed upon in instant disdain. It appeared to creep, cringing and apologetic, across the wide waters which felt the humiliation of its presence.

Yet he received a shock of elation as the train had moved slowly along the bridge, carrying him with it; and as he gazed downward upon flowing waters, again he marvelled at what men could do; at the power of men to build; to build a bridge so strong it would carry the weight of a great train, even with his own precious and conscious weight added thereto. And Louis mused about the bridge; why was it so mean, so ugly, so servile, so low-lived? Why could not a bridge perform its task with pride? Why was not a proud bridge built here? Was not New York a great state? Was it not called in his geography "The Empire State"? Was not Albany the Capital City of that state? Then why so shabby an approach? Was not the broad Hudson figuratively a great aqueous frontier between Massachusetts and New York, each state proud in sovereignty? And was not this bridge a presumptive greeting between sovereign states? For surely, the railroad train came straight from proud Boston to exalted Albany? And a veil lifted as there came to his mind a striking verse he had read:

> *"Why were they proud?*
> *Again I cry aloud*
> *Why in the name of glory*
> *Were they proud?"*

And there came up also to him the saying: "By their fruits ye shall know them," as, lost in imagery, he visioned forth the great Bay State, saluting the great Empire State, saying solemnly: The Sovereign State of Massachusetts greets the Sovereign State of New York. Let this noble bridge we herewith present you be a sign and a bond of everlasting amity between us, even as Almighty God proclaimed unto Noah of old and his sons: 'I do set my bow in the cloud, and it shall be for a token of a covenant between me and the earth.' Thus Louis, ruminating rather fiercely, wished to know what was behind the pestiferous bridge. He keenly felt that man's amazing power to do, should, in all decency and all reason, be coupled with Romance in the deed. And even more keenly he felt, as his eyesight cleared, that this venomous bridge was a betrayal of all that was best in himself, a denial of all that was best in mankind.

That day they took the New York Central train for Utica. After traversing the roughage, the Mohawk Valley opened to them its placid beauty as in welcome to a new land. And to Louis it was in verity a new land, known to him up to this very present hour as a

[133]

geographical name—an abstraction—unknown to him and wholly unimagined, in its wealth of open rarity, its beauteous immensity of atmosphere. Here was freedom; here was expanse! Louis ranged with his eyes from near to far, following the sweep of the valley floor from the Mohawk to the distant low-flowing hills, and to and fro caressingly; and as mile after mile of valley passed by, and again mile upon mile Louis's peaceful mind passed into wonder that such an open world could be; and now he marvelled, not at man's power and his works, but at the earth itself, and a reverential mood claimed him for its own, as he began in part to see with his own calm eyes what Mother Earth, in her power, had done in her varied moods, and to surmise as best he could what more she had done that he knew not of. And all this while the Mohawk wound its limpid way, gentle as all else; and Louis, softening into an exquisite sympathy, cast his burden upon the valley, and there he found rest; rest from overintrospection, rest from overconcentration; freed from suppression and taboo.

Thus Louis became freshened with new growth as a tree in spring, and a new resilience came to take the place of the old. He was cleansed as by a storm, and purified as by fire; but there was no storm, no fire, no whirlwind—there arose from the valley a still, small voice, and Louis heard the voice and recognized it as his own returning to him, and he was overjoyed and strengthened in his faith and became as one translated into the fresh, free joy of living; for in this valley, this wilderness of light and earth he had found surcease.

Louis turned to Grandpa, whom he found dozing.

The hills were coming together; a lurch of the train awakened Grandpa; he regarded Louis with a lazy smile and asked him if he had found the "big things," and how about the "shut-in life." Louis at once overflowed concerning the Berkshires, the Hudson, and the Bridge, but said not a word about the valley—*that* was sacred. When he had finished, Grandpa's face spread into one of those grimaces that Louis knew but too well as a preliminary to speech; and Grandpa said: "As to your bridge, young man, I know nothing; as to the Hudson, you know nothing; as to your Berkshires, they are an impertinence."

Grandpa was an incorrigible tease. With inward chuckle, with sweet, succulent sinfulness, he gazed his fill upon a crestfallen face, knowing the while how quickly and how well he could restore its color; then, having gloated long enough, he, as always, relented— but slowly, for effect, he began: "Louis, what good does the study of your stupid geography do you? Suppose you *can* bound all the states, you haven't an idea of what the states are. You see a crooked black line on your map and it is marked such or such a river; what do you know about that river? Have your teachers ever told you anything of value about a river? Any river? Have they ever told you that there are rivers and rivers each with its special character? Have they ever given you a word-picture of a river, so that you might at least summon up an image of it, however short of reality? They have not. They can not. They are not inspired. They are victims of routine, wearied on the daily treadmill until they can no longer see into the heart of a child. Now, I have watched you since you were a babe in arms, and I have mostly let you alone for fear of meddling with nature's work; for you were started right by my daughter, the mother who carried you and yearned for you. She is sound to the core. She alone of my children might fittingly wear the red cap of liberty. Yet you do not know your own mother. *I* know *you.* I know your abominable selfishness—come from your father; and your generosity and courage—come from my proud daughter. You have a God-given eye and a dull heart. You are at one and the same time incredibly industrious and practical, and a dreamer of morbid dreams, of mystic dreams, sometimes clean, brilliant dreams, but these are too rare.

"What you have said, from time to time, concerning man's power to do, has astounded and frightened me, coming from you. *That idea* you never got from any of us. *There* shines the light of the seer, of the prophet, leading where?—to salvation or destruction? I dare not think how that flame may grow into conflagration, or mellow into a world-glow of wisdom. But I know, worst of all, that adolescence is at hand; that you are in grave danger of a shake-up. Hard work and clear straight thinking may pull you through; that is my sincere hope. I regret, now, having spoken harshly: I did not intend to, but one thought led to another as a river flows. Now let us return to earth and I will tell you about the Hudson."

Then Grandpa, aroused to eloquence, made a splendid, flowing, word-picture of the Hudson, from Albany to the sea, that brought out all the rare qualities of his fine mind, and so aroused Louis that he made the journey with him—lost to all else. Just then the train slowed up and came to a full stop.

Louis looked out of the window. They were in a ravine, with high walls of rock, jagged and wild, and through this gorge came dashing, plunging, swirling, sparkling, roaring over the ledges in cascade after cascade, laughing and shouting in joy, the same Mohawk River that had flowed as gently as the footstep of a veiled nun, through the long, quiet valley they had traversed. Louis was exultant, he leaped from the train, waved his hat, and in spirit sang with the waters the song of joy. The bell clanged its warning note, Louis was aboard with a swing, and as the train moved on, from the rear platform he waved his farewell to Little Falls.

They soon arived at Utica; and Grandpa, who had begun to feel the fatigue of the journey; announced that they would spend the night there in order to be fresh on the morrow. Louis, still restless, took a long, evening stroll. Utica had not impressed him. It seemed staid and somnolent, giving out an air of old and settled complacence, differing however, in kind and quality, from that of New England. So he strolled; his thoughts reverting to Grandpa and his extraordinary monologue; and for the first time, since he had begun think such thoughts, he asked himself, what lies hidden behind Grandpa?

* * *

The Black River at that time flowed irregularly northward, as presumably it does today. Originating in hills not far northeast of Utica, it finally, after much argument with the lay of the land, debouched into Lake Ontario, not far beyond Watertown. About midway in its course it picked up the Moose River, and a short distance beyond their junction broke into a rough and tumble waterfall of perhaps forty feet descent, beyond which, its surface at first much ruffled, it went smoothly on its way as far as the eye could comfortably follow. The water-tumult was named Lyons Falls. Near the falls, on a narrow flat, close to the west bank of the river, sat dismally, in true American style, in the prevailing genius of ugliness, a hamlet or village, also called Lyons Falls. It was occupied at the time by what were then known as human beings and was the terminus of a canal, already in decay, that had somehow found its way from the city of Rome. At a level higher than the village flat, ran, substantially north and south, a railway, named, if memory serves, the Rome, Carthage & Watertown. During what time the village had served as the terminus of the railway, it flourished; when the line moved on, the village drooped and withered into what has eminently been set forth as a state of innocuous desuetude. At the station was a dirt road at right angles to the railroad, that quickly fell around a curve down to the village. To the westward, however, it ran straight as a section line over the hills and vanished.

From the railway station the ascent was gradual for a space, and at a distance, say of a hundred yards from the railway, and close to the northern side of the dirt road, rested the home of Walter Whittlesey, a rather modern structure for that day, surrounded by spruce trees that looked as though they had been dragged there and chained. Across the road from the family residence was the ice house, secreted in a lovely and refreshing glen of wildwood; at a decorous distance northeast of the "Mansion" was a big barn with its out-buildings, all in a state of dilapidation, and adjacent thereto was a worn and weary apple orchard, lichen-covered and rheumatic with age. Beyond this orchard was sheer stubble over a vast acreage.

Not very far west of the house, however, was a charming valley, quite incidentally berthed between the looming earth-billows. Throughout the length of this ever-to-be-hallowed spot busily ran a rivulet to the encouragement of a swath of herbage, and of thankful shrubbery clinging to its edges. Part way up the western slope was a long horizontal out-cropping of limestone ledge, along which, in comparative safety, grew a slender grove of tall, hardwood trees, with inviting undergrowth. One cannot drive a plow through a limestone ledge, and it is too much trouble to drain a low spot where there are plenty of hills. The groveland paid its rent in firewood, the rivulet paid no rent at all,—thus were they tolerated in their beauty. Hay was the general crop.

The Black River was crossed by a wagon bridge at a point between the Moose River and the falls. The road continued on to Lyonsdale. This same Black River gave an impression of performing a bold, high-handed deed. It split its territory sharply in halves. From its left bank rose wave upon wave of smooth hills mounting to a high plateau, while, as sharply from its right bank spread a huge, somber, primeval hemlock forest, mounting in turn upon its hills beyond the range of vision. Out of this forest rushed the Moose River, its waters icy and dark. Into this forest ran no road for long. The Black River appeared to have done this big, high-handed act; but the recurrence of the name Lyons, and the presence of a baronial seat at Lyonsdale, just within the edge of the forest, might have offered a diverging explanation to one intent upon what lies beyond appearances. However, such was the lay of the land.

The train bearing Grandpa and Louis, after the preliminary whistle and bell clanging of ceremony, slowed up at the station. Grandpa, clean shaven, erect, aglow, descended with dignity; Louis, somewhat begrimed because of his fixed belief that the place for his head lay outside the car window, jumped after him, already excited by the Black River. He wanted to investigate everything at once or immediately; oh, —yes—he must kiss *Tante Jennie*.

They were greeted at the station by Walter Whittlesey, a sizeable man, swarthy, grave, full bearded— black sprinkled with gray, wearing the wide felt hat of a landowner who knew horses. He had given instructions, and had so notified Grandpa, that all baggage and luggage would be cared for, extraneously, by menials. He was a calm, courteous man, whose bearing suggested a lineage of colonels on horseback, blue grass, bourbon, blooded stock, beauteous women, and blacks.

The three walked leisurely up the road, to the white house with green blinds where *Tante Jennie,* otherwise Mrs. Jenny List Whittlesey, awaited them with the reserve of a gentlewoman whom long practice had enabled to speak with delicate precision in a voice scarcely audible, and to inhale her smiles.

As the trio mounted the steps leading to the veranda, Louis in his rough and ready way casually noticed, not far from the doorway, a young lady reclining in an easy chair, quietly rocking, deeply absorbed in a book. Scarcely had he entered the open door but she had affirmed: "I'm going like that boy."

Within the "spare room" of the house, Grandpa folded his daughter in fervent arms, kissed her with the profound affection of an ageing father, and wept. Auntie did not weep; she amiably returned her father's greeting, and said something in very pure French that seemed to satisfy. Louis went through the performance, awkwardly, and as hastily as possible. Auntie gave him the dry kiss of superculture and assured him in very pure English of her gratification at his arrival within her home.

Louis at the earliest moment escaped to the veranda. He had forgotten all about the young lady, and was startled and abashed to find her still there, gently rocking, absorbed in her book. Before he could retreat she arose in greeting with a smile known otherwhere only in Paradise; she said in glee: "My name is Minnie! I am eighteen, and a 'young lady' now. Oh Louis! I have waited for you so impatiently, and here you are at last. I am sure we shall like each other; don't you think we will? I'm in society in Utica and I'm going to tell you lots of things. See, I wear long skirts and do up my hair, but I can't climb trees any more; isn't that a shame? But I'll run races with you and we'll have lots of fun; and I'll tell you all about the books I've read and all about society. Here I've been for a month reading French books and speaking French with Aunt Jenny and have grown weary of myself; now you and I are to be chums! Don't you think you'll like me?"

And Louis, taken thus unawares, and thus caressed with words, dared at last to look into gray Scotch eyes that seemed endowed with an endless fund of merriment, of badinage, of joy, of appeal, of kindness, and saturated with an inscrutable depth beyond all of these. He gazed steadily at a tender face, narrow, tapering, slender, and very pale, delicately freckled; at nostrils trembling; at a wide thin-lipped supersensitive mouth; at large ears; at thin, vagrant, dark, sandy hair; at a sprightly medium figure, all alive. She was clad in dark blue silk. He found in her not beauty but irresistible pervading charm. As he was thus absorbed Minnie said: "Sit down beside me, Louis dear, and watch me die. Sit very still and watch." Whereupon, leaning back in her easy chair, she closed her eyes, deepened her pallor, closed her nostrils, made a thin line of her mouth, elongated her face, and lay deathly still, as though in veritable *rigor mortis,* until Louis's nerves were on edge. Then, still dead and rigid, the fine line indicating her closed lips slowly widened across her face, the thin lips parting slightly as of themselves, cadaverously, the teeth also, a little later; after a seemingly endless wait, from this baleful rictus there came out moans, wails, gurgles, the ears began to crawl as of themselves. Then of a sudden the corpse sat bolt upright, with wide glaring eyes, grasped Louis by the shoulders and in fierce, frothy words forecast for him the direst of misfortunes by sea and land. Then she patted Louis's pale cheek, fell back into her chair and giggled softly, casting at Louis the funniest, merriest, glances. "How old are you, Louis?" "Fourteen." "Oh, I knew that. I asked your auntie. But isn't it lovely, fourteen and eighteen; fourteen and eighteen!—and to think that I have died for you, and have come back to you!

[142]

"Tomorrow we'll go to church. The new minister's a rather nice chap. I like to hear him pray, he's so genteel about it; and he's sound in doctrine, so your auntie says, and you know she's a blue Presbyterian." And Minnie immediately took Louis under her wing.

Next day she *took* him to church, leading him by a string, as it were, set him down beside her in the family pew, and their whisperings mingled with other whisperings in the repressive silence. Then the minister appeared in the pulpit, a fairly young man with mien and countenance betoking earnestness, piety and poverty. Louis thought he prayed well, as with quiet fervor he set forth his belief that God was within his temple, and assuredly within the hearts of his flock. When it came to the sermon, Louis sat up straight and took eager notice, for the good man had just read from the big Bible this text: "And the Lord went before them by day in a pillar of cloud, to lead them on the way, and by night in a pillar of fire, to give them light to go by day and night." Louis needed no sermon; in a flash he knew that all his life he had been led in by a pillar of gleaming cloud, and a pillar of fire; and his far-reaching instant vision forecast it would be thus until the end. Yet he took much heart in listening to the youngish man in the pulpit grasp the totality of this simple story, transmute it into a great symbol, and in impassioned voice lift it to the heights of idealism and of moral grandeur, refashioning it into a spiritual pillar of cloud and a pillar of fire ever present in the hearts, the minds, the souls of all humans, as he urgently, yea, piteously, besought the blind to see.

As they walked home Minnie remarked that it was

[143]

an extra-fine sermon, but as Louis did not reply she scented danger and tactfully chatted about little things, until her joyous sweetness detached him from his pillar of ravishing cloud and the pillar of wondrous fire. Soon she had him laughing as gaily as herself and plucking wayside flowers for her. For Minnie was intuitive to a degree. She knew that Louis had been deeply stirred, that he had been dreaming somberly as they left the church: and this she would not countenance. She believed that if one must dream it should be of happiness, and the dreamer wide awake to the joy of living. They sat for a while by the falls, but Louis was not content. There seemed to be something purposeless in this clumsy tumbling about of dark waters, losing their balance, falling helplessly over ledges and worn boulders, lost in their way among them, and reeling absurdly off at the bottom. It all seemed to lack order and singleness of purpose. Near the falls was a small wooden mill afflicted with the rickets, and this alone seemed in tune with the falls.

So they trudged home and Aunt Jenny said the blessing. Grandpa had just returned from a long walk, his favorite pastime—fifteen or twenty miles—nothing for him. It became his daily habit. He always went barehead, always got lost and always found his way back.

Next day Minnie told Louis, in confidence, she knew of a charming spot not very far away, where there were ledges of rock and tall trees, and a darling rivulet with green along its banks. She *took* him there, and would not even let him help her over the lichen and moss covered rocks. With Louis in tow she found a shady spot, with ferns and undergrowth forming a

[144]

nook, and the wide-branching trees a canopy. She had taken books with her, and on a large, ancient stone which she called her pulpit, she perched with her slave. Below them ran the rivulet, and above the opposite crest there showed a bit of the roof of the dwelling. Minnie clapped her hands with joy. "Louis, don't you think I'm good to bring you here? It is the solitary oasis in this desert of hayland. There is hay, hay, hay, for miles."

Presently she opened a book and read from Tennyson, making her selections carefully varied, feeling her way through Louis's responses to see where she could reach his heart, how she could bare it, and then keep her secret. She read from Byron, recited many other poems with a skill unknown to elocutionists, and a stealthy, comfortable look came into her eyes now turned green, her face wreathed in a Mona Lisa smile, as she said: "Louis, this is a great, beautiful, good world if but we knew it, and to this very spot I have often come in thankful mood, and from this very pulpit prayed to these trees to make me pure in heart." And then she told Louis about the many books she had read, largely French novels—for practice, she said; and then Louis told her he had read all of Captain Mayne Reid's books, all the Leather Stocking Tales, some by Maryatt, and some wonderful and beautiful stories in the Bible; and he recited for her, verbatim, the story of Elijah, the whirlwind, and the still small voice.

The smile on Minnie's pale face became luxurious, her gleaming eyes about to close, as she said half-warningly: "Louis, Louis, you are in danger!" and refused to explain. Then suddenly coming to herself she cried: "We must go back to the house at once; if we are late at supper, your auntie will give me just one look, and I will know exactly what that one look means; but *you* won't." And she took Louis by the hand, her books under the other arm, resumed her jaunty mood and led him to the house, delivering to his Auntie a human package not merely stirred, but churned into butter and whey.

Auntie again said grace; the thoughts of all bowed heads but hers were on supper. The evening was spent by the family on the dark veranda singing old-fashioned hymns; after which the peace of night came over all—but one.

Next day, Minnie, repentant of her wickedness, appeared as a fresh blown morning glory, gave hearty, cheerful greetings to all, and to Louis talked as might an ordinarily affectionate sister. Her eyes were crystalline, her carriage buoyant. Then, at the appointed time, she began her hour of French with Auntie; and as Louis, nearby, listened, he framed a desire and a resolve to learn the language which Minnie seemed to read and speak as easily as Auntie. The lesson over, Minnie came to Louis, took a place beside him and as one wooing, said, "Dear *protégé:* the hour is at hand. I have much to say. The woods are calling, the birds are waiting. Let us now repair to the pulpit and be two sensible humans." To the pulpit they repaired, that day and many a day. Once seated on the great stone, Minnie put Louis at his ease and began rapid-fire questions, about Louis's home and school life. She wished every detail; and Louis answered faithfully. He told her not only the story of his life, but the story of every one and everything therewith connected: Minnie saying: "Fine, fine, how well you tell it," in running comment. He even told Minnie one of Julia's fairy tales, the tale of the "Good People," and Minnie cried: "Oh, what a lovely brogue, isn't it sweet?" and Louis said yes, it was, and added that Julia had taught him some real Gaelic words, but he had forgotten the meaning of most of them. "That gives me a bright idea, Louis; you don't know French, so I will give you a pass-word, in French, that is better than any Gaelic. Say to me, once every day, *Je t'aime*"; and Louis said to her once every day *Je t'aime*—deeming it a secret. And Minnie would gravely say each time, in approval, that he pronounced it beautifully.

She told him conversationally about herself and her home. She described in detail her finishing school, and mimicked its follies. She raved over her adored brother Ed, fresh from Yale. Told of her coming out, of Utica society, and her set, and of the landed aristocracy, the old families, the exclusive, best people; said her father was a big grain forwarder, and had plenty of money, as far as her simple needs were concerned, and described minutely her trip to Europe. She travelled this ground to and fro with many a mimicry, flippancy, wise saw, and splendid enthusiasms.

So Louis began to see that people were graded. He was pained at many things Minnie casually described. She was revealing too much. She was unconscious of lifting many veils, as Louis was unconscious of repeating world-truth when he said, every day, *Je t'aime*. He was not lifting any veil for Minnie; this self-same Minnie having one small devil peeping through each eye. Their talk, throughout that live-long day, was gossip.

When Minnie came, through questioning, to a full sense of the depth of Louis's ignorance of the world, of social organization both in its ephemeral and its momentous inert and stratified aspects, that he was provincial, that he was honest, frank, and unsuspecting, she became alarmed at the new danger, and determined to prepare him; and in so doing, she lifted at least a corner of a sinister and heavy veil that lay behind appearances. This she did with skill, and a little at a time, proving her case in each instance, by direct illustration and remarks none too complimentary. But Minnie could not be serious for long at a time; she preferred frivolity, nonsense and high spirits—never for a moment neglecting to keep Louis dazed in her land of enchantment.

Minnie became Louis's precious teacher. She made him feel he was not being taught, but entertained with gossip. She knew that what she said in persiflage, would later sink in deep, and she knew why it would do so.

Minnie was both worldly and unworldly. With nature she was dreamy; but when it came to people, she became a living microscope, her sharp brain void of all illusion, for her true world was of the world of people—there she lived—as Louis's world had been a world of the wide open—of romance. Hence, with Louis she was ever gentle, even though she dangled him as though he were a toy balloon.

An aching in her guarded heart was soothed by him; and he became for her a luxury—a something to remain awhile a precious memory. Thus Minnie filled

the air with laughter, and with debonnaire delight—
meanwhile feeding honey drop by drop—just to see
upon a human face the rare, the precious witching
aspect of idolatry.

*   *   *

So came a day when Minnie, on the pulpit, talked
of things pertaining to herself. Among other words
she said the young men of her set were grossly stupid;
incapable of thought above the level of the sty. Their
outlook upon life she said was vapid, coarse and vain.
That they held women to be property, their appendage,
their vehicle of display. They were all rich, she said,
and this made matters worse. To be anchored to such
brutes, scarcely decent in their evening clothes, she said,
was horror. She would be owned, she said, by no
man rich or poor. She must be free, she said; free
as air. Knowing all this now, she had marked her
course in life, and she said that never would she marry
—the risk of sorrow was too great. All this she said
as lightly as a swallow on the wing.

At these last words, something fell away in Louis's
solar plexus, sometimes known as the sensorium, and
Minnie said: "Never mind, never mind, you'll outgrow
it, Louis, you are fourteen, I'm eighteen. While it
lasts, let us be dear friends together; the dearest comrades ever known. Your heart's in mine and mine in
yours, I know. Let these great oaks, as witnesses, be-
trothe us in such way, and prophesy a lovely memory."

Louis with unheard-of stoicism held back his tears.
And Minnie said: "Come now, let's be going; don't
refer to this again. Let's be as we've always been,
together, carefree—and let laughter ring again."

Such was Minnie's way of doing and of saying. She was Louis's loyal friend. She mothered him in sprightly malice and in tenderness alike. All her vagaries and sweetness came from one constant nature. She was ever thoughful of the needs of others. She was exquisitely human. To Louis, long adapted to the elderly, she was held by him as in a shrine, to be the only truly human he had ever known; and her kindness in adopting him, and making him her own, not for a day, but for all the glad summer long, made him feel as though his life, before her floating into it, had been but a blank. How could he ever repay! She had come, it seemed to him, out of the invisible that lies behind all things, all dreams, to be his faerie queen.

And now it seems as though a half a century had stood still.

PLATE 16. Wainwright Building, NW corner of Seventh and Chestnut Streets, St. Louis, Mo. 1890-91. Adler & Sullivan; Charles K. Ramsey, associate.

PLATE 17. Union Station, Illinois Central Railroad, New Orleans. 1892. Demolished in 1953-54.

CHAPTER IX

Boston—The English High School

WHILE at Lyons Falls, Louis made acquaintance of the sons of the tenant farmer; twins, two or three years older than he, and he appraised them accordingly. Broad shouldered, heavily built throughout, with large-featured homely faces evenly browned by the sun, they had big coarse hands which Louis envied. They swayed and lurched in talking, shifting their feet; good natured, heavy-minded fellows, taller than Louis. One day they said they were bound for Brown's Tract and would have as guide a trapper, a grown man; that they would head for a certain lake twenty miles away, where the trapper had a shack and a canoe; that they were after game; they asked Louis if he would like to come along. Louis jumped at a chance he had been aching for. Many a day he had wondered what a forest could be, within its depths, as he gazed at the mass of sombre and silentious green rising from the dark waters of the river and had seen no hope to solve the mystery. The boys warned him that it would be rough, heavy work, with some danger; but he said the rougher the better, and that as to the dangers he was curious.

Now, afoot, heavy laden, they have passed the fringe of the forest, and begun the ascent of a rough stony trail, climbing and descending the hills in a winding obscure way. Five miles in, they cross a "bark road," so called, a ragged gash through the woods with stumps of trees, loose boulders and corduroy for roadbed. Strewn along the way of the road lie huge naked hemlocks stripped of bark for the tanneries to southward. No trail beyond this road; the real hard work, the stern hardship begins in the utter wildness of ancient fallen trees, tangled wildwood, precipitous ravines, the crossing of raging torrents—feeders of the Moose River—roaring under masses of forest wreckage, involving high danger in the crossing, their waters dark brown, forbidding, foaming brown-white; detours to be made around impassable rock out-croppings; wadings through cedar swamps; a bit of smooth needle-carpeted floor, for relief at times; many panting rests, many restarts, grimly wending their way between close-set uprearing shafts of mighty hemlocks, and tamaracks, with recurring narrow vistas quickly closing as the trampers cross a plateau, and then again descent and climb and hardship, hidden danger of falling aged trees, no warning but the groan, then a crash and trembling earth; so pass four weary ones through a long August day, amid cathedral gloom, the roaring and the stillness of primeval forest.

By sundown they have made ten miles. A hasty camp—no tent, a quick fire—coffee, bacon, hardtack, water from canteens; a small tamarack felled, its delicate fragrant boughs laid thick for a bed, a circle of smudge-fires, and shortly, four humans, in soaking boots, and clothing soaked with sweat and spray, sleep the instant sleep of exhaustion, in the dark of the moon, in the pitch black forest, as the circle of smudge fires faintly smoulders.

At early dawn the trapper blows no horn, he rings no bell, but in bright good humor emits the awful siren of the screech-owl; the dead turn in their slumber-graves. Once more—the dead jump up. Campfire lighted, hurry-up, fires trod out, packs again on sore backs, stiff legs start and shortly limber. That day six miles of going, and again death-asleep. Next day four miles of easy going as they reach the margin of a wide basin or valley, with level floor and stop at one end of a sumptuous lake, resting placid and serene as a fathomless mirror upheld by forest walls. At this point is a limited natural clearing; nearby is the shack, a large rough-hewn affair of unbarked sapling logs; and, bottom up, in the deep shade are found canoe and paddles. It is early afternoon. They take their ease, lying awhile on the green sward, then spread boots and clothing in the sun to dry, bathe in the cool shallows safe from the icy spring-fed deep of the lake, resume half-dried boots and clothes and leisurely arrange the camp. Meanwhile the trapper, tall and lank, brings in a brace of partridge. Now all is joy, the pains forgot, the prize attained—they burst into raucous song to the effect that they are "dreaming now of Hallie."

Louis, musket in hand, walked to the edge of the shore, stopping not far from the timber wall. The lake, to his eye, appeared three miles long and three-quarters wide. He raised his gun and fired straight ahead. Instantly set in an astounding roar. It smashed, dashed and rolled sonorously along the mighty wall, suddenly fainting into an unseen bay, then rolling forth again into the open, passing on like subdued thunder; from the beginning scattering wild echoes, which in turn re-echoed criss-wise and cross-wise, an immense maze of vibrations, now passing slowly in decrescendo into a far away rumble and nearby trembling, fainting, dying, as the forest sternly regained its own, and primal stillness came. This display was too dramatic, even for Louis. Once was enough. It seemed too much like an eerie protest, the wildly passionate rejoinder of a living forest disturbed in its primal solitudes of contemplation. Yet the stupendous rhythm, the orchestral beauty of it all, sank deep in Louis's soul, now become as one with nature's mood. He wandered from the camp, wishing to be alone, where he might be himself, solitary, in nature's deep, and commune with venerable immensities that gave forth a voice of haunting stillness which seemed to murmur and at times to chant of an unseen, age-long, immanent, eternal power, which Louis coupled as one with a gentle, sensuous, alluring power to whose moving song of enchantment he had trembled in response, within a bygone springtime in the open.

The brief camp-life was much the usual thing. Game was scarce, but small speckled trout could be scooped up in quantity from a slow, deep rivulet in a nearby beaver meadow.

Came time to return. The trapper said he could lead them back by an easier way, but it meant a detour of thirty miles to Lyons Falls. They made the distance in three days. They had been away ten days all told; and Louis was exultant that he had made as good a showing as the farm-boy twins.

All too soon came the hour to begin the journey homeward. Good-byes were said—some of them wistful.

At Albany, Grandpa revealed a plan he had cherished in secret: They were to take the day-boat down the Hudson to New York. Louis was profuse in gratitude as he pre-figured coming wonders which he was to see with his very own eyes, and appraise with his own sensibilities. And so it was, as Louis passed almost directly from the sublimity of forest solitudes to the grandeur of the lower Hudson. As they passed West Point, Grandpa said that he had once taught French at the United States Military Academy, and that his pleasure there had been to swim the Hudson, across and back every morning before breakfast. Grandpa's stock immediately jumped many points, for Louis held prowess in high honor. As they passed the Palisades Louis was astounded as Grandpa explained their nature—huge basalt crystals standing on end. The life on the river all the way down had greatly entertained him; now he came in sight of greater shipping and entered an immense floating activity.

Of New York Louis saw but little; and when Grandpa said it was here they landed when he with his family came from Geneva, Louis took the information deafly, not even inquiring when and why they had moved to Boston. Grandpa felt the hurt of this indifference. Here was this boy, his own cherished grandson, whose fourteen living years had been filled to overflow with vivid episodes, with active thoughts, with dreams, mysteries, prophetic intuitions and rude industrious practicalities, all commingled; here was this boy, ignorant, grossly innocent and careless of the vicissitudes and follies of a seething human world. He shuddered momentarily at the chasm that lay between them. For Grandpa all too well knew the profound significance of a wholly truthful story of any human life, told continuusely, without a break, from cradle to old age, could it be known and recorded of any other than one's self. He knew that the key to the mystery of human destiny and fate lay wrapped and lost within these lived but unrecorded stories. He knew also that Louis was now paying in ignorance the penalty of a sheltered life. Then he told Louis another secret: They were to leave on a Fall River boat and traverse the length of Long Island Sound. Thus, Louis, in renewed joy and ecstasy made his first long trip on the salted sea. Then duly came Boston, Wakefield and the romantic journey's end.

*   *   *

Louis still had time to brush up rapidly for the high school examinations. He had chosen the English High rather than the Latin High. He was accustomed to thinking and acting for himself, seldom asking advice. His thoughts in mass were directed ever toward his chosen career; and he believed that the study of Latin would be a waste of time for him; the time element was present always as a concomitant of his ambitions. He wished always to advance in the shortest time compatible with sure results. He had no objection to Latin as such, but believed its study suitable only to those who might have use for it in after-life. He had a keen gift for separating out what he deemed essential for himself.

On September third, his birthday, he received a letter from Utica, filled with delicate sentiments, encouraging phrases, and concluding with an assurance that the writer would be with him in spirit through his high school days.

The English and Latin High Schools, in those days, were housed in a single building, rather old and dingy, on the south side of Bedford Street; a partition wall separating them, a single roof covering them. The street front was of granite, the side walls of brick. There were brick-paved yards for the recess half-hour with overflow to the street and a nearby bakery. It was a barn-like, repellant structure fronting on a lane as narrow as the prevailing New England mind of its day.

Louis passed the examinations and his name was entered in the year book 1870-71.

He was among those—about forty in all—assigned to a room on the second floor, presided over by a "master" named Moses Woolson. This room was dingy rather than gloomy. The individual desks were in rows facing north, the light came from windows in the west and south walls. The master's platform and desk were at the west wall; on the opposite wall was a long blackboard. The entrance door was at the north, and in the southwest corner were two large glass-paneled cabinets, one containing a collection of minerals, the other carefully prepared specimens of wood from all parts of the world.

The new class was assembled and seated by a monitor, while the master sat at his desk picking his right ear. Louis felt as one entering upon a new adventure, the outcome of which he could not forecast, but surmised would be momentous.

Seated at last, Louis glanced at the master, whose appearance and make-up suggested, in a measure, a farmer of the hardy, spare, weather-beaten, penurious, successful type—apparently a man of forty or under. When silence had settled over the mob, the master rose and began an harangue to his raw recruits; indeed he plunged into it without a word of welcome. He was a man above medium height, very scant beard, shocky hair, his movements were panther-like, his features, in action, were set as with authority and pugnacity, like those of a first mate taking on a fresh crew.

He was tense, and did not swagger—a man of passion. He said, in substance: "Boys, you don't know me, but you soon will. The discipline here will be rigid. You have come here to learn and I'll see that you do. I will not only do my share but I will make you do yours. You are here under my care; no other man shall interfere with you. I rule here—I am master here—as you will soon discover. You are here as wards in my charge; I accept that charge as sacred; I accept the responsibility involved as a high, exacting duty I owe to myself and equally to you. I will give to you all that I have; you shall give to me all that you have. But mark you: The first rule of discipline shall be SILENCE. Not a desk-top shall be raised, not a book touched, no shuffling of feet, no whispering, no sloppy movements, no rustling. I do not use the rod, I believe it the instrument of barbarous minds and weak wills, but I will shake the daylight out of any boy who transgresses, after one warning. The second rule shall be STRICT ATTENTION: You are here to *learn,* to *think,* to *concentrate* on the matter in hand, to hold your minds steady. The third rule shall cover ALERTNESS. You shall be awake all the time—body and brain; you shall cultivate promptness, speed, nimbleness, dexterity of mind. The fourth rule: You shall learn to LISTEN; to *listen* in *silence* with the *whole* mind, not part of it; to listen with your *whole heart,* not part of it, for sound listening is a basis for sound thinking; sympathetic listening is a basis for sympathetic, worth-while thinking; accurate listening is a basis of accurate thinking. Finally you are to learn to OBSERVE, to REFLECT, to DISCRIMINATE. But this subject is of such high importance, so much above your present understanding, that I will not comment upon it now; it is not to be approached without due preparation. I shall not start you with a jerk, but tighten the lines bit by bit until I have you firmly in hand at the most spirited pace you can go." As he said this last saying, a dangerous smile went back and forth over his grim set face. As to the rest, he outlined the curriculum and his plan of procedure for the coming school year. He stressed matters of hygiene; and stated that a raised hand would always have attention. Lessons were then marked off in the various books—all were to be "home lessons"—and the class was dismissed for the day.

Louis was amazed, thunder-struck, dumb-founded, over-joyed! He had caught and weighed every word as it fell from the lips of the master; to each thrilling word he had vibrated in open-eyed, amazed response. He knew now that through the years his thoughts, his emotions, his dreams, his feelings, his romances, his visions, had been formless and chaotic; now in this man's utterances, they were voiced in explosive condensation, in a flash they became defined, living, real. A pathway had been shown him, a wholly novel plan revealed that he grasped as a banner in his hand, as homeward bound he cried within: *At last a Man!*

Louis felt the hour of freedom was at hand. He saw, with inward glowing, that true freedom could come only through discipline of power, and he translated the master's word of discipline into its true intent: *Self Discipline of self power.* His eager life was to condense now in a focusing of powers: What had the words meant;—"silence," "attention," "promptness," "speed," "accurate," "observe," "reflect," "discriminate," but powers of his own, obscurely mingled, unco-ordinated, and, thus far, vain to create? Now, in the master's plan, which he saw as a ground plan, he beheld that for which, in the darkness of broad daylight, he had yearned so desperately in vain; that for which, as it were with empty, outstretched hands, he had grasped, vaguely groping; as one seeing through a film, that for which he had hungered with an aching heart as empty as his hands. He had not known, surely, what it was he wished to find, but when the master breathed the words that Louis felt to be inspired: "You are here as wards in my charge; I accept that charge as sacred; I accept the responsibility involved as a high exacting duty I owe to myself and equally to you. I will give to you all that I have, you shall give me all that you have,"—a veil was parted, as it were by magic, and behold! there stood forth not alone a man but a TEACHER of the young.

On board the train for Wakefield, Louis took account of himself; he viewed the long, loop-like journey he had but recently completed, still fresh and free in memory's hold. He had gathered in, as though he had flung and drawn a huge lassoo, the Berkshires, the Mohawk and its valley, Little Falls, the Black River, the Moose River, the primeval forest, and the Falls, the Hudson, the Catskills, the Palisades, New York Harbor, Long Island Sound; he had voyaged by rail, by river, and by sea. All these things, these acts, with their inspiring thoughts and emotions and reveries he had drawn into himself and shaped as one single imposing drama, ushering in a new and greater life. Or, in a sense reversed, his "child-domain," holding, within the encircling woods, his ravine, his rivulet, his dam, his lovely marsh, his great green field, his tall, beauteous, slender elm; land of his delight, paradise of his earth-love, sequestered temple of his nature-worship, sanctuary of his visions and his dreams, had seemed at first, and hopefully, to extend itself progressively into a larger world as far as Newburyport and Boston, there, however, to stop, to remain fixed and bound up for seven long years, held as by a sinister unseen dam, the larger, urgently growing Louis, held also back within it, impatient, repressed, confined, dreaming of power, storing up ambition, searching for what lies behind the face of things, agitated and at times morose, malignant. When, of a sudden, the dam gives way, the child-domain so far enlarged, rushes forth, spreading over the earth, carrying with it the invisible living presence of Louis's ardent soul, pouring its power of giving and receiving far and wide over land and sea, encompassing mountains and broad valleys, great rivers, turbulent waterfalls, a solemn boundless forest enfolding a lustrous lake, and again a noble river mountain-banked, an amazing harbor, and the great salt waves of the sea itself.

Thus were the boundaries extended; thus were the power and splendor of Mother Earth revealed in part; thus was provided deep and sound foundation for the masterful free spirit, striding in power, in the open, as the genius of the race of purblind, groping, striving, ever hoping, ever dreaming, illusioned mankind.

And thus it seemed to Louis that he was becoming stronger and surer of himself. Reverting to the words of the master, he dared affirm that this very power was within him, as a ward in his charge; that he must accept that charge as sacred; that he must accept the responsibility involved as a high exacting duty he owed to himself and equally to it; that he must give to it his all, to insure that it might give to him its all.

And Louis now saw clearly and in wonder, that a whim of his Grandpa, not the Rice Grammar School, had prepared him to meet Moses Woolson on fair terms. With confident assurance he awaited the beginning of what he foresaw was to be a long and arduous disciplinary training, which he knew he needed, and now welcomed.

That evening he told Grandpa what he thought of Moses Woolson and his plan; and Grandpa, with inward seeing eyes, smiled indulgence at his grandson seated on his knee, one hand about his neck, as he mused aloud: "My dear child, allowing for the rosy mist of romance through which an adolescent like yourself sees all things glorified, I will say that in the whole wide world it is true there may be found a few such men as you portray; but as a venerable and prudent Grandpa I shall reserve the right to wait awhile that we may see how the ideal and the real agree. But you go at it just the same, regardless of what may be passing in the back of my bald head." And Louis laughed, and kissed and hugged his Grandpa, and settled to his lessons, as grandma knitted by the student lamp, as uncle Julius thrummed away on a helpless guitar and sang the melancholy sentimental ditties of the day, and as Grandpa, in slippers, gazed with incredulity at a boy on the floor oblivious of them all.

As it has but little import in this story, we shall pass over the breaking-in period of Moses Woolson's class, and begin an exposition of Moses Woolson's plan and method, and Louis's responses thereto at that period the master himself had forecast as "when I have you firmly in hand at the most spirited pace you can go." Suffice it to say that with great skill in intensive training he had brought them to this point within three months.

The ground work of his plan was set forth in his opening address, and is now to be revealed in its workings in detail.

The studies on which Louis set the highest value were Algebra, Geometry, English Literature, Botany, Mineralogy and French language. All these subjects were to him revelations. Algebra had startled him; for, through its portal he entered an unsuspected world of symbols. To him the symbol x flashed at once as a key to the unknown but ascertainable. Standing alone, he viewed this x in surprise as a mystic spirit in a land of enchantment, opening vistas so deep he could not see the end, and his vivid imagination saw at once that this x, expanded in its latent power, might prove the key to turn a lock in a door within a wall which shut out the truth he was seeking—the truth which might dissolve for him the mystery that lay behind appearances. For this x, he saw, was manipulated by means of things unknown.

Thus he saw far ahead; looking toward the time

when he would be mature. Geometry delighted him because of its nicety, its exactitude of relationships, its weird surprises—all like fairy tales, fairy tales which could be proved, and then you said: Q.E.D. He began to see what was meant by a theorem, a postulate, a problem, and that *proof* was a reasoned process based on certain facts or assertions. It was well for him, at the time, that he did not perceive the Euclidian *rigidity,* in the sense that he had noted the fluency of Algebra. As to Botany, had he not always seen trees and shrubs and vines and flowers of the field, the orchard and the garden?

Now he was learning their true story, their most secret intimacies, and the organization of their world. He loved them all the more for this. Mineralogy was new and revealing, the common stones had begun as it were, to talk to him in their own words. Concerning French he was ardent, for he had France in view. English literature opened to him the great world of words, of ordered speech, the marvelous vehicle whereby were conveyed every human thought and feeling from mind to mind, from heart to heart, from soul to soul, from imagination to imagination, from thought to thought; and to his ever widening view, it soon arose before him as a vast treasure house wherein was stored, in huge accumulation, a record of the thoughts, the deeds, the hopes, the joys, the sorrows, and the triumphs of mankind.

Moses Woclson was not a deep thinker, nor was Moses Woolson erudite or scholarly, or polished in manners, or sedate. Rather was he a blend of wild man and of poet. But of a surety he had the art of teaching at his finger tips and his plan of procedure was scientific to a degree, so far beyond the pedagogic attainments of his day that he stood unique, and was cordially hated by his craft as lambs might fear and hate a wolf. Today men would speak of such a man as a "human dynamo," a man ninety-nine per cent "efficient." His one weakness was a temper he all too often let escape him, but his high strung, nervous make-up may be averred in part extenuation, for this very make-up was the source of his accomplishment and power: He surely gave in abundance, with overflowing hands, all that he had of the best to give.

His plan of procedure was simple in idea, and therefore possible of high elaboration in the steady course of its unfolding into action and results. For convenience it may be divided into three daily phases seemingly consecutive, but really interblended; first came severe memory drill, particularly in geometry, algebra, French grammar and in exact English; this work first done at home, and tested out next day in the school room. Second, (first, next day) a period of recitation in which memory discipline and every aspect of alertness were carried at high tension. At the end of this period came the customary half-hour recess for fresh air and easing up. After recess came nature study with open book. Chief among them Gray's "School and Field Book of Botany"—Louis's playground; then came a closing lecture by the Master.

Thus it may be said, there was a period of high tension, followed by a period of reduced tension, and this in turn by a closing period of semi or complete relaxation, as the master reeled off in easy, entertaining talk, one of his delightful lectures. It was in the nature studies, and in these closing lectures, particularly those in which he dwelt upon the great out-of-doors, and upon the glories of English literature, that the deep enthusiasms of the man's nature came forth undisguised and unrestrained, rising often to the heights of impassioned eloquence, and beauteous awakening imagery. These lectures, or rather, informal talks covered a wide range of subjects, most of them lying beyond the boundaries of the school curriculum.

Thus, in a sense, Moses Woolson's school room partook of the nature of a university—quite impressively so when Professor Asa Gray of Harvard came occasionally to talk botany to the boys. He did this out of regard for Moses Woolson's love of the science. The unfailing peroration of these lectures—every one of them, was an exhortation in favor of "Women's Rights," as the movement was called at the time; for Moses Woolson was a sincere and ardent champion of womankind. On this topic he spoke in true nobility of spirit.

But the talks that gripped Louis the hardest were those on English literature. Here the master was completely at his ease. Here, indeed, he revelled, as it were, in the careful analysis and lucid exposition of every phase of his subject, copious in quotatoin, delightfully critical in taking apart a passage, a single line, explaining the value of each word in respect of action, rhythm, color, quality, texture, fitness, then putting these elements together in a renewed recital of the passage which now became a living moving utterance. Impartial in judgment, fertile in illustration and expedient, clear in statement, he opened to view a new world, a new land of enchantment.

One day, to Louis's amazement, he announced that the best existing history of English literature was written by a Frenchman, one Hyppolite Taine by name. This phenomenon he explained by stating that the fine French mind possessed a quality and power of detachment unknown to the English; that Monsieur Taine further possessed that spiritual aspect of sympathy, that vision, which enabled him to view, to enter freely and to comprehend a work of art regardless yet regardful of its origin in time or place; and he rounded an antithesis of French and English culture in such wise as to arouse Louis's keenest attention, for the word *culture,* had hitherto possessed no significance for him; it was merely a word! Now his thoughts, his whole being floated o'er the sea to distant France, whereupon he arose from his seat and asked Moses Woolson what culture really meant, and was told it signified the genius of a people, of a race. And what was meant by the *genius* of a people? It signified their innate qualities and powers of heart and mind; that therefore their culture was their own expression of their inmost selves, as individuals, as a people, as a race. Louis was magnificently bewildered by this high concentration. He seemed to be in a flood of light which hid everything from view; he made some sheepish rejoinder, whereupon Moses Woolson saw his own mistake.

He came down from his high perch to which he had climbed unwittingly, for it was dead against his theory and practice to talk above the heads of his boys. He thereupon diluted the prior statement with a simply worded illustration, and Louis was glad to find his own feet still on the ground. Then Louis put the two aspects of the statement side by side again, and "culture" became for him a living word—a sheer veil through which, at first, he could but dimly see; but living word and sheer living veil had come from without to abide with him. It seemed indeed as though Moses Woolson had passed on to him a wand of enchantment which he must learn to use to unveil the face of things. Thus Louis dreamed.

By the end of the school year Moses Woolson through genius as a teacher, had turned a crudely promising boy into, so to speak, a mental athlete. He had brought order out of disorder, definition out of what was vague, superb alertness out of mere boyish ardor; had nurtured and concentrated all that was best in the boy; had made him consciously courageous and independent; had focussed his powers of thought, feeling and action; had confirmed Louis's love of the great out of doors, as a source of inspiration; and had climaxed all by parting a great veil which opened to the view of this same boy, the wonderland of Poetry.

Thus with great skill he made of Louis a compacted personality, ready to act on his own initiative, in an intelligent purposeful way. Louis had the same capacity to absorb, and to value discipline, that Moses Woolson had to impart it, and Louis was not a brilliant or showy scholar. He stood well up in his class and that was enough. His purpose was not to give out, but to receive, to acquire. He was adept in the art of listening and was therefore rather silent of mood. His object was to get every ounce of treasure out of Moses Woolson. And yet for Moses Woolson, the master and the man, he felt neither love nor affection, and it is quite likely that the master felt much the same toward him. What he felt toward the man was a vast admiration, he felt the power and the vigor of his intense and prodigal personality. It is scarcely likely that the master really knew, to the full extent, what he was doing for this boy, but Louis knew it; and there came gradually over him a cumulative reciprocity which, at the end, when he had fully realized the nature of the gift, burst forth into a sense of obligation and of gratitude so heartfelt, so profound, that it has remained with him in constancy throughout the years. There may have been teachers and teachers, but for Louis Sullivan there was and could be only one. And now, in all too feeble utterance he pleads this token, remembrance, to the memory of that ONE long since passed on.

*   *   *

Meanwhile a cloud no bigger than a man's hand arose into the clear blue above the horizon of Henri List's placid life. Early in 1871 Anna List, his wife, his prop, his anchor, his life's mainstay, was taken with her first and last illness. Louis was forbidden her room. All was quiet; furtive comings and goings; whispered anxious words. The cloud arose, darkened the world and passed on. One morning, it was told that he, Louis, might see her. He went directly to her room, opened the door, and entered. The white shades were down and all was light within. On the bed he saw extended an object fully covered by a sheet. He advanced, drew aside the sheet, rashly pressed his lips upon the cold forehead, drew back as though stung.

Standing erect he gazed steadfastly down upon rigid features that seemed of unearthly ivory.

Grandmamma had vanished!

What signified this cold menace he now scanned? This stranger in the house—whence Grandmamma had gone forever?

What meant this effigy, this ivory simulacrum that had come here in her stead?

It could not see, it could not hear, it could not feel, it could not move, it could not speak, it could not love!

Grandmamma had vanished!

She had passed on with a great cloud that had cast its shadow.

And here, now before him lay a counterfeit, where once she was.

An object, a nothing, a something and a nothing, which Louis could not think or name; an ivory mask which repelled, which instantly he rejected, as a ghastly intrusion.

And they had said that he would see his Grandmamma!

Ah! then, was this petrified illusion his Grandmamma?

They lied!

His true Grandmamma was in his heart and would remain there till his own end should come. Whatever this object before him might be, it was not Gran'ma!

His Grandmamma had vanished!

He replaced the shroud. Dry-eyed, and as one filled with a cold light, he left the room.

Never before had Louis seen what Death, the cloud no bigger than a man's hand, leaves behind it as it passes overhead and vanishes.

* * *

An upright white marble slab, in the cemetery, at the point of the promontory that juts into Lake Quannapowitt, says to the stranger wandering therein, that ANNA, wife of Henri List died 2 April, 1871, aged 66 years.

In this laconic statement the cynic hand of Henri List is clearly seen, even as at the funeral service in the "spare room" he was prostrate in an overwhelming flood of hysteria and tears, even as Louis stood by, gazing at him in wonder that a strong man could be so weak; even as Louis, cold and harshly irritated by the Baptist minister, whose sensuous words in praise of human bloodshed, he cursed. Driven to desperation by the whining quartet, he rushed into the open, sat under a tree and damned them all to perdition. Why had he been dragged into this gross orgy of grief? Could he not be left alone and in peace, to revere in memory that grandmamma who still lived on within his heart? The others with their noisy and their mercenary grief would soon forget. He, never. As thus he raged, a peach tree in full bloom in the garden caught his eye. He hastened to it as to a friend, in dire need. Its joyous presence in the garden gave him courage, for spring again was singing her great song. The air was vocal in a choir of resurrection. Here indeed was resurrection and the life. It seemed to him not in the least incongruous that his beloved had vanished into that great life whence she came—whence he had come; and that as Life was within him, so was his beloved within him as life within a life to be treasured evermore.

Thus near the peach tree in full bloom, Louis's tortured mind was stilled. He accepted death as an evanishment, he accepted Life as the power of powers. It seemed, indeed, as standing near his friend, gazing fondly round about and upward through the invisible firmament, that this great power, Life, in gesture and in utterance through the song of spring, had set its glowing rainbow in the passing cloud as a token of a covenant that the pure of eye might see. And indeed it seemed to him as quite lucid that the cloud with the glowing rainbow in its heart might well stand forever as a symbol of a token of a covenant between Life, and Man's proud spirit, and the Earth. Thus Louis dreamed. And it seemed as though a small voice coming from afar, said: "If one must dream let the dream be one of happiness."

*   *   *

For the second time the house of Henri List had collapsed and gone down. This time in fragments. Soon the farm was sold. Julia, she of flaming hair, bewitching fairy tales, and temper of Iseult, cook and companion for nine long years, vanished in turn; Julius, the son, now twenty-five, offered a place, "in Philadelphia," went there; his father followed.

Louis found welcome and shelter with the next door neighbors, the John A. Tompsons, whose son George for years had been his playmate. And the earth resumed its revolution about its own private axis as before; day following night as usual. Daily, George Tompson went to "Tech" to pursue his studies in railway engineering. Daily, Louis paid his renewed respects to Moses Woolson. Daily, John A. Tompson returned from Boston at an exact hour, removed his hat, walked to a glass cabinet, took exactly one stiff swig of Bourbon straight, smacked his lips, twinkled his eyes, sank into an easy chair which had remained in the same place for exactly how many years no one knows, dozed off for exactly ten minutes, arose, stretched his short muscular body, smiled widely, displaying false teeth, dyed-black side whiskers and moustache, a fine high forehead and dark fine eyes with as merry a twinkle as one could wish; then he went forth to see if each cultivated tree and shrub and bush and vine were exactly where they were in the morning. This man, gifted with extraordinary deftness of hand and a high-spirited intelligence, became a wonder and an inspiration to Louis, who spent the following two years in this charming household where epicureanism prevailed.

That spring and summer, Louis botanized and mineralized with incessant ardor, and he saw what it signified that each thing should have a name, and what order and classification meant in the way of organized intelligence, and increased power of manipulation of things and thoughts. His insight into the relationship of function and structure deepened rapidly. A thousand things now began to cohere and arrange into groups which hitherto had seemed disparate and wide apart. To be sure, Moses Woolson was the impelling cause and it was up to Louis to do the work and to search and find and see these things objectively and clearly for himself. Thus logical connections began to form a plexus in his growing mind, beside which also upgrew a sense of equal logic and order in action. Now, John A. Tompson had this faculty of order and delicate precision in so marked a degree that Louis kept a close eye on his doings. In the fall Louis returned to the English High School and entered the Second Class under a sub-master named Hale. Mr.

Hale was a scholar and a gentleman, a shining light of conscientious, conventional, virtuous routine.

With that clear and ruthless faculty, which boys possess, of spotting the essentials of their elders, Louis at the first session so sized up Hale; and dismay and despair swept through him in an awful wave of depression; it seemed as though the light of life had gone out. What was this tallow dip to the hot sun of Woolson. What could this mannikin accomplish? What could this respectable and approved lay figure do for one who had been trained intensively for a year by Moses Woolson? Let us therefore quickly draw the veil; and forget.

At the end of this school year, George Tompson asked Louis why he did not try for "Tech." And Louis replied that he supposed that he must first finish "High." "Nonsense," said George, "You can pass easily." And thus encouraged, Louis passed easily.

It should be mentioned that at the time of the great Chicago fire, Louis received prompt word that the family were safe and sound beyond the reach of its fearsome ravages. And also Louis's faithful correspondence with those far away must not be overlooked. Thus he now felt safe and strong to face in "Tech" his first adventure, as prelude to an architectural career.

PLATE 18. Transportation Building, World's Columbian Exposition, Chicago. 1893. Demolished. Photograph taken from "The Dream City."

PLATE 19. Stock Exchange Building, 30 North LaSalle
Street, Chicago. 1893-94.

CHAPTER X

Farewell to Boston

DURING the two years Louis dwelt in the home of the John A. Tompsons, in Wakefield, he was very busy in thought and deed. A certain materialistic clarification of intellect was proceeding within a new light which enabled him to see things superficially and to share in that state of illusion concerning realities which was the common property of the educated and refined. The dreams of childhood—that form of mystical illumination which enables the little one to see that upon which the eyes of its elders seldom focus—were thereby eclipsed; and, in one less romantic and willful by nature, would have vanished permanently from active consciousness in the usual and customary way. For this very period of imaginative childhood is by most adults relegated to obscurity; and if referred to at all, dismissed as inconsequential and "childish." But childhood, thus banished, remains sequestered within us unchanged. It may be obscured by an overlay of our sophistication, our pride and our disdain; we, the while, unaware that to disdain our fertile childhood is precisely equivalent to disdain of our maturity. Hence the illusion that we are no longer the child; the delusion that we are any other than grown children. For where lives the man who does not firmly believe in magic and in fairy tales; who does not worship something with a child-like faith, who does not dream his dreams, however sordid or destructive, however high, however nobly altruistic? And Louis thus dared to disdain and eclipse his own childhood.

For was he not rising now like a toy balloon into the rarefied atmosphere of intellect? And what had intellect to do with childhood? Intellect, indeed, was the cachet of manhood, in whose borderland he was now wandering, making ready to cross the frontier, some day to enter what men called "real life." This mood began when Louis was well settled in the Massachusetts Institute of Technology—familiarly known as "Tech"—pursuing his special course in Architecture.

To John A. Tompson's tutelage Louis owed many pirouettes, particularly some knowledge and some understanding and misunderstanding of the great oratorios. Under the sway of their beauty, the sensuous allure of the sacred music, Louis would return again and again to his childhood's sensibilities and faith. But there came a telling change when he had acquired from John A. some knowledge of their structure, some definition and labelling of the wondrous chords and modulations that had exalted him to an agony, and had borne him along in a great resplendent stream of song, which became a stream of wonder upon wonder, that men had made these things—had made them all out of their heads. And in this maze of hero-worship he had dreamed again and again his natal dream of power, of that power within man of which no one had told him; for he had heard only of the power of God. And in this special dream he had in truth and noble faith seen man as magician bringing forth from nothingness, from depths of silence of a huge world of sleep, as though, by waving of some unknown unseen wand, he had evoked this sublime, this amazing fabric; which equally would pass away and vanish with the sound of the last note, even as the bare thought of such passing left a haunt within.

It was then John A. Tompson, he of the precise, the articulate, the exact, the meticulous, the hard in· telligence—who bit by bit led Louis on. He dispelled for him the music-world of enchantment wherein simple faith had seen the true substance and value of results; he substituting therefor a world of fact and technique. It was all subtly done, bit by bit. The first effect of this was to arouse in Louis a new interest—an interest in technique—in the how. John A. Tompson, himself, indeed loved these oratorios, with a fanaticism pecu· liarly his own, somewhat as though he were impersonat· ing a machinist's vise. He clung to them indeed as though imagining he was a shipwrecked mariner and they a saving raft; yet he was quiet and gleeful amid the dangers of the open sea of sound.

He used to grit his teeth when he was pleased and he frequently was pleased when on shore he was giving Louis a hypodermic of technique. Louis's utter inno· cence of music's artful structure, form and content was John A.'s joy, his secret delight. Thus Louis learned, concerning chords, that the one in particular that had overwhelmed him with a sort of gorgeous sorrow was called the dominant seventh, and another that seemed eerie and that gave him a peculiar nervous thrill and chill was named the augmented fifth. Louis had been very curious concerning these two chords; and further· more he was insistent to know why certain parts of the music filled him with joyful, inspiriting and triumphant pleasure, while other parts made him sad even to mel· ancholy and despair. He was told that these opposites were known as the major and the minor modes and he was much concerned too, regarding what he later learned were the diatonic and the chromatic scales—and further concerning that strange swaying and turning of surging harmonies—that it was a movement technically known as a modulation from one key into another. Now Louis became avariciously curious concerning all the remaining technicalities and names, and amassed them as one might collect precious curios. It seemed to him that in giving names to all these sounds and movements he had heard and felt; it was much like giving names to the flowers and shrubs and trees he had loved so well. But this difference he marked: That while his plants and trees in spite of names lived on in mystery, and slept their winter sleep, to be again awakened by the call of Spring, giving names to music had dispelled the mystery, and had caused its sweet enchantments one by one to pass in defile into a group of words, which might mean much or nothing according as one first had felt the living power without their aid. That the danger was that music might become enslaved to the intellect and might nevermore be free. For as he began to see the full bulk of the mechanics, the mechanisms, and the tyranny of rules he became alarmed that music might die. For he could not yet see that here also, spite of names, the mystery, the enchantment would live on even though it be in winter sleep, and, at imagination's rousing call, again and again would renew its onward flow of rejuvenescence, and thus retain its magic power to stir the heart.

Thus Louis learned a modicum concerning music. A very trifle, to be sure. For he lived in Puritan New England where large utterances of joy and faith in the

Earth, of faith in Life, of faith in Man, were few and far between.

Nevertheless he had now definitely entered the cultural world, within which were the blest, without which were the damned. The world of intellectual dissection, surgery and therapeutics; the world of *theory,* of conjecture, of analysis and synthesis; the world of Idea, of Abstraction, of tenuity, of minute distinctions and nuances, filled with its specific belief in magic, its own superstitions, its aberrations, its taboos, denials and negations, and yet equally a world of vast horizons, of eagle-eyed range, of immense powers of ethereal flight to the far and the near, seeking the stars to know them, seeking the most minute to know it, searching the invisible to inquire what may be there, ever roaming, ever inquiring, inquisitive, acquisitive, accumulating a vast fund of the how and why, wherewith to record, to construct, to upbuild; and yet, withal, in giant service to the willful power of Imagination without whose vitalizing spark it could not stir; while in the fullness of its strength it can no more than carry on the heart's desire.

The living relationship of Intellect and Instinct has far too long been overlooked. For Intellect is recent, and neuter, and unstable in itself, while Instinct is primordial and procreant: It is a power so vast, so fathomless, so omnipresent, that we ignore it; for it is the vast power of all time that sleeps and dreams; it is that power within whose dream we dream,—even as in our practical aspect, our hard headed, cold-blooded, shrewd, calculating suspicious caution we are most obviously dreamers of turbid dreams, for we have pinned

[179]

our faith to Intellect; we gaze in lethal adoration upon a reed shaken by the wind.

About this time flamboyantly arose Patrick Gilmore with his band and his World Jubilee. Then Louis discovered there had been in existence music quite other than oratorio, hymn, sentimental songs of the hoi polloi and burnt-cork minstrels, or the classic grindings of the hurdy-gurdy.

He found it refreshing and gay, melodious above all. When he heard full bosomed Parepa sing in *coloratura,* he could scarcely keep his seat; never was such soprano heard in oratorio, and when the elder Strauss like a little he-wren mounted the conductor's stand, violin in hand, and dancing, led the orchestra through the lively cadence of the Blue Danube, Louis thought him the biggest little man on earth; and when it came to the "sextette" from Lucia, Louis roared his approval and listened just as eagerly to the inevitable encore. And the "Anvil Chorus"—oh, the Anvil Chorus! And so on, day by day, night by night from glorious beginning to glorious end. He had heard the finest voices in the world, great orchestral out-pourings, immense choruses. But he was, above all, amazed at the power of the single voice, when trained to perfection of control. He felt again with delight its unique quality, its range, its fluency, its flexibility, its emotional gamut, its direct personal intimate appeal; he felt a soul, a being, in the single voice, the heartful, the perfect instrument whereby to interpret and convey every state of feeling and of thought; and he was glad indeed.

This blossoming of music exotic to all he had known hitherto, made him glad, made him gay, relaxed his

[180]

sobriety, refreshed his outlook on life. It filled him with a new consciousness of beauty; of a beauty that seemed free and debonair, like a swan in the pool, like rain on the roof, like roses on a garden wall, with groves, and a turquoise sky; like bold and joyous horses, saying ha! ha!—and like unto furtive gentle creatures of wood and stream, and like curling breakers when close by, or the tossing of trees in a hearty gale.

*   *   *

More excitement: Came the great conflagration of 9 and 10 November, 1872. Louis saw this terror from its trifling beginning—a small flame curling from the wooden cornice of a building on the north side of Summer street. There were perhaps a half dozen persons present at the time. The street was night-still. It was early. No fire engine came. Horses were sick, "epizootic" was raging. Engines must be drawn by hand. All was quiet as the small flame grew into a whorl and sparks shot upward from a glow behind; the windows became lighted from within. A few more people gathered, but no engine came. Then began a gentle purring roar. The few became a crowd but no engine came. Glass crackled and crashed, flames burst forth madly from all windows, and the lambent dark flames behind them soared high, casting multitudes of sparks and embers abroad, as they cracked and wheezed. The roof fell, the floors collapsed. A hand-drawn engine came, but too late. The front wall tottered, swayed and crumbled to the pavement, exposing to view a roaring furnace. It was too late. The city seemed doomed. With this prelude began the great historic fire. Louis followed its ravages all night long.

It was a magnificent but terrible pageant of wrathful fire before whose onslaught row after row of regimented buildings melted away. As far as the eye could reach all was consuming fire, and dire devastation; an inferno, terrible and wonderful to look upon. Louis went here and there, retreating as the holocaust advanced ever northward. All the city seemed doomed, but it was not. All hope seemed lost, but it was not. The end came at last; courageous, weary and worn men triumphed, after agonies of hope and despair. What a terror, what a holocaust, what ruin of men, what downfall, what instant collapses of fortune, what a heavy load to meet and bear, what a trial and a test. Yet a proud spirit, the eternal spirit of man rose to the height of the call of calamity. The city was rebuilt. For Louis it was a terrifying experience; so sudden, so overwhelming, so fatalistic, so cruel.

When the ruins cooled Louis found it difficult to locate the streets. They seemed labyrinthine, lost in a maze of wreckage and debris; bit by bit he found his strange way about. At night he was put on guard duty as a member of the M. I. T. battalion. Clad in full uniform with Springfield rifle and fixed bayonet at right shoulder, he walked his beat from Tremont street to Pleasant street as far as opposite the tower of the Providence Depot, and return. For hours in the night, all alone, he walked his beat and saw not a soul. At first it was novel and exciting, but as nothing happened, he became weary from loss of sleep, bored by the monotonous to and fro, and glad to be relieved. He had two nights of this. Then came a show of order throughout the city and the great work of clear-

[182]

ing and upbuilding, in due time began. He returned to his studies in Tech.

He had liked military drill; he had had two years of it at "High." He liked the exercise, the sense of order and precision, the neat evolutions and the compact team work of the many cadets. But he considered it as discipline in play. He had no thought of war other than to loathe it, as the wild dream of madmen who stood safely behind the evil. For Louis, long since had begun to sense and to discern what lay behind the veil of appearances. Social strata had become visible and clear, as also that hypocrisy of caste and cant and "eminence" against which his mother, time and time again, had spoken so clearly, so vehemently in anger and contempt. Her ideal she averred was a righteous man, sound of head, clean of heart, a truthful man too natural to lie or to evade. These outbursts of his mother sank deep into the being of her son; and in looking back adown the years, he has reason justly to appraise in reverence and love a nature so transparent, so pure, so vehement, so sound, so filled with a yearning for the joy of life, so innocent-ecstatic in contemplation of beauty anywhere, as was that of the one who bore him forth, truly in fidelity, to be and to remain life of her life. Thus the curtain of memory ever lifts and falls and lifts again, on one to whom this prayer is addressed. If Louis is not his mother's spirit in the flesh, then words fail, and memory is vain.

* * *

Upon his entry into "Tech" Louis felt a marked change in atmosphere from that of "High." It was now an atmosphere of *laissez faire,* of a new sort of freedom. Tuition paid, the rest he found was up to him. There was no special regularity of hours or of attendance. He might exert himself or not as he saw fit. He might learn as much or little as he chose. There was no discipline further than this: That one was expected to conduct himself with decorum and with a reasonable degree of application. It was broadly assumed that the student was there in his own interest and would apply himself accordingly.

The school was housed in Rogers Hall, adjoining, on the south, the Museum of Natural History, at Boylston and Berkeley streets. The quarters were pleasant and airy, the long drafting-room or atelier facing broadside to the south. There was also a Library and a Lecture Room. At this date the school was comparatively new, having been opened in 1865. Louis therefore was among its early students. This one building housed the Institute entire.

The School of Architecture was presided over by Professor William R. Ware, of the Boston architectural firm of Ware & Van Brunt. Among the important works of this firm were the Memorial Building at Harvard, and the large Railway Station at Worcester. Professor Ware was a gentleman of the old school; a bachelor, of good height, slender, bearded in the English fashion, and turning gray. He had his small affectations, harmless enough. His voice was somewhat husky, his polite bearing impeccable and kind. He had a precious sense of quiet humor, and common sense seemed to have a strong hold on him. Withal he was worthy of personal respect and affection. His attainments were moderate in scope and soundly cultural as of the day; his judgments were clear and just. The words amiability and quiet common sense sum up his personality; he was not imaginative enough to be ardent.

His assistant, Eugene Letang, was a *diplomé* of the Ecole National des Beaux Arts, Paris, and specifically an *ancien* of the *atelier libre* of Emil Vaudremer, *architect,* a winner of the Grand Prix de Rome.

This man Letang was sallow earnestness itself; long and lean of face with a scanty student beard. Let us say he was thirty. He had no professional air; he was a student escaped from the Beaux Arts, a transplanted *massier* as it were of the *atelier,* where the *anciens,* the older students, help the *nouveaux,* the younger set, along. He was admirably patient, and seemed to believe in the real value of the work he so candidly was doing; and at times he would say: "From discussion comes the light." So here was a student absorbed in teaching students, while Professor Ware conserved the worldly pose and poise of the cultural Boston of the time,—creating and maintaining thus an air of the legitimate and approved.

There were perhaps not over thirty students, all told, in the architectural course, and Louis found them agreeable companions. Some of them were University graduates and therefore older than he and much more worldly wise, in their outlook. And there were as well a few advanced students. A few were there as rich men's sons, to whom the architectural profession seemed to have advantages of tone. Arthur Roche was one of these. A few were there as poor men's sons. They worked hard to become bread-winners. Among these was William Roche Ware, nephew of the Professor, and George Ferry of Milwaukee. What certain others were there for, including Louis, is a somewhat dubious surmise. But Louis began to like companionship for the first time. Hitherto he had been entirely neglectful of his school comrades, caring neither who nor what they were as persons. Here, however, there was space, freedom of movement and continued personal informal intercourse. So Louis began to put on a bit of swagger, to wear smart clothes, to shave away the down and to agitate a propaganda for inch-long side whiskers. A photograph of that date shows him as a clean-cut young man, with a rather intelligent expression, a heavy mop of black hair neatly parted for the occasion, a pearl stud set in immaculate white, and a suit up to the minute in material and cut. But inasmuch as in this photograph he neither moves nor speaks, we are free to infer that, being young, there may be either something or nothing of real value there. Louis, however, knew more about that picture than the picture knew or could convey of him. For memory, reviving, he knew all his past; and this does not in the least appear in the picture, nor what was of abiding significance in that past. So Louis posed a bit, sensing the reflected prestige and social value of a student at "Tech." But he did not altogether make a nuisance of himself, not a complete nuisance, for he was toppy rather than vain.

Louis had gone at his studies faithfully enough. He learned not only to draw but to draw very well. He traced the "Five Orders of Architecture" in a manner quite resembling copper plate, and he learned about diameters, modules, minutes, entablatures, columns, pediments and so forth and so forth, with the associated minute measurements and copious vocabulary, all of which items he supposed at the time were intended to be received in unquestioning faith, as eternal verities. And he was told that these "Orders" were "Classic," which implied an arrival at the goal of Platonic perfection of idea.

But Louis by nature was not given to that kind of faith. His faith ever lay in the oft-seen creative power and glory of man. His faith lay indeed in freedom. The song of Spring was the song in his heart. These rigid "Orders" seemed to say, "The book is closed; Art shall die." Then it occurred to him: Why five orders? Why not one? Each of the five plainly tells a different story. Which one of them shall be sacrosanct? And if one be sacrosanct the remaining four become invalid. Now it would appear by the testimony of the world of scholarship and learning that the Greek is sacrosanct; and of all the Greek, the Parthenon is super-sacrosanct. Therefore there was and has been in all time but the unique Parthenon; all else is invalid. Art is dead. And it should not be forgot that the unique Parthenon was builded by the ancient Greeks, by living men. It was physically upreared in an exact spot on the Acropolis at Athens, a timely demonstration of Greek thought concerning ideas.

Now after centuries of ruin the Parthenon is dead; therefore all is invalid, Art is dead. This line of reasoning amused Louis quaintly. It seemed to him romantic; much like a fairy tale. And this is all that he gathered from the "Orders"—that they really were fairy tales of the long ago, now by the learned made rigid, mechanical and inane in the books he was pursuing, wherein they were stultified, for lack of common sense and human feeling. Hence he spent much

time in the library, looking at pictures of buildings
of the past that did not have pediments and columns.
He found quite a few and became acquainted with
"styles" and learned that styles were not considered
sacrosanct, but merely human. That there was a difference in the intellectual and therefore social scale,
between a style and an order. Professor Ware did
not press matters thus; he did not go so far as to
apotheosize the cognoscenti and the intelligentsia. He
himself was quite human and in a measure detached.
The misfortune was that in his lectures on the history
of architecture he never looked his pupils in the eye,
but by preference addressed an audience in his beard,
in a low and confidential tone, ignoring a game of spit-
ball underway. Yet a word or a phrase reached the
open now and then concerning styles, construction and
so forth, and at times he went to the blackboard and
drew this and that very neatly. Louis picked up something of all this melange, but his thought was mostly
on the tower of the New Brattle Street Church, con-
ceived and brought to light by the mighty Richardson, undoubtedly for Louis's special delight; for was
not here a fairy tale indeed! Meanwhile there were
projets to be done and Eugene Letang surely earned
his pay in the sweat of his brow. Prof. William Ware
did the higher criticism and frequently announced he
had no use for "gim-crack" roofs.

Thus passed the days, the weeks, the months in a
sort of misch-masch of architectural theology, and
Louis came to see that it was not upon the spirit but
upon the word that stress was laid, even though it
were a weighty matter of sprinkling or immersion. He
began to feel a vacancy in himself, the need of some-

thing more nutritious to the mind than a play of mario-
nettes. He felt the need and the lack of a red-blooded
explanation, of a valiant idea that should bring life to
arouse his cemetery of orders and of styles, or at least
to bring about a *danse macabre* to explain why the
occupants had lived and died.

Moreover, as time passed he began to discover that
this school was but a pale reflection of the Ecole des
Beaux Arts; and he thought it high time that he go to
headquarters to learn if what was preached *there* as
a gospel, really signified glad tidings. For Louis felt
in his heart that what he had learned at "Tech" was
after all but a polite introduction to the architectural
Art,—as much as to say, "I am glad to meet you."
He reflected with a sort of despair that neither immaculate Professor Ware nor sweaty, sallow, earnest
Eugene Letang was a Moses Woolson. Ah, if but
Moses Woolson had been versed in the story of architecture as he was in that of English Literature, and
had held the professorship; ah, what glowing flame
would have come forth to cast its radiance like a rising
sun and illuminate the past. But why dream such
foolish dreams?

Louis made up his mind that he would leave "Tech"
at the end of the school year, for he could see no future
there. He was progressive, aggressive and impatient.
He wished to live in the stream of life. He wished to
be impelled by the power of living. He knew what he
wanted very well. It behooved him he thought before
going to the Beaux Arts, to see what architecture might
be like in practice. He thought it might be advisable
to spend a year in the office of some architect of
standing, that he might see concrete preparations and

results; how, in effect, an actual building was brought about. So he said a warm good-bye to Boston, to Wakefield (to his dear South Reading of the past), to all his friends, and made straightway for Philadelphia where he was to find his uncle and his grandpa. On the way he stopped over in New York City for a few days. Richard M. Hunt was the architectural lion there, and the dean of the profession. Louis called upon him in his den, told him his plans and was patted on the back and encouraged as an enterprising youngster. He listened to the mighty man's tale of his life in Paris with Lefuel, and was then turned over to an assistant named Stratton, a recent arrival from the Ecole to whom he repeated the tale of his projects.

Friend Stratton was most amiable in greeting, and gave Louis much time, receiving him in the fraternal spirit of an older student toward a younger. He sketched the life in Paris and the School—and in closing asked Louis to keep in touch with him and be sure to call on him on the way abroad. Thus Louis, proud and inflated, went on his joyous way to face the world. He arrived in Philadelphia in due time, as they say. He had noticed in New York a sharper form of speech, an increase of energetic action over that he had left behind, and also a rougher and more arrogant type of life Stratton had mentioned that Louis, on his arrival in Philadelphia, should look up the firm of Furness & Hewitt, architects, and try to find a place with them. But this was not Louis's way of doing. Once settled down in the large quiet village, he began to roam the streets, looking quizzically at buildings as he wandered. On the west side of South Broad street a residence, almost completed, caught his eye like a flower by the roadside. He approached, examined it with curious care, without and within. Here was something fresh and fair to him, a human note, as though someone were talking. He inquired as to the architect and was told: Furness & Hewitt. Now, he saw plainly enough that this was not the work of two men but of one, for he had an instinctive sense of physiognomy, and all buildings thus made their direct appeal to him, pleasant or unpleasant.

He made up his mind that next day he would enter the employ of said Furness & Hewitt, they to have no voice in the matter, for his mind was made up. So next day he presented himself to Frank Furness and informed him he had come to enter his employ. Frank Furness was a curious character. He affected the English in fashion. He wore loud plaids, and a scowl, and from his face depended fan-like a marvelous red beard, beautiful in tone with each separate hair delicately crinkled from beginning to end. Moreover, his face was snarled and homely as an English bulldog's. Louis's eyes were riveted, in infatuation, to this beard, as he listened to a string of oaths yards long. For it seems that after he had delivered his initial fiat, Furness looked at him half blankly, half enraged, as at another kind of dog that had slipped in through the door. His first question had been as to Louis's experience, to which Louis replied, modestly enough, that he had just come from the Massachusetts Institute of Technology in Boston. This answer was the detonator that set off the mine which blew up in fragments all the schools in the land and scattered the professors headless and limbless to the four quarters of earth and hell. Louis, he said, was a fool. He said Louis was an idiot to have wasted his time in a place where one was filled with sawdust, like a doll, and became a prig, a snob, and an ass.

As the smoke blew away he said: "Of course you don't know anything and are full of damnable conceit."

Louis agreed to the ignorance; demurred as to conceit; and added that he belonged to that rare class who were capable of learning, and desired to learn. This answer mollified the dog-man, and he seemed intrigued that Louis stared at him so pertinaciously. At last he asked Louis what in hell had brought him there, anyway? This was the opening for which Louis had sagaciously been waiting through the storm. He told Frank Furness all about his unaided discovery of the dwelling on Broad street, how he had followed, so to speak from the nugget to the solid vein; that here he was and here he would remain; he had made up his mind as to that, and he looked Frank Furness in the eye. Then he sang a song of praise like a youthful bard of old to his liege lord, steering clear of too gross adulation, placing all on a high plane of accomplishment. It was here, Louis said, one could really learn. Frank Furness admitted as true a part of what Louis had said, waving the rest away as one pleasantly overpraised, and said: Only the Greeks knew how to build.

"Of course, you don't want any pay," he said To which Louis replied that ten dollars a week would be a necessary honorarium.

"All right," said he of the glorious beard, with something scraggy on his face, that might have been a smile. "Come tomorrow morning for a trial, but I prophesy you won't outlast a week." So Louis came. At the end of that week Furness said, "You may stay another week," and at the end of that week Furness said, "You may stay as long as you like." Oh what a joy! Louis's first task was to retrace a set of plans complete for a Savings Institution to be erected on Chestnut street. This he did so systematically and in so short a time that he won his spurs at once. In doing this work he was but carrying out the impulsion of Moses Woolson's training in accuracy and speed; and Moses Woolson followed him thereafter everywhere.

The other members of the firm was George Hewitt, a slender, moustached person, pale and reserved, who seldom relaxed from pose. It was he who did the Victorian Gothic in its pantalettes, when a church building or something of that sort was on the boards. With precision, as though he held his elements by pincers, he worked out these decorous sublimities of inanity, as per the English current magazines and other English sources. He was a clean draftsman, and believed implicitly that all that was good was English. Louis regarded him with admiration as a draftsman, and with mild contempt as a man who kept his nose in books. Frank Furness "made buildings out of his head." That suited Louis better. And Furness as a freehand draftsman was extraordinary. He had Louis hypnotized, especially when he drew and swore at the same time.

But George Hewitt had a younger brother named John, and John was foreman of the shop. He was a husky, smooth-faced fellow under thirty. Every feature in his clean cut, rather elongated face, bespoke intelligence and kindness, in fact a big heart. He had taken a fancy to Louis from the start. He was the "practical man" and Louis ran to him for advice whenever he found himself in a tight place. John was patience itself and made everything clear with dainty sketches and explanatory notes. These drawings were beautiful and Louis frankly told him so. He begged John to teach him "touch" and how to make such sketches, and especially how to "indicate" so crisply. This John did. In fact, it was not long before he had made of Louis a draftsman of the upper Crust, and Louis's heart went out to lovable John in sheer gratitude.

In looking back upon that time Louis Sullivan gives thanks that it was his great good fortune to have made his entry into the practical world in an office where standards were so high—where talent was so manifestly taken for granted, and the atmosphere the free and easy one of a true work shop savoring of the guild where craftsmanship was paramount and personal. And again he goes back to the day of Moses Woolson and his discipline. We may say in truth that Moses Woolson put him there. For without that elastic alertness and courage, that grimness Moses Woolson imparted, it is sure that Louis would not have broken through the barrier of contempt in that first interview.

Louis worked very hard day and night. At first he had lived with his grandpa and uncle in West Philadelphia. But soon he decided to move into town to be nearer the office and to be freer to study into the small hours. His relaxation on Sundays was Fairmount Park and a walk up the rough road of the

PLATE 20. Prudential Building, SW corner of Church and Pearl Streets, Buffalo, N. Y. 1894-95. Formerly the Guaranty Building. Terra cotta defaced by cleaning, 1955.

PLATE 21. Prudential Building (see Plate 20). Doorway, east facade.

PLATE 22. Prudential Building (see Plate 20). Column
and capital, east facade.

PLATE 23. Gage Building (at right), 18 South Michigan Avenue, Chicago. 1898-99. Remodelled. Louis Henri Sullivan; Holabird & Roche, associates.

Wissahickon valley, a narrow beauteous wilderness such as Louis had never seen, and with which he was completely charmed. He loved the solitude through which the Wissahickon purled its way. The companionship of the wild was soothing to him. The isolation gave him comfort and surcease. Thus passed a hot summer.

*   *   *

The offices of Furness & Hewitt occupied the entire top floor of a new, brick, four-story building at the northeast corner of Third street and Chestnut.

One day in September, it was very warm, all windows were open for air, the force was wearily at work. As they worked, there came through the open windows a murmur, barely noticed at first; then this murmur became a roar, with wild shouting. Then, all to the windows. Louis saw, far below, not pavement and sidewalks, but a solid black mass of frantic men, crowded, jammed from wall to wall. The offices of Jay Cooke & Co. were but a short distance south on Third street. Word came up that Jay Cooke & Co. had just closed its doors. Louis saw it all, as he could see down both Chestnut street and Third. Chestnut westward from Third also was a solid mass. The run on the banks had begun. The devastating panic of 1873 was on, in its mad career. Louis was shocked, appalled at the sight. He was too young, too inexperienced, to understand what it really meant, even when told it was a panic in finance, that credit had crumbled to dust, that men were ruined, and insane with despair; that this panic would spread like wildfire over the land leaving ruin in its wake everywhere.

And still he could not understand what had brought it about.

The office held steady for a while; there was work on hand which had progressed so far that it must be completed.

One day in November Frank Furness said: "Sullivan, I'm sorry, the jig is up. There'll be no more building. The office now is running dry. You've done well, mighty well. I like you. I wish you might stay. But as you were the last to come it is only just you should be first to go." With that he slipped a bill into Louis's hand, and wished him farewell and better days.

Within a week Louis took the Pennsylvania train for Chicago. He saw the great valley of the Susquehanna; surmounted the huge Alleghenies; passed along the great descending Horse-Shoe Curve, the marvel of the day; and then night fell. He was aroused and broadened by what he had seen. It was all new. His map was enlarged. So was his breadth of view; his inner wealth.

Next morning he was utterly amazed and bewildered at the sight of the prairies of northern Indiana. They were startling in novelty. How could such things be! Stretching like a floor to the far horizon,—not a tree except by a watercourse or on a solitary "island." It was amazing. Here was power—power greater than the mountains. Soon Louis caught glimpses of a great lake, spreading also like a floor to the far horizon, superbly beautiful in color, under a lucent sky. Here again was power, naked power, naked as the prairies, greater than the mountains. And over all spanned the dome of the sky, resting on the rim of the horizon far away on all sides, eternally calm overhead, holding an atmosphere pellucid and serene. And here again was a power, a vast open power, a power greater than the tiny mountains. Here, in full view, was the light of the world, companion of the earth, a power greater than the lake and the prairie below, but not greater than man in his power: So Louis thought.

The train neared the city; it broke into the city; it plowed its way through miles of shanties disheartening and dirty gray. It reached its terminal at an open shed. Louis tramped the platform, stopped, looked toward the city, ruins around him; looked at the sky; and as one alone, stamped his foot, raised his hand and cried in full voice:

THIS IS THE PLACE FOR ME!

That day was the day before Thanksgiving in the year Eighteen Hundred Seventy-three.

CHAPTER XI

Chicago

HEARD and seen by all stands the word *PER-SONALITY,* in solitary and unique grandeur. Heard and seen by all stands the word *Personality,* eminent, respectable, much admired.

Heard and seen by all in the crowd it calls together, and through which it deftly wanders like a shrewd hunch-back, the word *personality,* now a dwarf grimaces salaciously.

And now it is a word on fire; a tiger in the jungle; a python hanging from the limb, very still.

How deep, how shallow is that which we call the soul.

How monstrous, how fluent, how vagrant and timorous, how alert are the living things we call words. They are the giants and the fairies, the hob-goblins and the sprites; the warrior and the priest, the lowly and the high; the watch-dog and the sheep; the tyrant and the slave,—of that wonder-world we call speech.

How like hammers they strike. How like aspens they quiver. How like a crystal pool, a rivulet therefrom, becomes a river moving sinuously between the hills, growing stronger, broader as its affluents pour in their tributary power; and now looms the estuary, and the Ocean of Life.

Words are most malignant, the most treacherous possession of mankind. They are saturated with the sorrows of all time. They hold in most unstable equilibrium the vast heritage of man's folly, his despair, his wrestling with the angel whose name is Fate; his vanity, his pride before a fall, his ever-resurrecting hope—arising as a winged spirit from the grave of disaster, to flit in the sunshine for a while, to return to the dust and arise again as his civilizations, so laboriously built up, have crumbled one by one. And yet all the beauty, all the joy, all the love that man has known, all his kindness, all his yearnings, all his dreams for better things; his passionate desire for peace and an anchorage within a universe that has filled him with fear and mystery and adoration; his daily round of toil, and commonplaces; his assumption of things as they are; his lofty and sublime contemplations, his gorgeous imageries; his valor, his dogged will, his patience in long suffering, his ecstacies, his sacrifices small and great—even to the casting aside of his life for a thought, a compassion, an ambition—all these are held bound up in words; hence words are dangerous when let loose. They may mean man's destruction, they may signify a way out of the dark. For *Light* is a word, *Courage* is a word, and *Vision* is another. Therefore, it is wise to handle words with caution. Their content is so complex and explosive; and in combinations they may work beautiful or dreadful things.

All these thoughts have flowed from the one word, Personality, with which we began.

At Louis's age upon reaching Chicago, personality meant little as a formal word. He recognized by sight and feeling, by observing action and appearances, many of the phases of the powers of man upon which a word is built for use.

For words in themselves he had come to form a passing aversion, since he had noted their tendency to eclipse the vibrant values of immediate reality. Therefore, he preferred to think and feel and contemplate without the use of words. Indeed, one of his favorite pastimes was deliberately to think and feel and contemplate without the use of words, to create thus a wordless universe, with himself, silent, at the center of it all. Thus came about a widening clarity; an increased sensitiveness to values; a separate isolation of the permanent and the ephemeral; and it seemed, also, as though within his small, self-created silence he listened to the strident noises of the world as coming from without. All this Louis did with buoyant jocularity, for fun, for "practice" as he called it. And yet now and then a word came to him of a sudden, in surprise, a sort of keyword that unlocked, that opened and revealed. Among such was the word *self-expression,* which gave him a rude shock of hilarity and wonder. He said: What!—which expressed quite well what he meant.

For the first week in the strange city, Louis was the prodigal returned; and the fatted calf was offered up in joy. The next week he spent in exploration. As everybody said: "Chicago had risen phoenix-like from its ashes." But many ashes remained, and the sense of ruin was still blended with ambition of recovery. Louis thought it all magnificent and wild: A crude extravaganza: An intoxicating rawness: A sense of big things to be done. For "Big" was the word. "Biggest" was preferred, and the "biggest in the world" was the braggart phrase on every tongue. Chicago had had the biggest conflagration "in the world." It was the biggest grain and lumber market "in the world." It slaughtered more hogs than any city "in the world." It was the greatest railroad center, the greatest this, and the greatest that. It shouted itself hoarse in *réclame*. The shouters could not well be classed with the proverbial liars of Ecclesiastes, because what they said was true; and had they said, in the din, we are the crudest, rawest, most savagely ambitious dreamers and would-be doers in the world, that also might be true. For with much gloating of self-flattering they bragged: "We are the most heavily mortgaged city in the world." Louis rather liked all this, for his eye was ever on the boundless prairie and the mighty lake. All this frothing at the mouth amused him at first, but soon he saw the primal power assuming self-expression amid nature's impelling urge. These men had vision. What they saw was real, they saw it as destiny.

The elevated wooden sidewalks in the business district, with steps at each street corner, seemed shabby and grotesque; but when Louis learned that this meant that the city had determined to raise itself three feet more out of the mud, his soul declared that this resolve meant high courage; that the idea was big; that there must be big men here. The shabby walks now became a symbol of stout hearts.

The pavements were vile, because hastily laid; they erupted here and there and everywhere in ooze. Most of the buildings, too, were paltry. When Louis came to understand the vast area of disaster, he saw clearly and with applause that this new half-built city was a hasty improvization made in dire need by men who did not falter. And again spread out in thought, the boundless prairie and the mighty lake, and what they meant for men of destiny, even as the city lay stretched out, unseemly as a Caliban.

In spite of the panic, there was stir; an energy that made him tingle to be in the game.

So he bethought him he would enter the office of some architect; for a few buildings showed talent in design, and a certain stability. Outstanding among these was the Portland Block, a four-story structure of pressed brick and sandstone at Washington and Dearborn Streets. So he inquired concerning the architect of this structure and was told the name was Jenney: Major Jenney; or in full, Major William Le Baron Jenney. There were still some buildings under way, or arranged for, on the momentum of pre-panic days, though the town was otherwise badly hurt. A great fire, and a panic in finance, certainly made load enough for any community to carry, but Chicago, hard hit, bore up bravely.

Louis learned incidentally that the Portland Block had in fact been designed by a clever draftsman named Cudell. This gave him a shock. For he had supposed that all architects made buildings out of their own heads, not out of the heads of others. His experience in the office of Furness & Hewitt, in Philadelphia, it seems, had given him an erroneous idea. Yet the new knowledge cheered him in this hope: That he might some day make buildings out of his head for architects who did not have any heads of their own for such purpose.

He had once supposed that the genius for creating ugliness was peculiarly a Yankee monopoly; but he later found in New York and Philadelphia that almost all the buildings in these cities were of the same crassness of type; a singularly sordid, vulgar vernacular in architectural speech. So when he found the same thing almost universally in evidence in Chicago, he assumed that this illiteracy was general, and a jargon peculiar to the American people at large. The only difference he could see between the vernacular of the East and that of the West was that one was older and staler; and he cited Fifth Avenue, New York, as an instance. It is true that, scattered through the east were architects of book-attainment in fair number, and a few of marked personality and red blood—particularly one Henry Richardson, he of the strong arm and virile mind—sole giant of his day. In Chicago there were two or three who were bookish and timid, and there were some who were intelligently conscientious in the interest of their clients. Among the latter may be mentioned Major Jenney. The Major was a free-and-easy cultured gentleman, but not an architect except by courtesy of terms. His true profession was that of engineer. He had received his technical training, or education at the *Ecole Polytechnique* in France, and had served through the Civil War as Major of Engineers. He had been with Sherman on the march to the sea.

He spoke French with an accent so atrocious that it jarred Louis's teeth, while his English speech jerked about as though it had St. Vitus's dance. He was monstrously pop-eyed, with hanging mobile features, sensuous lips, and he disposed of matters easily in the manner of a war veteran who believed he knew what was what. Louis soon found out that the Major was not, really, in his heart, an engineer at all, but by nature, and in toto, a *bon vivant,* a gourmet. He lived at Riverside, a suburb, and Louis often smiled to see him carry home by their naked feet, with all plumage, a brace or two of choice wild ducks, or other game birds, or a rare and odorous cheese from abroad. And the Major knew his vintages, every one, and his sauces, every one; he also was a master of the chafing dish and the charcoal *grille*. All in all the Major was effusive; a hale fellow well met, an officer of the Loyal Legion, a welcome guest anywhere, but by preference a host. He was also an excellent raconteur, with a lively sense of humor and a certain piquancy of fancy that seemed Gallic. In his stories or his monologues, his unique vocal mannerisms or gyrations or gymnastics were a rich asset, as he squeaked or blew, or lost his voice, or ran in arpeggio from deep bass to harmonics, or took octaves, or fifths, or sevenths, or ninths in spasmodic splendor. His audience roared, for his stories were choice, and his voice, as one caught bits of it, was plastic, rich and sweet, and these bits, in sequence and collectively had a warming effect. The Major was really and truly funny. Louis thought him funny all the time, and noted with glee how akin were the Major's thoughts to the vertiginous gyrations of his speech. Thus we have a semblance of the Major's relations to the justly celebrated art of architecture.

The Major took Louis in immediately upon application, as he needed more help. And to the fact that Louis had been at "Tech" he attached the highest importance—as alumni of any school are apt to do; so much for temperamental personality.

There was work enough in the office to keep five men busy and a boy, provided they took intervals of rest, which they did. In the Major's absences, which were frequent and long, bedlam reigned. John Edelmann would mount a drawing table and make a howling stump speech on greenback currency, or single tax, while at the same time Louis, at the top of his voice, sang selections from the oratorios, beginning with his favorite, "Why Do the Nations so Furiously Rage Together"; and so all the force furiously raged together in joyous deviltry, and bang-bang-bang. For a moment Louis quieted the riot and sang, "Ye people rend your hearts, rend your hearts, but not your garments," whereupon there followed a clamor of affronts directed toward Elijah the Prophet. The office rat suddenly appears: "Cheese it, Cullies; the Boss!", which in high English signifies: "Gentlemen, Major William Le Baron Jenney, our esteemed benefactor, approaches!" Sudden silence, sudden industry, intense concentration. The Major enters and announces his pleasure in something less than three octaves. Thus the day's work comes out fairly even. For "when they work they work; and when they don't they just don't."

On the stool next to Louis sat patient Martin Roche, now, and for many years, of Holabird & Roche. There was a tall, fleshy, mild-voiced American-German who had taught school; and a rachitic, sharp-faced, droll, nasal Yankee, who drawled comic cynicisms and did the engineering. "The old man," he would say, "is some engineer. . . . Like the Almighty, he watches the 'sparrow's fall,' but when it comes to the *tons* he's a l-e-e-t-l-e shy now and then, and sometimes then and now. You fellows work for glory, but I just work for coin." And then he rasped in song: "And as I said be-f-o-o-o-r, don't fall in love with a groceryman what keeps a grocery store," and thus he cackled on, as he figured strains; this time, he said, on a basis of three sparrows, while Louis hummed: "And as I said before, don't fall in love with a groceryman what keeps a grocery store."

John was the foreman. By nature indolent, by vanity and practice very rapid. He laughed to scorn and scattered to dust those that were slow; and would illustrate, in roseate tales, how fast he had done this and that. It speedily became evident that John was a hero-worshipper, as John blandly worshipped John in the presence of all; and Louis casually remarked that John's unconsciousness of his own personality was remarkable to the point of the fabulous and the legendary, whereupon they became fast friends.

Louis had instantly noted in John a new personality; brawny, twenty-four, bearded, unkempt, careless, his voice rich, sonorous, modulant, his vocabulary an overflowing reservoir. A born orator—he must talk or perish. His inveterate formula was, "I myself"—did —was—said—am—think—know—to the sixteenth decimal and the nth power of egoism. It gradually dawned upon Louis that he had run across a THINKER, a profound thinker, a man of immense range of reading, a brain of extraordinary keenness, strong, vivid, that ranged in its operations from saturnine intelligence concerning men and their motives, to the highest transcendentalisms of German metaphysics. He was as familiar with the great philosophers as with the daily newspapers. As an immediate psychologist, never before or since has Louis met his equal in vitality, in verity, and in perspicacity of thought. He, John, knew all that all the psychologists had written, and much, of his own discernment, that they but recently have begun to unveil. Louis found in John a highly gifted talker, and John found in Louis a practised listener, so their bond of union may be summed up in the token "I myself."

One day John explained his theory of *suppressed functions;* and Louis, startled, saw in a flash that this meant the real clue to the mystery that lay behind the veil of appearances. Louis was peculiarly subject to shock from unexpected explosion of a single word; and when the word "function" was detonated by the word "suppressed," a new, an immense idea came suddenly into being and lit up his inner and his outer world as one. Thus, with John's aid, Louis saw the outer and the inner world more clearly, and the world of men began to assume a semblance of form, and of function. But, alas, what he had assumed to be a single vast veil of mystery that might perhaps lift of a sudden, like a cloud, proved in experience to be a series of gossamer hangings that must slowly rise up one by one, in a grand transformation scene, such as he had viewed when, as a small boy, he saw "The Forty Thieves," where all was transformed into reality by a child's imagination. Now would it be possible for him, through the reverse power of imagination, to cause the veils of the hidden world to rise and reveal? On this threshold, for a passing moment, he faltered. Then resurging courage came.

Louis soon noticed that while *he himself* had a clear program in life, John had none. That all this talk, while of deep import to him, was for John merely luxurious self-indulgence and a luscious hour with parade of vanity; that he, the elder, regarded the younger with patronage, much as a bright child, but a tyro in the active world; while Louis saw that John was merely drifting. In this regard each kept his thoughts to himself, while encouraging the other.

In Philadelphia, one hot summer's evening, Louis had gone to the Academy of Music to hear a Thomas Concert. During the course of the program he had become listless, when of a sudden came the first bars of a piece so fiery, that, startled, all alert, he listened in amazement to the end. What was this? It was new—brand new. The program now consulted, said: *Vorspiel,* Third Act, Lohengrin—Richard Wagner. Who was Richard Wagner? Why had he never heard of him? He must look him up; for one could see at a glance that this piece was a work of genius.

He mentioned this episode to John Edelmann, shortly after they had become acquainted; and John said: Why, at the North Side Turner Hall, Hans Balatka and his fine orchestra give a concert every Sunday afternoon, and Hans is introducing Wagner to Chicago; let's go. They went.

Louis heard the Pilgrims' Chorus—and raved. They went every Sunday afternoon until Spring. There followed in course, the *Vorspiel* to Lohengrin, to Die Meistersinger, to the Flying Dutchman, the Ride of the Walkyrie, the amazing fabric of the overture to Tristan und Isolde, the immense solemnity of Siegfried's Tod, the exquisite shimmering beauty of the Waldweben.

Louis needed no interpreter. It was all plain to him. He saw it all. It was all as though addressed to himself alone. And as piece after piece was deployed, before his open mind, he saw arise a Mighty Personality—a great Free Spirit, a Poet, a Master Craftsman, striding in power through a vast domain that was

[208]

his own, that imagination and will had bodied forth out of himself. Suffice it—as useless to say—Louis became an ardent Wagnerite. Here, indeed, had been lifted a great veil, revealing anew, refreshing as dawn, the enormous power of man to build as a mirage, the fabric of his dreams, and with his wand of toil to make them real. Thus Louis's heart was stirred, his courage was ten-folded in this raw city by the Great Lake in the West.

Yet John had the good sense to caution Louis to let the philosophers alone for a while; to let them lie in possession — paraphrasing Siegfried's Dragon — as each had merely built an elaborate scaffolding, but no edifice within, and each was more concerned with the symmetry of his scaffold than with aught else, unless it be to scorn the flimsy scaffoldings of others. He said that Schopenhauer showed some intelligence, because he was a man of the world, while the others were more like spiders, weaving, in the gloom of obscurantism, festoons of cobwebs in their dens, far from the light of the world of men and things. That Louis had better let the *ding an sich*—the ultimate thing—alone, and keep his eyes on the world as it is; that he would find plenty to interest him there, and that if he had the eyesight he would find a great romance there, also a great tragedy. That—quoting Carlyle,—he said: "The eye sees that which it brings the power to see"; which again shocked Louis; for the thought rose up: Maybe the veil is not without, but covers my own eyes; as John went on, preaching of the world of men and their significance, for worth or ill, in the social order, Louis again was shocked at the words "social order."

But their talks were not always so strenuous and disturbing; for John was mercurial—an inventor of self-moods—a poseur, infatuated with the pessimistic attitudinizing he assumed at will, for the sake of the sensation of gazing into the mirror of his thoughts which reflected the image of one he deemed the greatest philosopher and psychic of all time, still unknown to the world. But John had many other moods, as many as he chose to summon, and on the whole, he was jolly bombastic, much alive, and in public, loud of speech in an over-weening beggary to attract attention, and thereby feed his hungry vanity. But withal he was Louis's warm friend, and showed it by a devotion and self-sacrifice singular in one so absorbed in self worship. And be this said here and now: The passing years have isolated and revealed John Edelmann, as unique in personality among fine and brilliant minds. Be assured he will not turn in his grave, unless in bliss, should he hear it said that he was the benefactor and Louis the parasite and profiteer.

They were both fond of exercise, and frequented the gymnasium. John, though not so very tall, was huge in bulk and over-muscled. He excelled in feats of strength, while Louis was dexterous and nimble in lighter work. As spring approached, John talked more and more about the "Lotos Club," whose members had boat houses on the bank of the Calumet, near the bridge where the I. C. R. R. crosses. He spoke of a "Great Chief," one William B. Curtis by name, who had founded the Club, who had beaten Dr. Winship at heavy lifting; was a champion all-round athlete, and had chosen the club name because of a bed of Lotus not far down the sluggish stream. He had said briefly, he preferred the Greek word *Lotos* to the Latin *Lotus*.

So in the spring the two went to live in John's boat-house. There were three other houses, one occupied by said William B. Curtis, who, when asked, said his middle name was Bill,—and "Bill" he was called. Louis was simply wild with joy over this new life. He was now actually a member of a real athletic club. He had never been a member of any club. And these young men, all older than he, were heroes in his eyes, if not demi-gods; they showed such skill in performance, and were so amiable toward a youngster. The mighty "Bill" was 38, so he said. He was the man of brains who never bragged. He was too cynical to brag, and deadly literal in speech. As a mathematician he had revised Haswell. His brain was hard, his manner human. He knew his anatomy, and had devised special exercises to develop each separate muscle in his body. So when in the sunlight he walked the pier for a plunge, he was a sight for the Greeks, and Louis was enraptured at the play of light and shade. He had won a barrel full of medals and he said he kept them there.

By a strange paradox he detested display. He had no vanity. He had a quizzical sense of humor which he displayed when he said the club was no club, because there were no dues, no entrance fees, no by-laws. All that was needed in an applicant was a sound constitution and a paper shell. And yet he said he had named the Club the Lotos because of his love of flowers, and the nearby presence of the lotos field. His brain was remarkably well stocked with varied information of the so-called higher sort, but he seldom talked of such, except briefly in derision. He was the exact opposite of John, but with an equal egoism which he kept under cover, and which passed as modesty—although he cared not in the least. All this interested Louis, who was beginning to observe men as individuals, and to study personalities; to observe in particular the working of men's brains; for he had begun to notice, with keen and growing interest, that the thoughts of a man corresponded exactly to his real nature. So Louis discerned in Bill a highly trained mind, self-centered and selfish in its nature. Louis guessed that the man had a past; that at least there was something hidden. So he spoke to John, who said: "You are right. Bill is not in athletics for fun, but for his health. Medals interest him only as tokens of condition. When he was a young man he was attacked by consumption. The doctors gave him up. Bill took to open air exercise. With his scientific brain you can imagine how systematically he went about it. He effected a cure; but now he has only one lung—would you guess it?" Briefly to complete the story of this man, the most remarkable that has ever appeared in the field of amateur athletics, —he became editor of "Wilkes Spirit of the Times" and remained such for years. At the age of 63 he, with a companion, was making the ascent of Mt. Washington when a blizzard overtook them near the summit. The bodies were found a quarter of a mile apart.

The effect of Bill Curtis upon Louis was not merely that of a magnificent athlete and man of brains, but primarily, and most valuably that of exemplar in the use of the imagination and the will, doggedly to carry out a program. That a consumptive should have risen to become a great athlete, was enough for him. The living fact profoundly and permanently strengthened Louis's courage in carrying out his own program. Though Louis did not especially warm up to the man, because their natures were not sufficiently alike, he has never forgotten what he then owed to the force of example of a clear brain. So Louis added "Bill" to his growing collection of personalities.

*   *   *

In the carrying out of his own program Louis's thoughts turned definitely towards France; which meant, specifically, the *Ecole des Beaux Arts*. He wished now to go to the fountain head of theory. Of practice he had enough for present purpose.

Thus on 10 July, 1874, he sailed from New York on the steamship Britannic, on her maiden trip eastward. Before she left her pier there were grand doings aboard —flowers, speeches, high society. For she was proclaimed "The Pride of the Seas." She displaced three thousand tons. She was headed for Liverpool.

Prior to leaving, Louis called again upon his friend Stratton in New York, and was given further pointers —first of all, to call at the American Legation.

Louis found the ocean trip disappointing and stupid, with exception of the ship's great vertical engines and deep stoke-hole, the various apparatus, and the working of the ship by officers and crew, which he studied carefully, as he had become much interested in engineering.

While Louis was leaning on the railing, watching, with vague emotion, his native land fade in the mist, and sink from sight, as though irrevocably lost, he felt a pang of nostalgia; the sea seemed so lonely—after brisk excitement. Near by at the rail were others also watching the land disappear. As it became dim, a grating voice spoke out: "Thank God we have seen the last of the damned Yankees." The words were said in savage bitterness and contempt. Another voice agreed. Louis turned to the left and saw two short swarthy men, black bearded, black eyed. For a moment Louis thought it would be nice to throw them both overboard. He looked at them, wide-eyed, with something of the sort in view, and they talked on in lower tones. Louis was puzzled by the speech. Why "damned Yankees" he asked himself. Why this hatred, this anathema? The phrase sounded racial; it stuck in his mind like a burr. It was said with such conviction as to seem impersonal; as though included in something larger. Never had he heard such virulence addressed to his own people. He pondered long over this; were the "Yankees" a hated people? If so, who hated them?

Louis did not know a soul aboard. He was proud of the ship, proud to be on it, but he was lonesome, and no one paid the slightest heed as he prowled up and down, in and out. The weather was fair all the way. The waves seemed eternally to roll and roll,— without crests. A vast expanse of water, dark blue, almost black; the circular horizon always present and only fifteen miles away. Never had his world seemed so small in fact, yet so limitless and grim in suggestion. He seemed to be always at the top of the world, always in the self-same spot, always in the midst of deadening monotony; day after day not a sail in sight, not a sign of a storm. Day after day confined to a solitary ship moving on through a wilderness of water, the vessel rhythmically rolling and heaving in its course, night and day, night and day; would it never end? Laughter, aboard, had long since ceased. Where was the romance of the high seas? The end came in a total lapse of ten days. The waters turned blue and then green. The boat came to a stop off Queenstown. Enshrouded in heavy mist, Louis saw a coast line of mountains or high hills. This is all he ever saw of Ireland.

The way along St. George's Channel seemed glorious. The clear, deep waters, and the glimpses of coast line restored his spirits as he felt his normal condition of clarity return. Here at last was an old world, which, as a new world he was to discover. How high his hopes, how buoyant his thoughts, as they swung into the Mersey. England came near to him, and nearer, then slowly nearer, then in contact, as the ship came to dock. Then came all the bustle and the joyous greetings about him, as Louis pressed his foot on English soil. Ah, what fluttering emotion, the overflow of bubbling youth. At last, at last, he had arrived where for years he had dreamed to come, and the broad Atlantic now lay between him and his native land. Now was to come that Great Adventure, which, as a joyous youth *sans peur* he faced with elation, and a confidence known only to pure fools. He stayed but a day or two in Liverpool, for his immediate objective was London. He was at pains to make it a daylight ride, for he wished to give his eyes all the treat of novelty.

And what he saw was a finished land—something that had ripened through the centuries. This finished land impressed him with a sense of the far-away. It did not seem to vibrate; and, *sub audite,* came to him a stream of ancient tales. He found quiet, unobtrusive charm in the countryside, he noted patches of crops arranged with a precision, an inch by inch economy of space, that gave him a feeling that the people of this Island must be crowded, as each small farm was pressed tight against its neighbors, and each crop pressed tight against the others. This tightness confirmed his impression of a finished land. It was a revelation to him, who had come from the middle west of America with its vast prairies sparsely settled. He noticed, too, the amazing solidity of the roadbed, and the smoothness with which the train flew on at high speed. He saw, too, that there were no grade crossings; that everything was immensely solid in contrast to the flimsiness with which he was familiar. And the country roads were wonderful, so sound, so smooth, as they wound their way; and the charming streams he crossed; the verdure, the lovely groves, the hamlets, the villages, the many church spires rising from masses of green; the rural air everywhere, charmed him with the softness, the velvet, the down of age and tradition. Surely it was a finished land, beautifully finished, sturdy, vigorous, solid, set, and he felt the power of this land, this tight-crowded land, and he thought as an inference it must be true that in such a crowded land its people must be tightly self-conscious and self-centered. But he did not as yet clearly discern the portrait of this Island crowded on all sides by the sea.

Arriving in London, he thought the roof of Euston Station would fall down upon him. It was so solid, so oppressively heavy, he was glad to escape to the street. In London he spent two weeks, most of the time joyfully. The weather, it appears, was extra fine. In this strange world called London, he walked many miles every day and examined most carefully

[216]

everything within reach, and he thrilled to the booming of "Big Ben," the like of which he had never heard. It seemed to be an old world sound, a remnant or an aftermath of the Age of Romance. The power of its stroke almost said to him: "I am that I am!"

One evening in his wanderings he found himself in the Haymarket and saw there shoals of wretches. He was rudely shocked, in horror, in pity and dismay. When he finally escaped from the many fingers clutching at his sleeve, he thought: Is *this* also London—does Big Ben boom in pride for these?—and a veil slowly lifted by degrees. And in the shops where he went to make his small purchases, the rudeness, the brutal rawness of the clerks, or "clarks," amazed him. At the Music Halls, he was equally astonished at the brilliance of the demi-monde. London was too much for Louis. He lacked the worldly wisdom to grasp its immensity, the significance of its teeming, struggling population, the cold reserve in certain places. But he noted the manifold variety, the surging crowds, the dismal hardness of so many faces, and a certain ruthlessness; and everywhere, in the jammed highways, the selfish push of those who must live. So he confined himself to the pleasanter aspects, such as Hyde Park, Rotten Row, and the Thames embankment. He was curious at the vast Houses of Parliament, vertical everywhere; and St. Paul's black with soot; and many structures in which he sensed, in their visages, the solemn weight of age. They did not appeal to him in their historic message so much as in the sense of that which is old. This massive oldness made a new sensation for him. So passed the days.

Louis left England with so many intermingling impressions thrust suddenly upon him, so many seeming contradictions and paradoxes, that time was needed for the turbid mixture to settle, to clarify, and to reveal a dominant idea.

Thus Louis reached the shores of France much puzzled as to England.

He had sailed from Dover to Dieppe.

In the course of the passage, all the transcendental curves, known and unknown to mathematics, were revealed to him by the packet, which distorted and twirled the very heavens, in its can-can with the sea.

As they moved into the little harbor of Dieppe, what was left of Louis gazed at the quaint city with acceptance and delight. How different from England. What a change in physiognomy. How cheerful the aspect—a delicate suggestion not so much of age as of mediaevalism; he had read about it in many books—a surviving fragrance of romance. But on the way through Normandy, Louis was equally startled, at the rigid spacing of trees, at the dinky chateaux, new-made, stuck here and there as though forming the heads of pins. All was clean, all was stiff. But the farms and the cattle were a revelation, especially the cattle— never had he seen such.

As the train passed through Rouen, twilight was under way, and the spire of the Cathedral seemed to float in the air as though there were no earth.

Arrived in Paris after night-fall, Louis saw the streets aglow. He boarded a *fiacre,* and shouted to the *cocher:*

Hôtel Saint Honoré!

PLATE 24. Carson Pirie Scott & Co., 1 South State
Street, Chicago. 1899-1904. Entrance at State
and Madison Streets.

PLATE 25. Carson Pirie Scott & Co. (see Plate 24). Detail of cast iron over entrance at State and Madison Streets.

Chapter XII.

Paris

AFTER a brief stay at the Hôtel St. Honoré, Louis found permanent quarters on the seventh floor of a rooming hotel, at the southeast corner Rue Monsieur le Prince and Rue Racine, in the Latin Quarter. Nearby were the "Boule Miche" toward the east, the Odeon, the Luxembourg Palace and its gardens to the southwest. From this lofty perch which he always reached on the run, two steps at a time, the City of Paris spread before him to the north, and on the small balcony, reached by casement doors, he would sometimes sit in the twilight and be caught by the solitary boom of the great bell of Notre Dame.

Early he had discovered that the French of his High School, for excellence in which he had taken first prize in a matter of course way, was not quite the colloquial French he now heard, spoken with exasperating rapidity and elision. As to the bill of fare, the *Menu,* at the first attempt he perspired awhile in anguish, then put his finger on a line at random, and set down the result in a special notebook. He must learn current French in a hurry. He engaged a teacher to come every day at a fixed hour. When on the streets, he walked close to the people ahead, to catch every word; in this way his ear caught up words, locutions, intonations, and emphasis; and soon he began to feel he was on the way, even though he did not understand a tenth of what he heard.

He early visited the American Legation, complied with requirements, received information and advice, was told to buy certain textbooks, and was referred to a certain Monsieur Clopet as the very best tutor in mathematics. At the Legation he made the startling discovery that the Beaux Arts entrance examinations were to begin in six weeks; and furthermore, he had scanned the Program of Admission, and was startled again at the range of subjects he was not up on. Was he downhearted? Not a bit. It was a *certainty* he would pass because he must *pass*. He had come to Paris from far-away Chicago with that sole end in view; so why argue? He knew it meant six weeks of the hardest work he had ever done. He figured on eighteen hours a day. He knew he was in physical condition. He would allot one hour each day to gymnasium work, and keep on simple diet. What stood uppermost in his mind and gave him self-reliance to face any task, was his assurance: Had he not been trained in discipline and self-discipline by Moses Woolson? Had he not been trained and tried by that great teacher in the science and the art of thinking, of alertness, of close attention and quick action, in economy of time, in sharp analysis, in the high values of contemplation?

He lost no time in calling upon Monsieur Clopet. He was greeted in simple gracious words, by a small dark man, who, to Louis's joy, spoke only French. The preliminaries over, Monsieur Clopet asked: "And what are the books you have under your arm?" Louis replied: "Books I was told at the American legation I would need." "Ah, yes, let me see them." He took the books, selected a large work on Descriptive Geometry, and began to turn the pages. "Now observe: Here is a problem with five exceptions or special cases; here a theorem, three special cases; another nine, and so on and on, a procession of exceptions and special cases. I suggest you place the book in the waste basket; we shall not need of it here; *for here our demonstrations shall be so broad as to admit of* NO EXCEPTION!"

At these amazing words Louis stood as one whose body had turned to hot stone, while his brain was raging. Instantly the words had flashed, there arose a vision and a fixed resolve; an instantaneous inquiry and an instant answer. The inquiry: If this can be done in Mathematics, why not in Architecture? The instant answer: It can, and it shall be! *no one has—I will!* It may mean a long struggle; longer and harder than the tramp through the forest of Brown's Tract. It may be years from now, before I find what I seek, but I shall find it, if otherwhere and otherwise, with or without guide other than my *flair,* my will and my apprehension. It shall be done! I shall live for that! —no one, no thing, no thousand shall deter me. The world of men, of thoughts, of things, shall be mine. Firmly I believe that if I can but interpret it, that world is filled with evidence. I shall explore that world to seek, to find. I shall weigh that world in a balance. I shall question it, I shall examine and cross-examine, I shall finally interpret—I shall not be withheld, I shall prevail!

During the immense seconds of this eidolon, Louis found himself shaking hands with Monsieur Clopet in parting, promising to join his class on the morrow. This he did. The class consisted of about twenty young men, mostly French, a few from other lands, no Englanders, no other American. Louis wished an exclusively French atmosphere—he was beginning feebly to think in French and wished no disturbance of the process. He had told his French tutor that he knew the grammar by heart and could conjugate all the irregular verbs; that what he wished, and he wished it done in a hurry, was to acquire the language of the man on the street first of all, to acquire what fluency he might in the short time before him, to increase his vocabulary, a hundred new words memorized every day. It must be talk, talk, talk, and read, read, read, to each other—daily papers, general history in particular, read aloud to each other, read and correct, talk and correct, and hammer away in the sweat of their brows. His tutor could not long stand the pace and begged to be excused. Louis got another, wore him out. The third one stuck. He saw into Louis's plan and it amused him greatly, so much so that he joined in, jovially, and made a play of it. A *petit verre* started him off nicely. He possessed a rare art of conversation, was full of anecdote, personal incident and reminiscence, knew his Paris, had the sense of comedy to a degree, looked upon life as a huge joke, upon all persons as jokes, and upon Louis as such in particular— he would amuse himself with this frantic person. At once he spoke to Louis *en camarade, vieux copain,* as one Frenchman to another. He made running comments on the news of the day, explained all sorts of things Louis was beginning to note in Paris life, put him in the running. He had a gift of mimicry, would imitate the provincial dialects and peasant jargon, with fitting tone and gesture, and, taking a given topic or incident, would relate it in terms and impersonations ranging in series from gamin to Academician. In these moods he was simply "killing." And when Louis told

[222]

a story, he would mimic it delightfully. But the man knew his French, and spread out the language before Louis in a sort of landscape which awoke imagination. At times he would wax eloquent concerning his mother tongue, as he revealed its resources and its beauty, its clarity, its precision, its fluidity, and he earnestly advised Louis that he must without fail go each Sunday to the Church of St. Roch, there to hear in the sermon the marvelous beauty of the language, as uttered there by one who, through life-long discipline, had attained to its perfection of form and vocal melody.

This tutor man suited Louis; he was wholly human, and well versed. Also well built, well under middle age, seldom sat for long, but paced the floor, or lolled here or there by moments. His voice was suave, his manner frank and free. He had an air, was well bred. He was either an unconscious or a crafty teacher, a *rara avis,* he knew how to get results. The daily lesson lasted one hour, and Louis daily plowed on, at high tension.

At Monsieur Clopet's class he was well received by the young gentlemen there. He returned their salutations and an atmosphere of *savoir faire* prevailed. All were hard put to it to keep up their notes as a lecture progressed. Monsieur Clopet was gentle, polished, forceful. "One must work; that is what one is here for." As a drill master he was a potent driver, as an expounder he made good his word to Louis in a method and a manner, revealing, inspiriting, as he calmly unfolded, step by step, a well reasoned process in his demonstrations which were so simple, so inclusive, so completely rounded as to preclude exception; and there was not a book in sight; but ever in sight was Monsieur Clopet, making something teachable out of what at first seemed an abstraction in three dimensions.

Louis was especially pleased at the novelty of saying *je dis*—"I say"—at the beginning of a demonstration. It humanized matters, brought them home, close up, a sort of challenge. How much more intelligent and lively to begin: "I say the sum of the angles of any triangle equals two right angles" than the formal impersonal statement: "The sum of the angles of any triangle equals two right angles." The latter statement one may take or leave. The former is a personal assertion and implies, "I will show you." In fact, it was this "I say" and this "I will show you" that made up the charm of Monsieur Clopet's teaching method. For Louis had but little use for what is called "proof." In his secret heart he did not believe that anything could be *proved,* but believed as firmly that many things might be *shown.* From long practice as listener and observer, he had reached this conclusion, and as time went on, in his studies he became convinced that all abstractions were assumptions—that abstract truth was a mirage. As Monsieur Clopet's course covered mainly descriptive geometry and the science of arithmetic, with plain and solid geometry as incidentals, Louis met his bugbear in this very science of arithmetic. He seemed to bump his head against invisible walls, a blockade which seemed to hold him a prisoner to inner consciousness, instead of the free open of outward consciousness — a working of the intellect detached from reality—therefore detached from life; but it was an examination requirement, so Louis stuck to the treadmill and learned how, by "rigorous logic," it might be proved that two and two make four. It was not that he lacked the sense that the study of numbers had its charm, and might exercise a fascination for those who had a mathematical career in view. It was against what he deemed the impertinence of rigid logic that he rebelled, for once we assume an abstraction to be real, he thought, we lose our anchorage which is in the real.

At the end of the first half hour Monsieur Clopet always called a recess. From his pocket he drew forth his pouch and his little book of rice papers; so did the others. There was sauntering, spectacular smoking and conversation. The cigarette finished, work was resumed. Louis thought this gay, immediately procured the findings, and learned to "roll his own." After recess the students were put through their paces at the blackboard for the final half-hour.

For Louis all this was exhilarating. He soon felt he was making sure headway. His fellow pupils were most amiable, and began to remark upon his improving French. Early in the game, however, they had taken him in hand regarding his attire, for Louis had made his first appearance clad in a flannel suit, a white cap and white canvas shoes. They were serious about it. "We would have you know, friend, you are not properly dressed. You are a student now, an aspirant for the Beaux Arts. Only the working classes wear the *casquette*. Gentlemen wear the *chapeau*, and only sporting people wear such clothes and shoes. You shall dress like a student and be one of us." As soon as it could be done, Louis appeared in tall silk hat, an infant beard, long tail coat, and trousers of dark material, polished shoes, kid gloves, and jaunty cane. Louis felt self-conscious, but he was met with so voluble a chorus of approval that he changed his tone, studied carefully the student manner so as to be one of them—they were such good fellows.

Swiftly fled the days; thus moved the work; nightly Louis sat in his room on the seventh, at his small desk, a candle at each side, black coffee and wet towel as aids. He codified the Clopet notes, arranged his French vocabulary, read history by the hour, for he knew this latter would be highly important; and so it went day and night—work, work, work. About midway in the game Louis's brain seemed to be overcome by a fog. Everything was blurred as in a mist, his memory lost its grip. His knowledge of athletics told him he had overtrained and run stale. A three days' change of scene and complete diversion put him right; memory returned, the mist lifted; after that, no trouble.

The great day of the Examinations was now near at hand. Louis's French tutor had cautioned him to be careful not to use slang when addressing the professors; and Monsieur Clopet had said in open class, "I don't know as to the rest of you, but there is one among you who will pass brilliantly in his mathematics, and he is an American."

So, several days before the examinations, which were to begin early in October, Louis stopped all work, relaxed completely, and, in a state of confidence amused himself with the sights and sounds of Paris, and enjoyed a few long sleeps. He wandered here and there and everywhere, immensely amused and satisfied. Paris seemed made for him. All was really new to him, but did not seem strange or alien as had England. The people seemed rather like his own people of the Middle West; more cultured, more polite, more refined, to be sure, but withal, a certain temperamental likeness he believed to exist between raw Chicago and finished Paris. He believed he had observed a similar affinity between Boston and London. To Louis's view the barrier of language was most unfortunate, for the two peoples at large appeared to possess the same light-hearted spirit of adventure. Paris, though filled with historic monuments did not seem old; it gave rather an impress of ever self-renewing youth and its people seemed light hearted.

Wherever he went he found the city well ordered and cleanly, with architectural monuments everywhere; and in the parks and gardens he went through the old experience of surprise that the children could speak French so well. In the Luxembourg Gardens he watched them in groups with their nurses and perambulators and toys, and to him the children were like flowers and the nurses stately flowers, and the babble and child laughter and twittering made delicate and merry music. Never had he seen such child-happiness, such utter joy in living; and he felt convinced this must be the child-key to France. Window-shopping also was his keen delight as he traversed the boulevards and the Rue de la Paix. He even ventured to enter, and was not met with scowls—nor did he hear a word equivalent to the "damned Yankees." The crowds upon the boulevards were varied, interesting and cosmopolite. Yes, there was an atmosphere; this atmosphere was Paris; Paris was to be his home; its air of hospitality, of world-welcomer and host, found in him a ready and a heartfelt response.

In the French language Louis had by now acquired a very fair degree of ease, and a vocabulary sufficiently covering the colloquial and the literary for his present purpose. His accent was good and on the way to becoming Parisian. Thus, prepared, with all his hard, gruelling work back of him, he felt at ease, but with a due sense of the close call he had had—six weeks! Had he been trained by any teacher other than Moses Woolson, in his high school days, and had he not all his life been in fine physical condition—which means no nerves —it is doubtful if he could have stood the strain of preparation.

The examinations were to be, severally, written, drawn, and oral. They were to cover a period of three weeks. The number of candidates for admission was large, covering all departments.

The great trial was now under way. The free hand drawing, the mechanical drawing, and an *esquisse en loge* of a simple architectural project, went smoothly enough for Louis; perhaps with some difficulty for others. The real test for him would lie in the oral examinations, which were conducted in little amphitheatres, a professor presiding, and all aspirants free to come and go, as they did in a steady stream. Louis himself had been one of these wanderers awaiting his turn. The candidate under fire thus was by no means lonely; indeed, he deeply wished to be alone with his inquisitor.

Came Louis's turn for mathematics. For audience he had some twenty strange faces, all rather scared. The examining professor, elderly and of quiet poise, received him most courteously as a stranger in the land, a guest of France, and an aspirant to the Beaux Arts; that it was a pleasure to welcome him, that he need not feel in the least embarrassed, that the inquisition would proceed at a moderate pace, and that Louis was free to solve any problem in any way he liked, the objective being solely to discover the extent of his understanding, not of his memory. Then the examining professor settled to the work. For over an hour—Lord knows how long it was—he put Louis through a steady gruelling—always kindly, however—such as Louis had never known, never dreamed of, never believed could be so. In the midst of it he recalled Monsieur Clopet's "I don't know about the rest of you" and he came of a sudden into his true stride, which he held to the end. For, after a heart-breaking crisis, he suddenly found himself actually *thinking* in terms of mathematics, and, accordingly, lost all fear, relaxed and let his mind go free. From beginning to end he did not make a fluke. At the close, the examining professor, who had become quite interested when he found he could increase the difficulties, pressed Louis's hand and said: "I felicitate you, Monsieur Sullivan: you have the mathematical imagination which is rather rare. I wish you well."

Now, of all things Louis might have said he did *not* possess, the mathematical imagination would head the list in a large way. He knew, in a small way, he had been charmed in his high school by the novelties of the ideas set forth in geometry and algebra. But there they were simply discipline, founded categorically on the books. And in the books was no imagination that he could discern. Perhaps, after all, it was the freedom of Monsieur Clopet's classroom and Louis's enthusiasm at each beautiful demonstration, and the many pointed questions he asked of Monsieur Clopet, that had led the latter to speak as he did concerning "an American." However this may be, Louis found the open world of mathematics; that it was possible to think in such terms as it was possible to think in French—for doing this latter, also, was an act of imagination. And now from the secret places of this new world there came a Siren call which perturbed Louis sadly for many years. Toward this new world Louis turned many a wistful thought thereafter: It was a land of Romance.

Now came the questioning in History, and Louis was equally startled at the method. He was well prepared according to the books, which he had visualized into a moving picture, but he was not prepared for the shock.

Three questions only, were asked—the replies covered one hour and a half of constant talking. Louis had supposed that questions and answers would be categorical, after the manner of procedure he had been taught in America, where, to epitomize, it might be said the chief interest centered around the exact date of the discovery of America. Now Louis felt the earth leave him, as the first question came: "Monsieur, will you be kind enough to tell me the story of the Hebrew People?" Then the earth came back, but the question remained immense. Still the situation was not altogether infelicitous, for Louis had read considerably in the Bible, and had heard far more than he had read—in spite of the fact that John Edelman had cautioned him that no one should read the Bible before the age of mental maturity, which he had placed at forty, and was reserving that treat for himself. So Louis began safely with the desert tribes, the sojourn in Egypt, the wandering in the desert, carrying the story down to the destruction of Jerusalem, and the captivity. He also sketched the patriarchal age, the prophets in captivity, the final triumph of ritual over inspiration and righteousness. The charm of this examination lay in the fact that Louis was encouraged by the examining professor to give a pictorial and rather dramatic recital, and the professor's frequent questioning concerning what Louis had said and as to why he thought thus or so. He, for instance, asked Louis what had impressed him most vividly in the story of the Jews, and Louis said: The emergence and vivid personality of Jehovah, their God.

The next question now followed: "I would like an account of the ten emperors of Rome." Another half-hour of talk as Louis covered the ground, from the bookish point of view, and made a few remarks on his own account, which led the professor to say: "You do not seem to be in sympathy with Roman civilization." "No," said Louis, "I feel out of touch with a civilization whose glory was based on force."

Then came the third question: "Monsieur, I see you have a certain faculty, a bit crude as yet, of making word pictures, of discerning something real beneath the glamour of the surface, which it is the particular business of the true historian to uncover. Now, therefore, as this is to be the last question, do your best and give me an intimate account of the times of Francis First." Louis did this with joy. On account of Leonardo's part in it, he had studied the period with especial care and devotion. He had seemed to live in this time, and with its people, its manners, its customs, its thoughts, it stood forth for him as a very present picture of the past.

At the close the examining professor smiled. He

said: "The object of these examinations is not to ascertain an array of facts devoid of shaping context, but to discern the degree of intelligence possessed by the candidate; to ascertain his capacity for interpretation, and if he possess, to any perceptible degree, the faculty of constructive imagination—without which the pursuit of history is merely so much wasted time. I am agreeably surprised at times to find this latter quality present, and in you it is vivid, amazing and rash. To be sure you are not expected to be profound in historic knowledge, but you have shown me, in your faithful way, that instinctively, you know how to go about it, so I say: Continue, continue. After some years you will begin to understand a little, and as you mature, you may perhaps feel inclined to turn the teachings of history upside down. I can now do no less for your gratification and as well my own, than to give you the highest rating, and to wish you happiness. I shall doubtless have been long gone hence before your studies shall have matured into a valuable and personal idea; a contribution to the knowledge of mankind, but courage, courage,—and *Adieu!*"

Thus Louis, in Paris, spent an hour and a half answering three history questions. At home he would have been asked perhaps five times as many questions, all categorical in nature, and would have been through with them in a half an hour. It was this immense difference in matter and manner, especially as applied to mathematics and history, that opened Louis's eyes to the quality and reach of French thought; to its richness, its firmness, its solidity, and above all, the severity of its discipline beneath so smooth a surface.

Examinations over, Louis received his card of admission to the school, good until the age of thirty. Then he made his *entrée* into the atelier of Monsieur Emil Vaudremer, practicing architect. He much preferred an atelier *libre*—or free—independent—to the official ateliers of the Ecole. There were a number of such ateliers, under the care of architects of distinction, men who had been winners of the *Grand Prix de Rome,* —veritable Polar Star of the Ecole. As Eugene Letang had come from the *Atelier Vaudremer,* it seemed but natural that Louis should feel at home there.

The Director of the Ecole gave out the program of a three-months *projet;* the twenty-four-hour sketches were made *en loge,* and filed as briefs; whereupon, to Louis's surprise, everybody vanished. So Louis bethought him to vanish.

During his preparatory work he had discovered three small volumes by Hippolyte Taine devoted to the Philosophy of Art in Greece, in Italy, and in the Netherlands. From these works he derived three strong impressions, novel shocks: First, that there *existed* such thing as a Philosophy of Art; second, that according to M. Taine's philosophy the art of a people is a reflex or direct expression of the life of that people; third, that one must become well acquainted with that life in order to see into the art. All this was new and shining. He knew it was true of Boston and Chicago. In the volume on Italy, however, occurred a statement which struck Louis as of most sinister import for him: It alarmed him. It was to this effect: That, concerning the work of Michael Angelo in the Sistine Chapel, the Last Judgment was *obviously* done on *momentum,* as compared with the vigor of the ceil-

ing. Now Louis had never trusted the care of his eyesight to anyone, nor did he now propose to entrust it
in M. Taine's keeping. He was averse to taking things
on say-so. It was his pride that he could see. But,
could his eye detect so subtle a change in the work of
a great artist as was implicated in the word *momentum*
and which M. Taine had said was *obvious?* He had
many sinkings at the heart because of this. He must
go to Rome, to verify; for the worth of his whole
scheme seemed to rest in this delicate balance. It was
vital. There must be no doubt. He *must,* beyond
question, be sure of the quality of his eyesight. To
Rome he went, quaking but courageous.

The Sistine Chapel! One steady sweep of the eye!
It was easy—oh, so easy! So self-evident! Thus a
cumulating agony ended forever in a supreme moment
of relief; and Louis knew, once and for all, that he
could see anything that eye could see. He would not
have used the word *momentum*—an academic word—
he would have called it the work of a man powerful
even in old age. Louis spent three days in Rome—two
of them in the Sistine—alone there, almost all the time.
Here he communed in the silence with a Super-Man.
Here he felt and saw a great Free Spirit. Here he
was filled with the awe that stills. Here he came face
to face with his first great Adventurer. The first
mighty man of Courage. The first man with a Great
Voice. The first whose speech was Elemental. The
first whose will would not be denied. The first to cry
YEA! in thunder tones. The first mighty Craftsman.
The man, the man of super-power, the glorified man,
of whom he had dreamed in his childhood, of whom
he prophesied in his childhood, as he watched his big,

strong men build stone walls, hew down trees, drive huge horses—his mighty men, his heroes, his demigods; a powerful presentiment which he had seen and felt in the glory of the sunrise; which he had heard in the voice of spring; and which, personified through the haze of most mystical romantic trances, he believed in, he had faith in—that faith which is far removed from fancy, that faith which is near its source and secure.

Now was he in that veritable dreamed-of Presence. Here was that great and glorious personality. Here was power as he had seen it in the mountains, here was power as he had seen it in the prairies, in the open sky, in the great lake stretching like a floor toward the horizon, here was the power of the forest primeval. Here was the power of the open—of the free spirit of man striding abroad in the open. Here was the living presence of a man who had *done things in the beneficence of power.* And Louis gazed long and long, as one enthralled. And with his own eyes, with his own responses, he discerned more and more. There seemed to come forth from this great work a mystery; he began to *see into it,* and to discern the workings of a soul within. From beneath the surface significance there emerged˙ that which is timeless, that which is deathless, that which in its immensity of duration, its fecundity, its everpresent urge, we call LIFE. And in this great outpouring which encompassed him, he saw the Dreamer at his work. For no hand, unaided, could do this; no intellect unaided could do this; Imagination alone could do this; and Imagination, *looked into,* revealed itself as uncompromising faith in Life, as faith in man, and especial faith in his wondrous powers. He saw that Imagination passes beyond reason and is a consummated act of Instinct—the primal power of Life at work. Thus Louis pondered as he viewed o'er and o'er the Persian Sibyl. Forty-nine years have come and gone since a youth of eighteen thought these thoughts without words; alone in the Sistine.

"There was a Child went forth every day."

* * *

Louis saw Florence and does not know how he came to break the golden chains that bound him there, a too willing captive. It needed full six weeks to part a net that seemed but of gossamer; or was it the fragrance of Lotus Land?

And the rocky coast of the Riviera, alive with beauty and with color implanted by the hand of man near the water's edge, on the crags which came down from the foot of the mountains to indent the sea—precious spots in memory's hold. And the solid blue sea, with sky as solid blue—ineffable blue—wondrous blue—Mediterranean and Riviera—sea and mountain range, a revelation and a piercing joy—how could such things be? Then on to Nice, to Paris—and hard work again.

Louis was keyed for every form of anticipated effort; keen and anxious to observe, to analyse, to compare; to start on the second phase of his program, the purport of which was to ascertain what the Great School had to give, what Monsieur Vaudremer had to give, and to get close to the glowing heart of French Culture, as nearly as he might. It was his purpose to *live,* in fact; to absorb, to contemplate. He felt he had no time to lose, that he must press on. Insatiable curiosity urged him.

He went back to his old quarters on the seventh, with its northward spreading view. Nightly he sat long at his desk, a candle at each side, and, pondering his books of history slowly he persuaded the peoples of the past to come forward to meet him until they seemed of his own day, and he of theirs, in a dramatic moving present, a spectacle, a processional of the races and the nations, whose separate deeds seemed to flow from their separate thoughts, and whose thoughts and deeds seemed, as he himself progressed, toward them, to coalesce into a mass movement of mankind, carrying the burden of a *single* thought. What was that thought? He did not know. He could not see. But he knew it was there, he could feel it in the atmospheric depths of the centuries, a single ever-present thought, which since the beginning had been the Lodestar of the Man of the past. Thus became vaguely outlined an image of Man as a vast personality, within which were gathered all the powers, all the thoughts of the races, all vicissitudes of the civilizations—a presence which seemed to move steadily, silently, across the depths, onward into the modern day, indistinct but real, following the turn of each leaf of the Calendar. This strange presence he had evoked Louis could not banish, it seemed to be immense and to stir immediately behind the veil of appearances. He would some day locate this phantasm, he said, and meet it as real; for in it, he said, was that secret men called truth. Thus history became for Louis a moving drama, and he sole spec-tator. And it was in this sense that he studied the history of architecture—not mreely as a fixation here

and there in time and place, but as a continuous outpouring never to end, from the infinite fertility of
man's imagination, evoked by his changing needs.
These were hours of deepest contemplation, the beginning of his self-education.

*   *   *

The Atelier Vaudremer gave on a courtyard,
reached by a passageway leading from the Rue de Bac,
about a mile west of where Louis lived. It was at
the ground level, a rough affair, like a carpenter's shop,
large enough to accommodate about twenty young
ruffians. Here it was the work was done amid a cross
fire of insults, and it was also here that Monsieur Emil
Vaudremer came to make his "criticisms." He was
one of the dark Frenchmen, of medium size, who carried a fine air of native distinction; a man toward whom
one's heart instantly went out in respectful esteem bordering on pride and affection. His personality was
calm, deliberate yet magnetic, a sustained, quiet dignity
bespeaking a finished product. His "criticisms" were,
therefore, just what one might expect them to be, clear,
clean-cut, constructive, and personal to each student,
in each case, with that peculiar sympathy with the
young which comes from remembrance of one's own
youth. Always, however, he was disciplinarian, and
one felt the steady pressure. Louis thought the exigent
condition that one hold to the original sketch in its
essentials, to be discipline, of an inspired sort, in that
it held one firmly to a thesis.

Monsieur Vaudremer—otherwise *Le Patron,* had to
his credit as executed works, the Church of the Sacred
Heart, of Mont Rouge, and the Prison Mazzas. He

was considered, therefore, a rising and highly promising young member of his profession—he was forty-five. This condition may be better understood when it is made known that winners of the *Grand Prix* are usually close under thirty.

Louis entered heart and soul into the atelier life, with all its tumult and serious work, and its curious exacting etiquette at the times of arrival and departure. He now spoke French well enough to be treated *en camarade,* and the package of thieves' slang, which he carried in his sleeve and sprinkled on occasions, raised his standing to one of esteem, to such extent that he no longer was required to carry wood for the stove or clean the drawing boards. The intimate life of the atelier with its free commingling of the younger and the older students seemed to Louis invaluable in its human aspects, so much so that he became rather more absorbed in the work of others than in his own, for he always felt himself to be in the position of observer. The Atelier, the School, came to be for him but part of a larger world called Paris, and Paris but a part of a larger world called France, and France but a part of a larger world called Europe, all in contradistinction to his native land; the continuously finished as against the raw or decadent. The sense of stable motion he noted everywhere. As time went on it became clearer and clearer to him what the power of culture meant. He began to realize that Paris was not of a day, but of busy and sad centuries. He studied carefully all its monuments and each seemed to speak to him of its own time. He attended unforgettable midnight masses at Notre Dame; he spent many hours in the museums; he followed closely the exhibits at the School, especially the exhibits of the second or higher class. He familiarized himself thoroughly with the theory of the School, which, in his mind, settled down to a theory of *plan*, yielding results of extraordinary brilliancy, but which, after all, was not the reality he sought, but an abstraction, a method, a state of mind, that was local and specific; not universal. Intellectual and æsthetic, it beautifully set forth a sense of order, of function, of highly skilled manipulation. Yet there was for him a fatal residuum of artificiality, which gave him a secret sense of misery where he wished but too tenderly to be happy. And there came the hovering conviction that this Great School, in its perfect flower of technique, lacked the profound animus of a primal inspiration. He felt that beneath the law of the School lay a law which it ignored unsuspectingly or with fixed intention—the law he had seen set forth in the stillness of the Sistine, which he saw everywhere in the open of life. Thus crept over him the certitude that the book was about to close; that he was becoming solitary in his thoughts and heart-hungry, that he must go his way alone, that the Paris of his delight must and should remain the dream of his delight, that the pang of inevitable parting was at hand.

PLATE 26. St. Trinity Russian Greek Orthodox Church, Exterior.
1121 North Leavitt Street, Chicago. 1903.

PLATE 27. St. Trinity Church (see Plate 26). Interior
view toward the altar.

CHAPTER XIII

The Garden City

THERE was a time a city some three hundred thousand strong stood beside the shore of a great and very wonderful lake with a wonderful horizon and wonderful daily moods. Above the rim of its horizon rose sun and moon in their times, the one spreading o'er its surface a glory of rubies; its companion, at the full, an entrancing sheen of mottled silver. At other times far to the west in the after-glow of sunset the delicate bright crescent poised in farewell slowly dimmed and passed from sight. Around this city, in ever-extending areas, in fancied semi-circles, lay a beauteous prairie, born companion of the lake; while within this prairie, at distances of some seven to twelve miles from the center of the Garden City, were dotted villages, forming also an open-spaced semi-circle, for each village nestled in the spacious prairie, and within its own companionable tree growth. To the north and west of the city there grew in abundance lofty elms and oaks; to the south the section-line dirt roads were double rowed with huge willows all swayed toward the northeast as the summer winds year by year had set them when sap was flowing strong; while scattered through this tract were ancient cottonwoods rising singly or in groups, in their immense and venerable strength. Further to the south, where the soil becomes sandy, there appeared fantastic dwarf pines and scrub oaks, while at the Lake Shore, neighboring them, stretched a mile or more of heavy oak groves that might be called a forest. Within it were winding trails; within it one seemed lost to the world.

The city itself was more than a large village—it was a village grown robust with an impelling purpose. In and near its central business district, residences held their own, and churches sent up their spires on Court House Square. There were few tramways. Horse-and-buggy was the unit; and on the Grand Boulevard fine victorias, blooded high-steppers noisily caparisoned in shining brass, liveried driver and footman, were daily on view to the populace—wealth was growing breathlessly. The business section passed insensibly into the residential, then began tree growth and gardens —the city bloomed in its season. In winter was the old time animation which came with heavy, lasting snows, with cutters, jangling bells, and horses of all shades and grades, and the added confusion of racing; for everybody who was anybody owned at least one horse.

And then again came equinoctial spring; crocuses appeared; trees, each after its kind, put forth furtive leaves; for "April Showers" all too often were but chilling northeast rains. Indeed there was no Spring— rather a wave-motion of subsiding winter and protesting summer. But in June the Garden City had come again into its own. From a distance one saw many a steeple, rising from the green, as landmarks, and in the distances the gray bulk of grain elevators.

The Garden City was triparted by a river with two branches; thus it had its three back yards of urgent commerce, where no gardens grew; and as well, its three shanty-towns.

On occasion, when a spell of hard weather had held the lumber fleet in port, one on watch might see the schooners pour in a stream from the river mouth, spread their wings, and in a great and beautiful flock, gleam in the sunlight as they moved with favoring wind, fan-like towards Muskegon and the northern ports.

The summer was dry. During September the land winds blew hot and steadily.

The legend has it that a small flame, in shanty town, destroyed the Garden City in two awful nights and days. The high winds did their carrier's work. The Garden City vanished. With it vanished the living story, it had told in pride, of how it came to be. Another story now began—the story of a proud people and their power to create—a people whose motto was "I will"—whose dream was commercial empire. They undertook to do what they willed and what they dreamed. In the midst of the epic of their striving, they were benumbed by the blow of a great financial panic, and when Louis returned from Paris the effect of this blow had not wholly passed—though the time was nearing. The building industry was flat. Finding thus no immediate use for his new-fangled imported education, and irking at the prospect of idleness, he bethought him to see what others might be doing in their lines, and at the same time get the lay of the land, something he had not found time to do during his first visit. Daily he made his twenty miles or more in the course of a systematic reconnaisance on foot. When this adventure had come to its end, he knew every nook and corner of the city and its environs, and had discovered undisturbed all that had formed the prairie setting of the living Garden City, and all that had remained undestroyed.

Curiosity seemed to be Louis's ruling passion; always

he was seeking, finding something new, always looking for surprise sensations, always welcoming that which was fresh and gave joy to the sight. He had a skill in deriving joyful thoughts from close observation of what is often called the Commonplace. To him there was nothing commonplace—everything had something to say. Everything suggested it be listened to and interpreted. He had followed the branches of the Chicago River, had located the lovely forest-bordered River Des Plaines, and the old-time historic portage. Had read Parkman's vivid narrative of La Salle and the great Northwest, and his wonder stories of Marquette and Joliet, and he shared in mind the hardships of these great pioneers. Thus he came to know the why and wherefore of the City; and again he said: *This is the Place for me!* This remnant scene of ruin is a prophecy!

In a while the pulse of industry began the slow feeble beat of revival, and the interrupted story of imagination and will, again renewed its deep refrain in arousing energy. The Garden City had vanished with its living story. That tale could not be twice told; that presence could not be recalled. It had gone forever with the flames. Hence a new story must be told. Naught else than a new story could be told. Not again would the city be the same. It could not be the same—men could not now be what they were. It was the approach of this new story that excited Louis; he would bide his time. He worked briefly now, at intervals, in the office of this or that architect, until he had nearly covered the field. These men were mostly of the elder generation, whose venerable clients clung to them for Auld Lang Syne. They were men of homely make-up, homely ways. Louis found them very human, and enjoyed their shop-talk, which was that of the graduate carpenter. He did not demur because they were not *diplômés* of the Beaux Arts. He preferred them as they were; much of their curious wisdom stuck to him. They were men of their lingering day. To them Louis was a marvel of speed. Indeed one of the younger of them, who laughed like a goat, remarked to his partner: "That Irish-*man* has ideas!"

He was a caustic joker and a man of brains, this same Frederick Baumann. Educated in Germany to the point of cynicism, he was master of one idea which he embodied in a pamphlet entitled "A Theory of Isolated Pier Foundations," published in 1873. The logic of this essay was so coherent, its common sense so sound, that its simple idea has served as the basis of standard practice continuously since its day. All honor therefore to Frederick Baumann, man of brains, exploiter of a new idea, which he made up out of his head. His vigorous years reached on to ninety-five, and as each one of them passed him by in defile, the world and its people seemed to his sharp, mirthful eye, to grow more and more ridiculous—a conviction that gave him much comfort as his vertebrae began to curve. Louis met him frequently of evenings, at the gymnasium, and liked to talk to him to get his point of view, which he found to be not bitter, but Mephistophelian. He was most illuminating, bare of delusion, and as time went on Louis came to regard him as a goat-laughing teller of truths out of school—but he, Louis, did not forget.

Reliable text books were few in those days. Due to this fact Louis made Trautwine's "Engineers' Pocket Book" his Bible, and spent long hours with it. The engineering journals kept close track of actual current doings, and thus Louis found himself drifting towards the engineering point of view, or state of mind, as he began to discern that the engineers were the only men who could face a problem squarely; who knew a problem when they saw it. Their minds were trained to deal with real things, as far as they knew them, as far as they could ascertain them, while the architectural mind lacked this directness, this simplicity, this singleness of purpose—it had no standard of reference, no bench-mark one might say. For he discerned that in truth the science of engineering is a science of *reaction,* while the science of architectural design—were such a science to be presupposed—must be a science of *action.* Thus Louis arranged in his mind the reciprocal values of the primary engineering and the primary architectural thought, and noted the curious antagonism existing between those who professed them. The trouble as he saw it was this: That the architect could not or would not understand the real working of the engineering mind because it was hidden in deadly literal attitude and results, because of the horrors it had brought forth as misbegotten stigmata; while the engineer re garded the architect as a frivolous person of small rule-of-thumb consequence. And both were largely right; both professions contained small and large minds— mostly small or medium. Nevertheless they were all human beings, and therefore all ridiculous in the Mephistophelian sense of Frederick Baumann.

About this time two great engineering works were under way. One, the triple arch bridge to cross the Mississippi at St. Louis, Capt. Eades, chief engineer; the other, the great cantilever bridge which was to cross

[246]

the Chasm of the Kentucky River, C. Shaler Smith, chief engineer, destined for the use of the Cincinnati Southern Railroad. In these two growing structures Louis's soul became immersed. In them he lived. Were they not his bridges? Surely they were his bridges. In the pages of the Railway Gazette he saw them born, he watched them grow. Week by week he grew with them. Here was Romance, here again was man, the great adventurer, daring to think, daring to have faith, daring to do. Here again was to be set forth to view man in his power to create beneficently. Here were two ideas widely differing in kind. Each was emerging from a brain, each was to find realization. One bridge was to cross a great river, to form the portal of a great city, to be sensational and architectonic. The other was to take form in the wilderness, and abide there; a work of science without concession. Louis followed every detail of design, every measurement; every operation as the two works progressed from the sinking of the caissons in the bed of the Mississippi, and the start in the wild of the initial cantilevers from the face of the cliff. He followed each, with the intensity of personal identification, to the finale of each. Every difficulty encountered he felt to be his own; every expedient, every device, he shared in. The chief engineers became his heroes; they loomed above other men. The positive quality of their minds agreed with the aggressive quality of his own. In childhood his idols had been the big strong men who *did* things. Later on he had begun to feel the greater power of men who could *think* things; later the expansive power of men who could *imagine* things; and at last he began to recognize as dominant, the will of the Creative Dreamer: he who possessed the power of vision needed to harness Imagination, to harness the intellect, to make science do his will, to make the emotions serve him—for without emotion nothing.

This steadfast belief in the power of man was an unalloyed childhood instinct, an intuition and a childhood faith which never for a day forsook him, but grew stronger, like an indwelling dæmon. As day by day passed on, he saw power grow before his eyes, as each unsuspected and new world arose and opened to his wonder eyes; he saw power intensify and expand; and ever grew his wonder at what men could do. He came in a manner to worship man as a being, a presence containing wondrous powers, mysterious hidden powers, powers so varied as to surprise and bewilder him. So that Man, the mysterious, became for him a sort of symbol of that which was deepest, most active in his heart. As months passed and the years went by, as world after world unfolded before him and merged within the larger world, and veil after veil lifted, and illusion after illusion vanished, and the light grew ever steadier, Louis saw power everywhere; and as he grew on through his boyhood, and through the passage to manhood, and to manhood itself, he began to see the powers of nature and the powers of man coalesce in his vision into an IDEA *of power*. Then and only then he became aware that this idea was a *new idea,*—a complete reversal and inversion of the commonly accepted intellectual and theological concept of the Nature of man.

That IDEA which had its mystical beginning in so small a thing as a child's heart, grew and nurtured itself upon that child's varied consistently continuing and metamorphosing experiences in time and place, as has been most solicitously laid bare to view in detail, in the course of this recital. For it needs a long long time, and a rich soil of life-experience, to enable a simple, single idea to grow to maturity and solid strength. A French proverb has it that "Time will not consecrate that in which it has been ignored," while the deep insight of Whitman is set forth in the line, "Nature neither hastens nor delays."

Louis's interest in engineering as such, and in the two bridges in particular, so captivated his imagination, that he briefly dreamed to be a great bridge engineer. The idea of spanning a void appealed to him as masterful in thought and deed. For he had begun to discern that among men of the past and of his day, there were those who were masters of ideas, and of courage, and that they stood forth solitary, each in a world of his own. But the practical effect of the bridges was to turn Louis's mind from the immediate science of engineering toward science in general, and he set forth, with a new relish, upon a course of reading covering Spencer, Darwin, Huxley, Tyndall, and the Germans, and found a new, an enormous world opening before him, a world whose boundaries seemed destined to be limitless in scope, in content, in diversity. This course of reading was not completed in a month, or a year, or in many years; it still remains on the move.

What Louis noted as uppermost in the scientific mind, was its honest search for stability in truth. Hitherto he had regarded his mathematics as an art; he had not followed far enough to see it as a science. Indeed he had hitherto regarded every constructive human effort as an art, and to this view he had been held through the consistent unfolding of the Idea. Inevitably this view was to return in time; through the channels of science itself. For that which at once impressed Louis as new to him and vital, was what was known as *"The Scientific Method."* He saw in it a power of solution he long had fruitlessly been seeking. His key to an outlook took shape in the scientific method of approach to that which lay behind appearances; a relentless method whereby to arrive at the truth by tireless pursuit. He now had in his hands the instrument he wanted. He must learn to use it with a craftsman's skill. For the scientific method was based on exact observation from which, by the inductive system of reasoning, an inference was drawn, an hypothesis framed, to be held tentatively in "suspended judgment" until the gathering of further data might raise it to the dignity of a theory, which theory, if it could stand up under further rigorous testing, would slowly pass into that domain of ordered and accepted knowledge we fondly believe to be Truth. Yet science, he foresaw, could not go either fast or far were it not for Imagination's glowing light and warmth. By nature it is rigid and prosaic—and Louis early noted that the free spirits within its field were men of vision—masters of imagination, men of courage, great adventurers—men of one big, dominant idea.

*   *   *

In the course of Louis's daily working life, conditions were steadily improving. His engagements in offices grew longer, he began to prosper. The quality of work was improving. He had passed the day of his majority, and was now looking out for himself. His success in this regard made him proud. He was a man now, and he knew it. He knew he was equipped to hold his own in the world. He had made a reputation as a worker, and consorted now with a small aristocratic group of the highest paid draftsmen. They met at lunch in a certain favored restaurant. They talked shop; but Louis kept his major thoughts to himself. His plan was, in due time to select a middle-aged architect of standing and established practice, with the right sort of clientele; to enter such an office, and through his speed, alertness and quick ambitious wit, make himself so indispensable that partnership would naturally follow. But this was merely a broad plan. He had no direct selection in mind, but was looking the field over from the corner of his eye. He was in no hurry. He believed in the motto: "Be bold but prudent." He wished events to shape themselves.

Now John Edelmann returned. During the dull spell he had been away in Iowa trying to play the game of farming. The game played him instead. He showed up at lunch one winter day, clad *à l'outrance* as a farmer, for his usual theatrical effect. Instantly the room was filled with sound as he lustily proclaimed the joys of farming in Iowa, twenty miles from nowhere.

He entered the architectural office of a firm named Burling & Adler. The single, very large square office room he flooded with language; he literally "ate up" the work, as he spouted. Naturally he joined the aristocratic lunch-club, and made things lively. As usual he monopolized the conversation, unless rudely interrupted. One need not surmise to whom the sound of his voice was music from the spheres. He cut loose on his latest fad—single tax—and lauded Henry

George in superlatives. He drew the long bow, he colored all things rosy, told Irish stories well in the broad brogue, and on the whole was a nuisance—entertaining and agreeable.

One day, after lunch, John asked Louis to come over to the office to meet Adler, of whom he had spoken at times. Louis went along to please John. They entered the large bare room, drawing tables scattered about; in the center were two plain desks. Those who had business came and went unceremoniously. Both partners were present and busy. Louis thus had time to size them up. Burling was slouched in a swivel chair, his long legs covering the desk top; he wiggled a chewed cigar as he talked to a caller, and spat into a square box. He was an incredible, long and bulky nosed Yankee, perceptibly ageing fast, and of manifestly weakening will—one of the passing generation who had done a huge business after the fire but whom the panic had hit hard.

Further away stood Adler at a draftsman's table, full front view, well lighted. He was a heavy-set short-nosed Jew, well bearded, with a magnificent domed forehead which stopped suddenly at a solid mass of black hair. He was a picture of sturdy strength, physical and mental.

Louis was presented first to Burling who reached out a hand and said "Howdy," in the distrait manner age so frequently bears toward strangely sprouting incomprehensible youth, separated by the gulf of years. Next, John led Louis to Adler whose broad serious face, and kindly brown efficient eyes, joined in a rich smile of open welcome. It did not take many ticks of the clock to note that Adler's brain was intensely active and ambitious, his mind open, broad, receptive, and of an unusually high order. He was twelve years Louis's senior, and in the pink of condition. Louis was of the exuberant age. Adler thought highly of John. The talk was brief and lively; Adler said nice things, questioned Louis as to his stay at the Beaux Arts. The little talk ended, Louis left; John remained in his preserve. This was the last that Louis saw of Adler for many moons. He was pleased to have met him and to have reason heartily to respect his vigorous personality. But he was no part of Louis's program, hence he soon faded from view, and became almost completely forgotten. Louis was satisfied with things as they were going. He was ambitious but cautious; he was waiting for the right man to show up. He did not remain too long in any one place, and each time increased his salary.

Meanwhile his days were for work; his nights for study, for reflection, and gradual formulation of ideas subsidiary to the main Idea he was consciously now working out alone. This form of solitude did not disturb him. He saw that a *Clopet demonstration* meant a matter of years of work and growth. He was disturbed, however, by the elusive quality of the main thought he was pursuing, which seemed to recede and grow larger even as he grew abler to deal with it.

On a recent Christmas his father had given him a copy of John Draper's work on "The Intellectual Development of Europe," in two volumes; still a notable work of the day. This he read and reread with absorbing interest, passing over its controversial trend, for the "war between science and religion" as it was called, was still raging. The broad division of the work into an "Age of faith," and an "Age of reason" held his interest, as he saw set forth the emergence and the growth of science as the spirit of man sought and found freedom in the open. This coincided with his own belief, that man's *spirit* must be free that his *powers* may be free to accomplish in beneficence. He had discovered, to his annoyance, that in the architectural art of his day, the spirit of man was not free, nor were his powers so liberated and so trained that he might create in beneficence. Not only this, but that for centuries it had been the case that art had been belittled in superstitions called traditions— and lived on by virtue of a thin and baseless faith— and John Edelmann's theory of *suppressed functions,* recurred to him as broadly set forth, in confirmation, in Draper's heavy work. Further than this, Louis felt as a result of reading Draper, that his thoughts concerning architecture must broaden into a perfected sympathy with mankind. That Man, past and present, must and would become more and more significant, would be found to have filled a greater rôle than any art, than any science. That man, perhaps and probably was the only real background that gave distinction to works appearing in the foreground as separated things,—or perhaps was it the invisible spirit of mankind that pervaded all things, all works, all civilizations, and informed them with the sense of actuality? That his, Louis's true work, was now and henceforth to lie in the study of what man now thought, and had thought through the centuries. Thus the task for him grew larger, and the time required, longer— for he was still in the plastic formative groping stage.

In Darwin he found much food. The Theory of

Evolution seemed stupendous. Spencer's definition implying a progression from an unorganized simple, through stages of growth and differentiation to a highly organized complex, seemed to fit his own case, for he had begun with a simple unorganized idea of *beneficent power,* and was beginning to see the enormous complexity growing out of it, and enriching its meaning while insistently demanding room and nurture for further growth, until it should reach that stage of clarity through the depths of which the original idea might again be clearly seen, and its primal power more fully understood. Thus, Louis, while still in a haze, felt the courage to go on. He had been reading the works of men of matured and powerful thought, 'way beyond his years; but what he could grasp he hung on to. He felt the enthusiasm of one who is on the way, and who senses that his goal is real.

* * *

One day John Edelmann, who meanwhile had entered into partnership with a man named Johnson, who did school work, sent for Louis to come over that evening—said he had something to say. And this was his story: That Adler had cut loose from Burling, set up independently, and, in collaboration with George A. Carpenter, a resourceful promoter, had put through the New Central Music Hall, now nearing completion, and had other work on hand. The time was early in 1879. John urged that this was Louis's opportunity. That Adler had all the strong points, but was feeble in design and knew it. That he had talked the matter over several times with Adler, that Adler was cautiously and eagerly interested, but timid in making advances.

Louis saw the point at once. So they made a second call on Adler. There ensued a mutual sizing up at close range, very friendly indeed. And it was then and there agreed that Louis was to take charge of Adler's office, was to have a free hand, and, if all went well for a period, and they should get along together, there was something tangible in the background. Louis took hold and made things hum. Soon there came into the office three large orders; a six-story high grade office building—the Borden Block; an up-to-date theatre, and a large substantial residence. Louis put through this work with the efficiency of combined Moses Woolson and Beaux Arts training. It was his first fine opportunity. He used it. He found in Adler a most congenial co-worker, open-minded, generous-minded, quick to perceive, thorough-going, warm in his enthusiasms, opening to Louis every opportunity to go ahead on his own responsibility, posting him on matters of building technique of which he had a complete grasp, and all in all treating Louis as a prize pet—a treasure trove. Thus they became warm friends. Adler's witticisms were elephantine. He said one day to Louis:

"How would you like to take me into partnership?" Louis laughed.

"All right," said Adler, "draw up a contract for five years, beginning first of May. First year you one third, after that, even."

Louis drew up a brief memorandum on a sheet of office stationery, which Adler read over once and signed.

On the first day of May, 1880, D. Adler & Co.

moved into a fine suite of offices on the top floor of the Borden Block aforesaid. On the first day of May, 1881, the firm of Adler & Sullivan, Architects, had its name on the entrance door. All of which signifies, after long years of ambitious dreaming and unremitting work, that at the age of 25, Louis H. Sullivan became a full-fledged architect before the world, with a reputation starting on its way, and in partnership with a man he had least expected as such; a man whose reputation was solidly secured in utter honesty, fine intelligence and a fund of that sort of wisdom which attracts and holds. Between the two there existed a fine confidence and the handling of the work was divided and adjusted on a temperamental basis—each to have initiative and final authority in his own field, without a sharp arbitrary line being drawn that might lead to dissension. What was particularly fine, as we consider human nature, was Adler's open frank way of pushing his young partner to the front.

Now Louis felt he had arrived at a point where he had a foothold, where he could make a *beginning* in the open world. Having come into its responsibilities, he would face it boldly. He could now, undisturbed, start on the course of practical experimentation he long had in mind, which was to make an architecture that fitted its functions—a realistic architecture based on well defined utilitarian needs—that all practical demands of utility should be paramount as basis of planning and design; that no architectural dictum, or tradition, or superstition, or habit, should stand in the way. He would brush them all aside, regardless of commentators. For his view, his conviction was this: That the architectural art to be of contemporary immediate value must be *plastic;* all senseless conventional rigidity must be taken out of it; it must intelligently serve—it must not suppress. In this wise the forms under his hand would grow naturally out of the needs and express them frankly, and freshly. This meant in his courageous mind that he would put to the test a formula he had evolved, through long contemplation of living things, namely that *form follows function,* which would mean, in practice, that architecture might again become a living art, if this formula were but adhered to.

The building business was again under full swing, and a series of important mercantile structures came into the office, each one of which he treated experimentally, feeling his way toward a basic process, a grammar of his own. The immediate problem was increased daylight, the maximum of daylight. This led him to use slender piers, tending toward a masonry and iron combination, the beginnings of a vertical system. This method upset all precedent, and led Louis's contemporaries to regard him as an iconoclast, a revolutionary, which was true enough—yet into the work was slowly infiltrated a corresponding system of artistic expression, which appeared in these structures as novel and to some repellent, in its total disregard of accepted notions. But to all objections Louis turned a deaf ear. If a thousand proclaimed him wrong, the thousand could not change his course. As buildings varying in character came under his hand, he extended to them his system of form and function, and as he did so his conviction increased that architectural manipulation, as a homely art or a fine art must be rendered completely plastic to the mind and the hand of the designer; that

PLATE 28. Mrs. Josephine Crane Bradley residence, 106 North Prospect Street, Madison, Wis. 1909. Now Sigma Phi Fraternity House.

materials and forms must yield to the mastery of his imagination and his will; through this alone could modern conditions be met and faithfully expressed. This meant the casting aside of all pedantry, of all the artificial teachings of the schools, of the thoughtless acceptance of inane traditions, of puerile habits of uninquiring minds; that all this mess, devoid of a center of gravity of thought, and vacant of sympathy and understanding, must be superseded by a sane philosophy of a living architecture, good for all time, founded on the only possible foundation—Man and his powers. Such philosophy Louis had already developed in broad outline in the course of his many dissatisfactions and contemplations. He wished now to test it out in the broad daylight of action, and to perfect its form and content. This philosophy developed will be set forth in these closing chapters.

It is not to be supposed that Louis arrived directly at results as though by magic. Quite the contrary, he arrived slowly though boldly through the years, by means of incessant thought, self correction, hard work and dogged perseverance. For it was his fascinating task to build up a system of technique, a mastery of technique. And such a system could scarcely be expected to reach its fullness of development, short of maturity, assuming it would reach its fullness then, or could ever reach it; for the world of expression is limitless; the theory so deep in idea, so rich in content, as to preclude any ending of its beneficent, all-inclusive power. And we may here recall Monsieur Clopet, the book of descriptive geometry that went into the waste basket, and the thunderclap admonition: "Our demonstrations shall be such as to admit of no exception."

CHAPTER XIV

Face to Face

IF with open mind one reads and observes industriously and long; if in so doing one covers a wide field and so covering reflects in terms of realism, he is likely, soon or late, to be brought to a sudden consciousness that Man is an unknown quantity and his existence unsuspected.

One will be equally amazed to note that the philosophers, the theologians, of all times turned their backs upon Man; that, from the depths of introspection, fixing their gaze in all directions save the real one, they have uniformly evolved a phantasm, or a series of phantoms, and have declared such to be man in his reality—and such reality to be depraved. A small feature, however, was overlooked by them in the neglect to observe that their man, in his depravity, had created the gods. Their insistent view of man—a further product of their phantasy—lay in the dogma, protean in form, that man is creature.

Meanwhile the real man was always at their elbow, or moving in groups or multitudes about them, or even looking them in the eyes and holding converse with them. But they did not see him; he was too near, too commonplace—too transparent. The gods were far away and could be understood.

The mighty man of war also turned his back. Yet the wise man, the warrior and the priest differed in no valid sense from the multitude enfolding them as in a genesis; for man in his state of depravity as creature, created these also, as his demigods.

Thus man, not knowing himself, and none else knowing him, lived as a mirage, within a world of mirage which he fancied real. It was real for him; for such is the habit of man's imagination in playing tricks with him in his credulity.

The careful reader and observer again may be astonished to note that to the multitudes imagination, as such, is unknown—that the multitudes are unconscious of this power within themselves. Hence the reader, the observer, who is not so completely unconscious of himself, becomes aware of the imposing phenomenon that the huge and varied superstructures of the civilizations of all times have rested for support on so tenuous a foundation as the fabric of the radiant dream of the multitudes. That in such dream he will clearly see Imagination playing its clandestine rôle. The mass imagination of the multitudes is thus seen to be the prime impelling and sustaining power in the origins and growth of the civilizations. Let the mass imagination withdraw its consent, withhold its nourishing acquiescence and faith, then the civilization founded thereon begins to wither at the top, emaciates, atrophies and dies. One will further note that such changes in the mass imagination, in the mass dream, are of highly varied origins; but once under way, are beyond recall.

One also minutely notes that the tricks of imagination are universal and beyond numbering in variety, permeating all phases of the social fabric. Hence man's vagaries and follies and cruelties are beyond computation; yet all these betrayals and cajolings and trickeries flow from the same single source, namely the individual, unconscious that his imagination is incessantly at work. Because he is not acquainted with its nature, and unaware that he is its puppet, his waking hours are a continuing dream of inverted Self.

It is the mass dream of inverted self, populous with fears overt and secret, that forms the continuous but gossamer thread upon which are strung as phantom beads all civilizations from the remotest past of record to that of the present day and hour. As we follow back upon this thread—one end of which is delicately attached to our own inverted secret thoughts, we find it unchanging from end to end, regardless of environment; the civilizations it passes through and upholds on its way are but local manifestations and exhibits.

This intense and continuing preoccupation with inverted self makes it clear why man has turned his back on man, and why man is still unknown to himself—and unsuspected.

So long as imagination slyly tricked him into self deprecation, self debasement and the slavery of the creature conviction, or into the opposite, megalomania, with its unquenchable thirst for blood, for plunder, and dominion; or with siren song beguiled him through the portals of a closed world of abstraction,—he could not know himself, and the neighbor must remain a stranger to be feared, despised, or placated.

Indeed, until we come as pioneers, to seek out and know imagination as such, to view it clearly defined as an erratic and dangerous power, to be controlled; until we have observed with realistic clarity its multifarious doings from black magic upward to mighty deeds of hand and head and heart, we shall remain remote from man's reality, and from the splendor of his native powers.   *   *   *

One who has made the rough pilgrimage through the jungled infirmities of philosophy, of theology, and through the wilderness of turbid dream-words uttered by the practical man who deals in cold, hard facts; one who as pioneer worked his troubled way through the undergrowth of culture with its acceptances, its preconceptions and precious finalities; one who, led on by a faith unfaltering, at last arrives at the rendezvous with Life, here testifies the natural man as sound to the core and kindly, yet innocent of himself as the seat of genius, as container of limitless creative powers of beneficence.

Solely on the strength of this faith was begun the story of a child-dream of power.

* * *

Wherefore we may now inquire: What are these powers, and what is the reality we affirm to be man?

He is none other than ourselves divested of our wrappings. If we in imagination divest ourselves of our wrappings we may see that he is ourselves. If we remove our blinders we shall see more clearly. If we look out between the bars of our self-imprisonment, we may note him nearby, walking familiarly in the Garden of Life. Undoubtedly he is ourselves, he is our youth, he is our spirit, he is that within us which has yearned for frank utterance—how long—and still yearns.

It is appalling to think he is ourselves; to wake from our dreams and see him. Yet will it not be inspiriting to find him at our elbow—no longer a stranger—no longer to be feared? To know that he is like us all? To feel the widening sense, as we regard him, that he stands not only as our explanation, but as our self-revelation. True, he is not at all what we had supposed and what we have affirmed. Yet will he be grimly recognized as he comes into view—to our amaze, for he is precisely that which we have denied.

We may be shocked at first, retreat, and disclaim; for denial of the power of life is our habit of old. We have other habits of old woven into weird grotesqueries. These are among our wrappings.

*   *   *

Inasmuch as man has been affirmed herein as sound and kindly, let us examine him. Rest assured we shall find naught in him that is not truly in ourselves and was not there in latency at birth.

To begin: He is a *Worker* and a *Wanderer* in varied ways. With his bodily powers he may go here and there, he may move objects about, he may change the order of things. Here at the onset we find a portentous power—the power to change situations; he can make *new situations*. With his ten fingers he can do wonderful things, make things he needs, make accessory things to extend his muscular powers. Thus he *manipulates*—he further changes situations. He changes his own situations, he creates an environment of his own. One sees here the Adventurer, the Craftsman, the Doer,—ever growing in power. Thus man's first collective power within himself is the power to aspire, to work—to wander—to go from place to place near and far—to return to his home.

Now comes into view that power we call *Curiosity*— and coupled with it the power to *inquire*. Man's power to inquire we call a mental power, to distinguish it from his somatic power. It may have had a beginning, it can have no end. The result of inquiry we call knowledge; its high objective we call science. The objective of science is more knowledge, more power; more inquiry, more power.

Now, if to the power to do we added the power to inquire, Man, the worker, grows visibly more compact in power, more potent to change situations and to make new situations for himself. The situation may be a deep gorge in a wilderness; the new situation shows a bridge spanning the chasm in one great leap. Thus it is that man himself, as it were, leaps the chasm, through the adventurous co-ordination of his power to inquire and his power to do. And thus the natural man ever enlarges his range of beneficence. His life experiences are real. He reverses the dictum "I think: Therefore I am." It becomes in him, *I am: Therefore I inquire and do!*

It is this affirmative "I AM" that is man's reality.

Wherefore warrior, philosopher and priest turned their backs. This "I am" they could not see, could not suspect, even as it stood at their elbow regarding them with ordinary human eyes. For it had been settled long ago on abundant evidence that man is creature and depraved.

In the history of mankind there are recorded two great INVERSIONS. The first, set forth by the Nazarene to the effect that love is a greater power and more real than vengeance. The second, proclaimed the earth to be a sphere revolving in its course around the sun. These affirmations were made in the face of all evidence sacred to the contrary. Who could feel the earth revolving? Who could fail to see the sun rise and set? What but blood could satisfy, or an eye for an eye?

Hence man's powers were not seen as himself, nor himself as his powers. Such recognition would involve a reversal and inversion both of sacred lore and common sense.

In reactive consequence of age-long self-repression and self-beguilement the world of mankind is now preparing its way for a Third Inversion. The world of heart and head is becoming dimly sentient that man in his power is Free spirit—Creator. The long dream of inverted self is nearing its end. Emerging from the heritage of mystical unconsciousness and phantasy, the world of mankind is stirring. Man's deeds are about to become conscious deeds in the open. The beauty, the passion, the glory of the past shall merge into a new beauty, a new passion, a new glory as man approaches man, and recognizing him, rejoices in him and with him, as born in power.

* * *

Never in man's time has there been such sound warrant for an attitude of Optimism as in our own, the very present day. Yet to him who in myopic fear looks but at the troubled surface, there appears equal warrant in the phantasy of Pessimism. What a price man shall have paid for freedom! For freedom from the thrall of his parlous imagination! For freedom from the strangle hold of his own phantasmal self!

* * *

He who has lived, alive, during the past fifty years has viewed an extraordinary drama. He who starting young, shall live through the coming fifty years will move within the action and scene shifting of a greater drama.

The gravitation of world thought and dream is shifting. Out of the serial collapses of age-long feudalism is arising a new view of man. For man's powers in certitude, approach the infinite. They are bewildering—amazing in diversity. They unfold their intimate complexity to our view as an equally amazing solidarity, as we hold, steadfast, to the realistic concept of man as free spirit—as creator—even as the vast complexity in the outworking of the feudal thought simplifies into a basic concept of self-delusion and self-fear.

* * *

Our portrayal is not yet wholly clear. Let us go on. There lies another power in man. That power is MORAL: Its name is CHOICE! Within this one word, Choice, lies the story of man's world. It stands for the secret poise within him. It reveals as a flashlight all his imagings, his phantasies, his wilful thoughts, his deeds, from the greatest to the least, even in this gliding hour we call today. *This one word, Choice, stands for the sole and single power; it is the name of the mystery that lies behind the veil of all human appearances.* A word that dissolves the enigma of men's deeds. A word, a light that not only illuminates all his obvious works, all the inner springs and motives of his civilizations, but a light whose rays reach within the sanctuary of the secret thought of each and all, thus revealing the man of the past and the man of today, starkly in personal status as a social factor of beneficence or woe. Need we know man's thoughts? View his works, his deeds; they tell his choice.

Implicit in true freedom of spirit lies a proud and virile will. Such glorious power of free will to choose, envisages beneficent social responsibility as manifest and welcome. Here now stands in full light Man erect and conscious as a moral power. The will to choose aright lifts him to the peak of social vision whence he may forecast new and true situations.

* * *

The Free Spirit is the spirit of Joy. It delights to create in beauty. It is unafraid, it knows not fear. It declares the Earth to be its home, and the fragrance of Earth to be its inspiration. It is strong, it is mighty in beneficence. It views its powers with emotions of adventure. Humility it knows not. It dreams a civilization like unto itself. It would create such a world for mankind. It has the strength. It sees the strength of the fertile earth, the strength of the mountains, the valleys, the far spreading plains, the vast seas, the rivers and the rivulets, the great sky as a wondrous dome, the sun in its rising, its zenith, and its setting, and the night. It glories in these powers of earth and sky as in its own. It affirms itself integral with them all. It sees Life at work everywhere—Life, the mysterious, the companionable, the ineffable, the immensest and gentlest of powers, clothing the earth in a pattern of radiant sublimity, of tenderness, of fairy delicacy—ceaselessly at work. Thus the free spirit feels itself to be likewise clothed as with a flowing shoulder-garment, symbol of power akin to the fluent mystery and fecundity of Life. Thus it moves in the open with vision clear. Thus is man the wonder-worker bound up in friendship with the wonder-worker—Life.

* * *

Now the real man begins to shape within our vision.

Consider his primary powers: He, the *worker,* the *inquirer,* the *chooser.* Add to these the wealth of his emotions—also powers. Think how manifold they are, how colorful; how with them he may dramatize his works, his thoughts, his choosings; how he may beautify his choice. Think of his power to *receive;* to receive through the channels of his senses, to receive through his mystic power of sympathy which brings understanding to illumine Knowledge. Think of what eyesight means as a power, the sense of touch, the power to hear, to listen; and the power of contemplation. Add these to his cumulating interblending power; then think again of his enlarging power to act. Deep down within him lies that power we call Imagination, the power instantly or slowly to picture forth, the power to act in advance of action; the power that knows no limitations, no boundaries, that renders vivid both giving and receiving; the inscrutable dynamic power that energizes all other powers. Think of man as Imagination! Then think of him as Will! Now enrich the story of his prior-mentioned powers with the flow of imagination and the steadiness of will. Think anew of his power to act; of the quantity and quality of this power.

Now think of the freedom such power brings!

Think of the power we call Vision; that inner sight which encompasses the larger meanings of its outer world, which sees humanity in the broad, which beholds the powers without itself, which unifies its inner and its outer world, which sees far beyond where the eye leaves off seeing, and as sympathetic insight finds its goal in the real.

Now see Man go forth to work, inspired by his vision

of the outer world, himself made eager by the passion to live and worthily to do!

See him go forth in certitude as seer, as prophet, as evangelist, proclaiming his faith — in certitude as worker, to build a new home.

See him, as poet, as troubadour, as he goes forth, singing the new song, the refreshing song—calling in carols: Awake! ye dreamers all, lift up your heads, and be your hearts lifted up that Life in splendor may come in: Ye who dream in the shadows and are sore perplexed.

Thus the multitudes vibrate, as they dream—at the sound of a song in their dream.

It is the richness of the soul-life of the multitudes that inspires and at times appalls the observer. For the multitudes are compact of human beings—a vast ceaseless flow of individuals, each a dreamer, each latent in power, the mass moving noiselessly through time—slowly changing in its constancy of renewal.

* * *

Thus though Man now appears before us in glamor as a maze of powers, we have not yet made his image clear in full, and in diversity.

While it is plain, when all wrappings are removed, we shall find all men to be alike in native possession of essential powers, we are at once confronted by this paradox: That all men obviously are different; that no two are alike. In plain words we find each human being unique. When we say unique, we mean *the only one*. Thus each one is the only one. If we have mused long upon the immense fecundity and industry of Life, the paradox vanishes: The only one and the all coalesce. The individual and the mass become *one,* in a new phase of power whose stupendous potency of creative art in civilization stuns the sense of possibility.

Now opens to our view the Democratic Vista!

Now see unfold the power of the *only one* in multiple, and the *One* become a vast complex of unique powers inspired of its free spirit and its power of beneficence—its works now solidly founded on the full emergence of courage—the evanishment of fear!

* * *

Alas, the world has never known a sound social fabric, a fabric sound and clean to the core and kindly. For it has ever turned its back on Man. Through time immemorial it has, in overt and secret fear of self, been impotent to recognize the only one, the unique. Hence wars and more wars, pestilence, famine and desolation; the rise and crumbling of immense fabrics.

The feudal concept of self-preservation is poisoned at the core by the virulent assumption of master and man, of potentate and slave, of external and internal suppression of the life urge of the only one—of its faith in human sacrifice as a means of salvation.

The *only one* is Ego—the "I am"—the unique—the most precious of man's powers, their source and summation in diversity. Without Ego, which is Life, man vanishes. Ego signifies Identity. It is the free spirit. It is not a tenant, it is the all in all. It is present everywhere throughout man's wondrous being. It is what we call the spiritual, a term now becoming interchangeable with the physical. It is the sign and symbol of man's immense Integrity—the "I am that I am." To it the Earth, the world of humanity, the multitudes, the universe—become an Egocosm.

Thus to the eye of the earnest watcher, the dual man of legend and of present mythical belief fades, incorporeal as a ghost. Departing it leads the ghostly feudal scapegoat with its burden of sin.

It is man's manifest integrity that reveals him valid —sound to the core. It is this spiritual integrity that defines him human, that points true to his high moral power—the power of valid choice.

This new vision of man is the true vision of man.

Toward this new truth, this inversion, the world of mankind slowly turning, vaguely conscious, strives to articulate that which is as yet too deep, too remote, too new for its words. But it is not too deep, too remote or too new for its aspirations.

* * *

Thus in portrayal stands *Man the Reality:* Container of self-powers: A moving center of radiant energy: Awaiting his time to create anew in his proper image.

Are then the multitudes infertile? Is genius rare? Has our traditional education and culture left us wholly blind? Have we forgotten the children—Egos at our elbow? The springtide of genius there! Shall we continue to destroy? What is our *Choice?* How have we exercised it? How shall we exercise it? Is our moral power asleep? Are we without faith in our own?

Whence, then, this story of a child's dream of power? What shall *our* dream be?

* * *

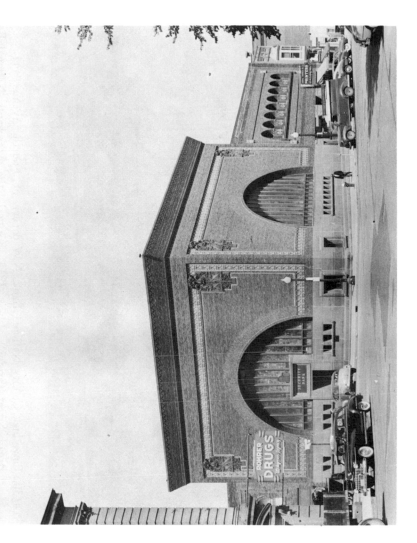

PLATE 29. Security Bank, NE corner of Broadway and Cedar Streets, Owatonna, Minn. 1907-08. Formerly the National Farmers' Bank.

PLATE 30. Poweshiek County National Bank, NW corner of Fourth Avenue and Broad Street, Grinnell, Iowa, 1914. Formerly the Merchants' National Bank.

Our dream shall be of a civilization founded upon ideas thrillingly sane, a civilization, a social fabric squarely resting on man's quality of virtue as a human being; created by man, the real, in the image of his fruitful powers of beneficence; created in the likeness of his aspirant emotions, in response to the power and glory of his true imagination, the power of his intelligence, his ability to inquire, to do, to make new situations befitting his needs. A civilization that shall reflect man sound to the core and kindly in the exercise of his will to choose aright. A civilization that shall be the living voice, the spring song, the saga of the power of his Ego to banish fear and fate, and in the courage of adventure and of mastership to shape his destiny.

Such dream is the vigorous daylight dream of man's abounding power, that he may establish in beauty and in joy, on the earth, a dwelling place devoid of fear. That in the so doing he shall establish an anchorage within his universe, in courage, in the mighty spirit of adventure, of masterful craftsmanship, as he rises to the heights of the new art of all arts,—the art of upbuilding for the race a new, a stable home.

*   *   *

Plainly the outworking of so sublime a conception as that of rearing the fabric of a worthwhile civilization upon the basic truth of man's reality as a sure foundation, implies the inversion of a host of fixed ideas "consecrated by the wisdom of the ages." The time has come to place the wisdom of the ages in the balance of inquiry; to ascertain, when weighed, wherein it may be found wanting in the human sense. One sure

[273]

test is sanity, for to be unkind is to be dangerously unbalanced.

It is also time to test out the folly of the ages, the multifarious corruption involved in abstract and concrete irresponsibility, the abuse of power, the abuse of the useful, the successive collapses and ruin, the ever present sense of instability, the all-pervading fear, the lack of anchorage.

So testing, we shall find that alike the wisdom and folly of the ages rest in utter insecurity upon a false concept of the nature of man. For both "wisdom" and folly have committed and still commit the double folly of turning away from man in contempt.

Glancing at our modern civilization we find on the surface crust essentially the same idea at work that has prevailed throughout the past. Yet if we search beneath the surface we discern a new power of the multitudes everywhere at work. It is the power of a changing dream, of a changing choice; of Life urging upward to the open the free spirit of man—so long self-suppressed under the dead weight of the "consecrated wisdom of the ages" and its follies.

*   *   *

The fabricating of a virile, a proud and kindly civilization, rich in its faith in man, is surely to constitute the absorbing interest of the coming generations. It will begin to take on its functional form out of the resolve of choice, and the liberation of those instincts within us which are akin to the dreams of childhood, and which, continuing on through the children and the children of the children, shall be a guide evermore. For who shall say the child is not the unsullied wellspring of power!

The chief business now is to pave the way for the child, that it may grow wholesome, proud and stalwart in its native powers.

So doing we shall uncover to our view the amazing world of instinct in the child whence arises genius with its swift grasp of the real.

The great creative art of upbuilding a chosen and stable civilization with its unique culture, implies orderly concentration and organization of man's powers toward this sole end, consciously applied in each and every one of his socially constructive activities in the clear light of his understanding that the actualities of good and evil are resident in man's choice—and not elsewhere. Thus will arise a new *Morale* in its might!

And let it be well understood that such creative energy cannot arise from a welter of pallid abstractions as a soil, nor can it thrive within the tyranny of any cut and dried system of economics or politics. It must and will arise out of the heart, to be nurtured in common honesty by the intelligence, and by that sense of artistry which does not interfere with the growth of a living thing but encourages it to seek and find its own befitting form. Thus the living idea of man, the free spirit, master of his powers, shall find its form-image in a civilization which shall set forth the highest craftsmanship, the artistry of living joyously in stable equilibrium.

Thus widens the Democratic Vista!

* * *

The historic Feudal thought, sought and found its form in a series of civilizations resting upon a denial of man by the multitudes themselves, who sought cohesion in mutual fear of life, and out of the culture of fear they created their tyrants. Their unsafe anchorage lay in the idea of force, in its convincing outward show of domination, splendor and glory.

In terror of the unknown, in appeal for mediation, the multitudes passed their immense unconscious power to those they raised aloft—gods or men, and as value received they created and accepted the status of servitude. Those thus raised aloft became enormously parasitic, capping and sapping the strength of the multitudes. As the latter grew in self-sacrifice and poverty, they became luxurious in that they gave their all in the name of glory that their children, the great, might flourish. They staggered beneath the weight of the mighty they upheld aloft and who came to know them not—other than as beasts to toil or fight. Thus has the feudal super-power ever undermined its own foundation, ever, in recurring cycle, collapsing and renewing —renewing and collapsing. Times, places, names, local colors, mechanisms, countenances, change. The idea, the thought, the fear, persists through the ages.

*   *   *

For us the chief impress of the self-revealing story of mankind lies in the perception that all sanctioning power comes from below. From the vast human plenum we have called the multitudes, it arises gently, massively, step by step, stage by stage, height upon height; all of which but signifies the peoples' dreams of glory taking shape vicariously in their times and places. The spectacular and imposing groups and summits of the feudal superstructure have no other base, no other sanction. Like towering cumulus clouds they float upon thin air.

As there are truths that lie within truths, so are there dreams that lie within dreams. The most ancient of dreams lies indeed within the feudal dream. This dream is none other than the dream of the reality of man.

As truths one by one appear above the surface, ever more powerful, farther reaching as they come from greater depths of life, so the great deep dream of man's free spirit has been moving upward through the feudal dream. The flair of his powers is now sensing in the thought of the man of today.

*   *   *

With the great inversion of the Earth and the Sun, brought definitely about by so small an object as a telescope which man in his curiosity invented—created —to extend his power of eyesight and the daring thought—the dream—it stood for; with this shock of inversion definitely began the greatest of man's adventures upon his Earth.

We in present sense and in retrospect call it the MODERN.

The feudal flow poured on, the germ of the modern growing in embryo apace and inexterminable. Inquiry upon inquiry followed; invention upon invention, discovery upon discovery; and wars and more wars, tremors, and the downfall of mighty superstitions; cunning and betrayal raged in abuses of delegated power, institutions rocked, dogma came forth in the open, knife and torch in hand the feudal flow went on in stealth, the modern power grew and ramified; there was calm and there was turbulence; onward flowed the feudal stream with its new arrangements, its new col-

lapses, its new horrors, its new deaths, its new resur-
rections, as the power of man's self-determination, the
assertion of his free spirit, none too articulate as yet,
none too sane, clarified in growing strength, its inventions seized upon, its uses turned to abuse, yet goading
the feudal power into titanic writhings, fears and
dreads, desperations, ruses and stratagems, wars and
more wars—the dread phantom of awakening multitudes—the resolve to foster hate.

Yet man the worker, the inquirer, ever pushed onward in hope. Came the printing press, the mariner's
compass, the power of steam, railroads, great ships, the
discovery and development of new vast hidden riches
of earth, the harnessing of the mystical power of elec-
tricity, the land telegraph, the ocean cable, the telephone, the growth of libraries, the daily papers, the
public schools, the technical schools, the automobile,
vast systems of transportation of all kinds, the radio,
the aeroplane, the mastery of the air, the mastery of
the seas, the mastery of the earth, the increasing mastery of ideas. The immense growth in power of constructive imagination and of the will to do. And all
to what end? What may tomorrow and tomorrow
bring forth out of blood-stained yesterday and the flowing yesterdays since History's dawn?

The great drama we herein have called the Modern,
unique in the story of mankind, beginning with a small
telescope, advancing to the radio, to the measurement
of the stars, to the searching out of the utterly minute
in Life's infinitude of variety, to enormous strides in
developments of utility, we may say is in character so
eye-opening as to constitute the first act in the drama
of the universal education of mankind through a series

of imposing object lessons, changing situations, shifting scenes. Also, in that act begins the lifting of veils revealing object lessons coming closer up, and closer, from beneath the surface of feudal repression, and of the savage inertia of superstitions born of the habit of fear, and of unawareness, of dread of the reality of man; object lessons—ever object lessons—crowding upon us.

Among the most startling of these object lessons we are coming to apperceive the significance of choice—its dire or its joyous man-made results. Slowly in consequence comes forth from the hitherto invisible, and shapes before us, a presence no gesture can debar, no noise of words deter,—the sublime, the warning, the prophetic image of man as Moral Power.

Thus clarifies in the dawning light of our modern day the fuller meaning, the effulgence of the Democratic Vista; the super-power of Democratic Man.

Moral Power, in the intensity of its choice, in the full exercise of its purpose to create a world of sanity, of beauty and of joy, alone can cause to dissolve and fade into thin air as though it had never been, the baleful feudal superstition of dominion and blood-sacrifice.

This moral power residing in the multitudes and awakening to voice, is what Democracy means.

To envisage Democracy as a mechanical, political system merely, to place faith in it as such,—or in any abstraction, is to foster an hallucination, to join in the Dance of Death; to confuse the hand of Esau with the voice of Jacob. The lifting of the eyelids of the World is what Democracy means.

*   *   *

The implications of the Democratic Idea branch into endless ramification of science, of art, of all industrial and social activities of human well-being, through which shall flow the wholesome sap of its urge of self-preservation through beneficence, drawn up from roots running ever deeper and spreading ever finer within the rich soil of human kindness and intelligence. For kindness is the sanest of powers, and by its fruits shall Democracy be known. It is of the antitheses that Feudalism has prepared the way for kindness. Kindness, seemingly so weak, is in fact the name of a great adventure which mankind thus far has lacked the courage, the intelligence, the grit to undertake. Its manly, its heroic aspect has been unknown, by reasons of inverted notions of reality. This form of myopia is of the feudal view.

In place of myopic ideas, democratic modern thought uses clear vision. Clear vision leads to straight thinking, sound thinking to sane action, sane action to beneficent results that shall endure.

In this sense of sound thinking and clean action all sciences, all arts, all activities, become sentimentally, emotionally, dramatically and constructively imbued with the stirring, the self-propelling impulse of the democratic idea. Therefore they will all hold in common a thought whose inexhaustible power will shape a common end which shall signify in the solidity of its logic fruitful peace and joy on earth, as equally the romance of good-will toward men.

*   *   *

Now that we have a clarifying idea of the nature of man and his powers; now that we behold in him that which lies deepest and surest in ourselves, we may suggest the nature of a democratic education.

These things it shall do:

It shall regard the child body, the child mind, the child heart, as a trust.

It shall watch for the first symptom of surviving feudal fear and dissolve it with gentle ridicule while it teaches prudence and the obvious consequences of acts. No child that can toddle bravely is too young to know what choice means, when presented objectively and humanly. Thus it shall teach the nature of choice at the beginning.

It shall allow the child to dream, to give vent to its wondrous imagination, its deep creative instinct, its romance.

It shall recognize that every child is the seat of genius; for genius is the highest form of play with Life's forces.

It shall allow the precious being to grow in its wholesome atmosphere of activities, giving only that cultivation which a careful gardener gives—the children shall be the garden.

It shall utilize the fact that the child mind, in its own way, can grasp an understanding of things and ideas, supposed now in our pride of feudal thought to be beyond its reach.

It shall recognize that the child, undisturbed, feels in its own way the sense of power within it, and about it. That by intuition the child is mystic—close to nature's heart, close to the strength of Earth.

The child thus warded will be a wholesome, happy child. It will forecast the pathway to its maturity.

As from tender age the child grows into robust

demonstrative vigor, and ebullition of wanton spirits, the technic of warding will pass by degrees into the technic of training or discipline—bodily, mentally, emotionally; the imagination, the intellect, organized to work together; the process of co-ordination stressed. The idea of the child's natural powers will be suggested a little at a time and shown objectively.

The child by this time is passing out of its reveries; life is glowing, very real, very tangible. So shall its awakening powers be trained in the glowing real, the tangible, the three R's, made glowing and real to it as a part of its world. It is here the difference between welcome work and a task comes into play; the difference between a manikin and a teacher.

Now arrives the stage of pre-adolescence—unromantic urge of hastening vegetative growth; the period of the literal, the bovine, disturbed at times by prophetic reverie. This is the time for literal instruction.

Now comes the stage of adolescence, when the whole being tends to deliquesce into instability, vague idealisms, emotions hitherto unknown or despised, bashfulness, false pride, false courage, introspection, impulsiveness, inhibitions, awkward consciousness of self, yet with an eye clairvoyant to that beauty which it seeks, a stirring in the soul of glory, of adventure, of romance. The plastic age of impressionability, of enthusiasms. Also the Danger Age; the age of extreme susceptibility under cover of indifference in self-protection: The age when thoughts and musings are most secret. The age that makes or breaks.

This is the crisis where democratic education, recognizing it as such, shall attain to its first main objective in fixing sound character, in alert intensive training of the native power to feel straight, to think straight, to act straight, to encourage pride in well-doing, to make so clear the moral nature of choice that the individual may visualize the responsibilities involved in the consequences of choice. To train the imagination in constructive foresight, in the feeling for real things, in the uses of sentiment, of emotion, in the physical and the spiritual joy of living; to stabilize the gregarious into the social sense; to set forth the dignity of the ego and all egos.

This is the time to put on the heavy work, to utilize to the full this suddenly evolving power, the recrudescent power of instinct, to direct this power into worthwhile channels, to prepare adolescents to become worthwhile adults, free in spirit, clean in pride, with footing on the solid earth, with social vision clear and true.

The later technical trainings shall be imbued of the same spirit. The varied kinds shall all be set forth as Specialized yet Unified social activities. Science shall be thus understood and utilized, the fine arts shall be thus understood and utilized, the industrial arts, the arts of applied science, and most urgently the science and the art of education, all shall thus be understood and utilized as social functions, ministering to the all-inclusive art of creating out of the cruel feudal chaos of cross purposes, a civilization, in equilibrium, for free-men conscious of their powers, and with these powers under moral control.

Such civilization shall endure, and even grow in culture, for it shall have a valid moral foundation, understandable to all. It will possess a vigor hitherto undreamed of, a versatility, a virtuosity, a plasticity as yet unknown, for all work will be done with a living purpose, and the powers of mankind shall be utilized to the full, hence there shall be no waste.

No dream, no aspiration, no prophecy can be saner. Man shall find his anchorage in self-recognition.

Thus broadens and deepens to our comprehension the power and the glory of the Democratic Vista!

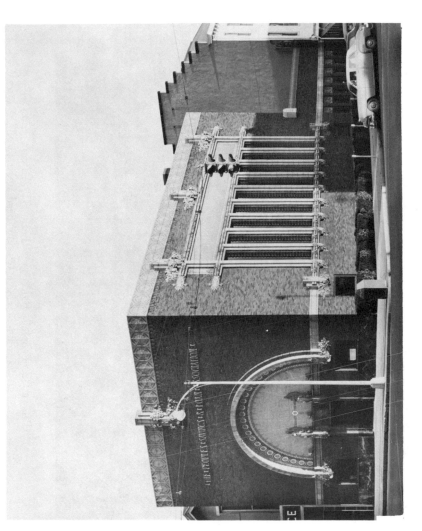

PLATE 31. People's Savings and Loan Association Bank, SE corner of Court Street and Ohio Avenue, Sidney, Ohio. 1917-18.

Plate 32. People's Bank (see Plate 31). Terra cotta ornament above window head, west facade.

PLATE 33. People's Bank (see Plate 31). Terra cotta ornament at window sill level, west facade.

CHAPTER XV

Retrospect

WHEN Louis Sullivan was in his eighteenth year, his mind a whorl of ambitious ideas, and at a time somewhat prior to his departure for Paris, he had occasion one day to pass in the neighborhood of Prairie Avenue and Twenty-first Street, Chicago. There, on the southwest corner of the intersection, his eye was attracted by a residence, nearing completion, which seemed far better than the average run of such structures inasmuch as it exhibited a certain allure or style indicating personality. It was the best-designed residence he had seen in Chicago. He crossed over to examine it in detail, and in passing around the corner of the building to analyze the other frontage he noticed a fine looking young man, perhaps ten years his senior, standing in the roadway absorbed in contemplation of the growing work. Louis, without ceremony, introduced himself, and the young man said: "Yes; it seems to me I've heard of you. Glad to meet you. My name's Burnham: Daniel H. Burnham; my partner, John Root, is a wonder, a great artist; I want you to meet him some day; you'll like him. The firm is Burnham and Root. We only started a few years ago. So far we've done mostly residences; we're doing this one for my prospective father-in-law, John Sherman; you know him—he's a big stockyards man—it's the most expensive one yet. But I'm not going to stay satisfied with houses; my idea is to work up a big business, to handle big things, deal with big business men, and to build up a big organization, for you can't handle big things unless you have an organization." And so the chat went on for an hour. They exchanged enthusiasms, prophecies, ambitions, and even confidences. Louis found Burnham a sentimentalist, a dreamer, a man of fixed determination and strong will—no doubt about that—of large, wholesome, effective presence, a shade pompous, a mystic—a Swedenborgian—a man who readily opened his heart if one were sympathetic. Soon they were calling each other Louis and Dan, for Dan said he did not feel at ease when formal; he liked to be man to man. He liked men of heart as well as brains. That there was so much loveliness in nature, so much hidden beauty in the human soul, so much of joy and uplifting in the arts that he who shut himself away from these influences and immured himself in sordid things forfeited the better half of life. It was too high a price to pay, he said. He averred that romance need not die out; that there must still be joy to the soul in doing big things in a big personal way, devoid of the sordid. In parting he said spaciously: "Come around and see John. You two men must have much in common; he'll welcome you as a kindred spirit. I'm proud of John as one man can be of another."

Years later, probably in the early eighties, Louis met John and grew to know him well. At once he was attracted by Root's magnetic personality. He, Root, was not of Burnham's type, but red-headed, large bullet-headed, close-cropped, effervescent, witty, small-nosed, alert, debonair, a mind that sparkled, a keen sense of humor—which Burnham lacked—solidly put together, bull-necked, freckled, arms of iron, light blue sensuous eyes; a facile draftsman, quick to grasp ideas, and quicker to appropriate them; an excellent musician; well read on almost any subject; speaking English with easy exactitude of habit, ready and fluent on his feet, a man of quick-witted all-round culture which he carried easily and jauntily; and vain to the limit of the skies. This vanity, however, he tactfully took pains should not be too obtrusive. He was a man of the world, of the flesh, and considerably of the devil. His temperament was that of the well groomed free-lance, never taking anything too seriously, wherein he differed from his ponderous partner, much as dragon fly and mastiff. Nor had he one tenth of his partner's settled will, nor of said partner's capacity to go through hell to reach an end. John Root's immediate ambition was to shine; to be the center of admiration, pitifully susceptible to flattery; hence, a cluster of expensive sycophants and hangers on, in whose laps it was his pleasure to place his feet by way of reminder, as he allowed himself to be called "John" by the little ones. Nevertheless, beneath all this superficial nonsense Louis saw the man of power, recognized him, had faith in him and took joy in him as a prospective and real stimulant in rivalry, as a mind with which it would be well worth while to clash wits in the promotion of an essentially common cause. Louis, true to his form of appropriating to himself and considering as a part of himself the things and personalities he valued —as he had done with Moses Woolson, Michael Angelo, Richard Wagner, *et alii*—immediately annexed John Root to his collection of assets; or, if one so wills to put it—to his menagerie of personalities great and small.

Architecturally, John Root's mania was to be the first to do this or that or the other. He grasped at novelties like a child with new toys. He thought them efficacious and lovely—then one by one he threw them away. And the while, Burnham's megalomania concerning the largest, the tallest, the most costly and sensational, moved on in its sure orbit, as he painfully learned to use the jargon of big business. He was elephantine, tactless, and blurting. He got many a humiliating knock on the nose in his quest of the big, but he faltered not—his purpose was fixed. Himself not especially susceptible to flattery except in a sentimental way, he soon learned its efficacy when plastered thick on big business men. Louis saw it done repeatedly, and at first was amazed at Burnham's effrontery, only to be more amazingly amazed at the drooling of the recipient. The method was crude but it worked.

Thus, there came into prominence in the architectural world of Chicago two firms, Burnham & Root, and Adler & Sullivan. In each firm was a man with a fixed irrevocable purpose in life, for the sake of which he would bend or sacrifice all else. Daniel Burnham was obsessed by the feudal idea of power. Louis Sullivan was equally obsessed by the beneficent idea of Democratic power. Daniel chose the easier way, Louis the harder. Each brooded incessantly. John Root was so self-indulgent that there was risk he might never draw upon his underlying power; Adler was essentially a technician, an engineer, a conscientious administrator, a large progressive judicial and judicious mind securing alike the confidence of conservative and radical, plenty of courage but lacking the dream-quality of Burnham; and such he must remain—the sturdy wheel-horse of a tandem team of which Louis did the prancing. Unquestionably, Adler lacked sufficient imagination; so in a way did John Root—that is to say, the imagination of the dreamer. In the dream-imagination lay Burnham's strength and Louis's passion.

So matters stood in the early eighties and onward. The practice of both firms grew steadily.

Meanwhile, throughout all the activities of professional life, Louis never ceased in steady contemplation of the nature of man and his powers, of the mystery of that great life which enfolds and permeates us all; the marvel of nature's processes which the scientists call laws; and the imperturbable enigma of good and evil. He was too young to grasp the truth that the fair-appearing civilization within which he lived was but a huge invisible man-trap, man-made. Of politics he knew nothing and suspected nothing, all seemed fair on the surface. Of man's betrayal by man on a colossal scale he knew nothing and suspected nothing. He had heard of the State and had read something about the State, but had not a glimmering of the meaning of the State. He had dutifully read some books on political economy because he thought he had to, and had accepted their statements as fact. He had also heard vaguely something about finance and what a mystery it was. In other words, Louis was absurdly, grotesquely credulous. How could it be otherwise with him? He believed that most people were honest and intelligent. How could he suspect the eminent? So Louis saw the real world upside down. He was grossly ignorant. He prospered, so the world was fair. Later he sent forth his soul into the world and by and by his soul returned to him with an appalling message.

For long Louis had lived in a fool's paradise; it was well he so lived in illusion. For had the hideous truth come to him of a sudden, it would have "dashed him to pieces like a potter's vessel." So he kept on with his innocent studies, becoming more and more enamoured of the sciences, particularly those dealing with forms of life and the aspects of life's urging, called functions. And amid the immense number and variety of living forms, he noted that invariably the form expressed the function, as, for instance, the oak tree expressed the function oak, the pine tree the function pine, and so on through the amazing series. And, inquiring more deeply, he discovered that in truth it was not simply a matter of form expressing function, but the vital idea was this: That the function *created* or organized its form. Discernment of this idea threw a vast light upon all things within the universe, and condensed with astounding impressiveness upon mankind, upon all civilizations, all institutions, every form and aspect of society, every mass-thought and mass-result, every individual thought and individual result. Hence, Louis began to regard all functions in nature as powers, manifestations of the all-power of Life, and thus man's power came into direct relationship with all other powers. The application of the idea to the Architectural art was manifest enough, namely, that the function of a building must predetermine and organize its form. But it was the application to man's thought and deeds; to his inherent powers and the results of the application of these powers, mental, moral, physical, that thrilled Louis to the depths as he realized that, as one stumbling upon a treasure, he has found that of which he had dreamed in Paris, and had promised himself to discover,—a universal law admitting of no exception in any phase or application whatsoever.

Thus Louis believed he had found the open sesame, and that his industry would do the rest. But this innocent and credulous young person was not yet cynical in inquiry; he was too much of an enthusiastic boy to suspect that within the social organism were mask-forms, counterfeit forms, forms with protective coloration, forms invisible except to those in the know. Surely, he was an innocent with his heart wrapped up in the arts, in the philosophies, in the religions, in the beatitudes of nature's loveliness, in his search for the reality of man, in his profound faith in the beneficence of power. So he lived in his world, which, to be sure, was a very active world indeed. And yet, withal, he had a marked ability to interpret the physiognomy of things, to read character, to enter into personalities. He knew a dishonest man as readily as he knew a snake if he came in contact with him. *Per contra* he knew an honest man—and there were many. What delighted him was to observe the ins and outs of personality—wherein he was especially sensitive and keen to the slightest rhythms.

One day Louis dropped in to see John Root in his office in the "Montauk," a large office building recently completed by his firm. John was in his private room at work designing an interesting detail of some building. He drew with a rather heavy, rapid stroke, and chatted as he worked. Burnham came in. "John," he said, "you ought to delegate that sort of thing. The only way to handle a big business is to *delegate, delegate, delegate*." John sneered. Dan went out, in something of a huff. Louis saw the friction of ideas between the artist and the merchant; a significant mismating which made him ponder. And he watched through the years the growing of Daniel Hudson Burnham into a colossal merchandiser. Louis at that time had not grasped the significance of choice, much less its social and anti-social phases, the ramification of its effects as a cause, its complete explanation of things that seemed veiled. Dan Burnham had chosen.

John Root also had chosen, and he had a temper. He knew at least the value of social prestige. To be the recognized great artist, the center of acclaim and *réclame* was his goal. But John did not live to carry out his program to the full, though he had a full grown moral courage that in Burnham was rudimentary. He departed this vale of tears, and this best of all possible worlds, 15 January, 1891, at the age of 41, leaving in Louis's heart and mind a deep sense of vacancy and loss. For John Root had it in him to be great, as Burnham had it in him to be big. John Wellborn Root in passing left a void in his wake.

For several years there had been talk to the effect that Chicago needed a grand opera house; but the several schemes advanced were too aristocratic and exclusive to meet with general approval. In 1885 there appeared the man of the hour, Ferdinand W. Peck, who declared himself a citizen, with firm belief in democracy—whatever he meant by that; seemingly he meant the "peepul." At any rate, he wished to give birth to a great hall within which the multitude might gather for all sorts of purposes including grand opera; and there were to be a few boxes for the *haut monde.* He had a disturbing fear, however, concerning acoustics, for he understood success in that regard was more or less of a gamble. So he sought out Dankmar Adler and confided.

The only man living, at the time, who had had the intelligence to discern that the matter of acoustics is not a science but an art—as in fact all science is sterile until it rises to the level of art—was Dankmar Adler, Louis's partner. His scheme was simplicity itself. With his usual generosity he taught this very simple art to his partner, and together they had built a number of successful theatres. Hence Peck, the dreamer for the populace, sought Adler, the man of common sense. Between them they concocted a scheme, a daring experiment, which was this: To install in the old Exposition Building on the lake front, a vast temporary audience room, with a huge scenic stage, and to give therein a two-weeks season of grand opera, engaging artists of world fame.

This was done. The effect was thrilling. An audience of 6,200 persons saw and heard; saw in clear line of vision; heard, even to the faintest pianissimo. No reverberation, no echo,—the clear untarnished tone, of voice and instrument, reached all. The inference was obvious: a great permanent hall housed within a monumental structure must follow. This feeling marked the spirit of the Chicago of those days.

Ferdinand W. Peck, or Ferd. Peck as he was generally known—now "Commodore" at 75, took, on his slim shoulders, the burden of an immense undertaking and "saw it through." To him, therefore, all praise due a bold pioneer; an emotionally exalted advocate of that which he, a rich man, believed in his soul to be democracy. The theatre seating 4,250 he called the Auditorium, and the entire structure comprising theatre, hotel, office building, and tower he named the Auditorium Building—nobody knows just why. Anyway it sounded better than "Grand Opera House."

For four long years Dankmar Adler and his partner labored on this enormous, unprecedented work. Adler was Peck's man. As to Louis he was rather dubious, but gradually came around—conceding a superior æsthetic judgment—which for him was in the nature of a miracle. Besides, Louis was young, only thirty when the task began, his partner forty-two, and Peck about forty; Burnham forty—Root thirty-six.

Burnham was not pleased; nor was John Root precisely entranced. It is said the ancient Egyptians held a belief that man's shadow is a fifth or residual element of his soul. About this time—the earlier days—Burnham's shadow seemed to precede or follow him on all fours with its nose to the ground, as if perturbed. Mr. Peck had an able board of directors; among them was a man named Hale, William E. Hale. Mr. Hale's shadow seemed also perturbed and quadruped. Then came our old friend of "Tech" and Columbia, Prof. William R. Ware, whose shadow seemed serene. Then all shadows disappeared from the scene.

The unremitting strain of this work doubtless shortened Adler's life. He did not collapse at the end as Louis did; rather the effect was deadly and constitutional. Louis's case was one of utter weariness. He went to central California. The climate irritated him. Then he moved to Southern California—the climate irritated him. This was during January and February, 1890. He had friends in San Diego and stayed there awhile. There he learned, at four o'clock one morning, what a "slight" earthquake shock is like. Then on to New Orleans. That filthy town, as it then was, disillusioned him. Here he met Chicago friends. They persuaded him to go with them to Ocean Springs, Mississippi, eighty odd miles to the eastward on the eastern shore of Biloxi Bay. He was delighted and soothed by the novel journey through cypress swamp, wide placid marsh with the sails of ships mysteriously moving through the green, and the piney woods; Bay St. Louis, so brilliant; more piney woods, then Biloxi Bay's wide crossing; then, as dusk neared, the little frame depot with its motley platform crowd; the crippled hacks, the drive to the old hotel, pigs and cows wandering familiarly in the streets, all passing into silhouette, for night comes fast. Ah, what delight, what luxury of peace within the velvety caressing air, the odor of the waters and the pines.

With daylight there revealed itself an undulating village all in bloom in softest sunshine, the gentle sparkle of the waters of a bay land-locked by Deer Island; a village sleeping as it had slept for generations with untroubled surface; a people soft-voiced, unconcerned, easy going, indolent; the general store, the post office, the barber shop, the meat market, on Main Street, sheltered by ancient live oaks; the saloon near the depot, the one-man jail in the middle of the street back of the depot; shell roads in the village, wagon trails leading away into the hummock land; no "enterprise," no "progress," no booming for a "Greater Ocean Springs," no factories, no anxious faces, no glare of the dollar hunter, no land agents, no hustlers, no drummers, no white-staked lonely subdivisions. Peace, peace, and the joy of comrades, the lovely nights of sea breeze, black pool of the sky oversprinkled with stars brilliant and uncountable.

Here in this haven, this peaceful quiescence, Louis's nerves, long taut with insomnia, yielded and renewed their life. In two weeks he was well and sound. By day interesting rambles, little journeys of discovery in nook and byway, a growing desire to buy, which speedily floated as gossip concerning these Chicago millionaires, to the sharp ears of a Michigan Yankee who had settled there a while before, some miles to the eastward. He called. He said his name was Newcomb Clark, that he had been Speaker of the House in his State, and a volunteer Colonel in the Civil War.

"I came here for my health. I've cleared part of my land and built a house, but my wife is lonely, so far from town; we need neighbors more than trees. I've a fine piece of woodland. It's pretty wild, now. But if you clear it of pines and undergrowth the live oaks will show. You can set your houses close to the road that runs along the shore. I'll make the price right. Would you folks like to see it?"

Us folks certainly would like to see it right away. The trail wound up and down, crossed a bayou, then followed the shore, ascended a low bluff, following its edge, passing by some second growth at the left which gradually changed character, increased in height and density. Louis was becoming excited. At last the Colonel stopped, rose in his light wagon, and with a broad gesture as though addressing the House, he said: "This is my land."

Louis clasped his hand to his heart in an ecstasy of pain. What he saw was not merely woodland, but a stately forest, of amazing beauty, utterly wild. Noncommercial, it had remained for years untouched by the hand of man. Louis, breathless, worked his way as best he could through the dense undergrowth. He nearly lost his wits at what he discovered; immense rugged short-leaved pines, sheer eighty feet to their stiff gnarled crowns, graceful swamp pines, very tall, delicately plumed; slender vertical Loblolly pines in dense masses; patriarchal sweet gums and black gums with their younger broods; maples, hickories, myrtles; in the undergrowth, dogwoods, Halesias, sloe plums, buckeyes and azaleas, all in a riot of bloom; a giant magnolia grandiflora near the front—all grouped and arranged as though by the hand of an unseen poet. Louis saw the strategy. He knew what he could do. He planned for two shacks or bungalows, 300 feet apart, with stables far back; also a system of development requiring years for fulfillment.

The Colonel made the price right, not over ten times what he paid. The deed ran thus: Beginning at a cross on a hickory tree at the beach, thence north, so many chains (a quarter mile), then east, etc., and south to the beach, with riparian rights, etc. The building work was let to a local carpenter. On 12 March, 1890, the comrades light-heartedly looking toward the future, made their way toward Chicago.

This reverie is written in memoriam. After eighteen years of tender care, the paradise, the poem of spring, Louis's other self, was wrecked by a wayward West Indian hurricane.

'Twas here Louis did his finest, purest thinking. 'Twas here he saw the flow of life, that all life became a flowing for him, and so the thoughts the works of man. 'Twas here he saw the witchery of nature's fleeting moods—those dramas gauged in seconds. 'Twas here he gazed into the depths of that flowing, as the

mystery of countless living functions moved silently
into the mystery of palpable or imponderable form.
'Twas here Louis underwent that morphosis which is
all there is of him, that spiritual illumination which
knows no why and no wherefor, no hither and no hence,
that peace which is life's sublimation, timeless and
spaceless. Yet he never lost his footing on the earth;
never came the sense of immortality: One life surely
is enough if lived and fulfilled: That we have yet to
learn the true significance of man; to realize the destruction we have wrought; to come to a consciousness
of our moral instability: For man is god-like enough
did he but know it—did he but choose, did he but remove his wrappings and his blinders, and say good-bye
to his superstitions and his fear.

Arrived in Chicago, Louis at once went to work
with his old-time vim. Important work was at hand
in other cities as well as in Chicago. The steel-frame
form of construction had come into use. It was first
applied by Holabird & Roche in the Tacoma Office
Building, Chicago; and in St. Louis, it was given first
authentic recognition and expression in the exterior
treatment of the Wainwright Building, a nine-story
office structure, by Louis Sullivan's own hand. He felt
at once that the new form of engineering was revolutionary, demanding an equally revolutionary architectural mode. That masonry construction, in so far as
tall buildings were concerned, was a thing of the past,
to be forgotten, that the mind might be free to face
and solve new problems in new functional forms. That
the old ideas of superimposition must give way before
the sense of vertical continuity.

Louis welcomed new problems as challenges and

tests. He had worked out a theory that every problem contains and suggests its own solution. That a postulate which does not contain and suggest its solution is not in any sense a problem, but a misstatement of fact or an incomplete one. He had reached a conviction that this formula is universal in its nature and in application. In this spirit he continued his aggressive research in creative architecture, and, simultaneously—it may seem a far cry—his studies in the reality of man. For he had reached the advanced position that if one wished to solve the problem of man's nature, he must seek the solution within man himself, that he would surely find the suggestion within man's powers; but, that to arrive at a clear perception of the problem, he must first remove the accumulated mythical, legendary overlay, and then dissolve the cocoon which man had spun about himself with the thread of his imaginings. This, in considerable measure, he had succeeded in doing.

The work of the firm had taken Louis over a large part of the country, as Adler did not care much for travel. Louis, on the contrary, retained his boyhood delight in it, and took pains to do as much of it as possible by daylight. For there was fascination in the changing scene, in the novel aspects of locality. Thus in time, and on his own account, he had acquired a bird's-eye view of the broad aspects of his native land, having been in all the States except Delaware, Oklahoma, and the northern parts of New England. And he came to wonder how many people could visualize their country as a whole, in all its superb length and breadth, in its varied topography, its changing flora, its mountain ranges, its hilly sections, its immense prairies and plains, vast rivers and lakes, deserts and rich soils, immense wealth within the soil and above and below it. He visualized its main rhythms as south to north, and north to south; that in crossing the continent at various parallels from east to west, or west to east, one obtained superb cross-sections.

And he dramatized the land and the seasons.

He saw, as a vast moving picture, Spring, coming from the Gulf, moving gently northward, its Vanguard awakening that which sleeps; with its joyous trumpets sounding the call of rejuvenescence, luring forth the multicolored blossoming of tree and shrub, and herb, the filigree of verdure growing into opulence; setting the plow in motion, and the sowing of crops; its vast frontage, sweeping northward, ever northward toward the arctic.

In its wake follows sober Summer, ripening the procreative ecstasy of Spring—soon the waving grain, the laden bough, the hour of maturity of Nature's lavish gifts to Man.

Then the menopause.

Then the reversal, as Winter begins its vast migration from the polar spaces. It, too, heralds its coming with trumpets, sonorous in major chords, as the woods burst into painted flames as the Vanguard moves on, creeping toward the south with its fires.

And then the modulation into melancholy; grey skies, leafless trees, brown faded stubble; a modulation into the minor mode, as winter trombones and violins sigh and moan with the winds over hill and dale, mountain and plain, and the frost glimmers in the moonlight, all sap sinks into the ground, a *miserere* chants, shrill fifes announce sharp winds, snow flurries, as nature passes into somber resignation. Winter, in mass, moving south, ever southward, its Vanguard now lost in the blue waters; its serried ranks sifting snow flakes in the air till the sleeping earth lies still under beauteous coverlet of white within the vast brooding power that came from the north.

Again the menopause.

Again the call of Spring.

Again a menopause.

Again the flaming banners and the field of white. Northward and southward, southward and northward, moving in superb rhythms of alternate urging, o'er the expanse of what was once a virgin sleeping continent, now peopled by millions with one language in common, but no soul, a people unaware, their shadows rummaging like swine in the muck of cupidity. A people of enormous power—and devil take the hindmost. A time of *laissez faire* and unto him that hath, if he can grab it, shall be given; with here and there a soul pleading for kindness, and peace, and sanity.

Louis, through the years, had become powerfully impressed by two great rhythms discernible alike in nature and in human affairs, as of the same essence. These two rhythms he called Growth and Decadence; and in 1886 he wished to say something about them. He wished, for the first time, to put his thoughts in writing; and a convention of The Western Association of Architects furnished the pretext and occasion. He called his essay "INSPIRATION." The thesis fell into three parts: "GROWTHS: A Spring Song"; "DE-CADENCE: An Autumn Reverie"; "The INFINITE: A Song of the Sea"; the transition from part to part effected by two interludes; the thought sustained to the point of rhapsody, in utterance, lyric and dramatic, of flowing prose: The Poet in solitude, alone with nature's moods; first ecstasy, then sorrow and bewilderment, then tragic appeal that the sea might give answer:

> Deny me not, Oh sea! for indeed I am come to thee as one aweary with long journeying returns expectant to his native land.

> Deny me not that I should garner now among the drifted jetsam on this storm-wash shore, a fragmentary token of serenity divine. For I have been, long wistful, here beside thee, my one desire floating afar on meditation deep, as the helpless driftwood floats, and is borne by thee to the land.

With the exception of John Root, Paul Lautrup, Robert Craik McLean, then editor of *The Inland Architect,* now the *Western Architect,* and perchance a few others, the effusion did not take. The consensus of opinion was to the effect that "they" did not know what Louis was talking about and did not believe "he" did; that he was plainly crazy, for what had al this flowery stuff to do with architecture anyhow? Louis fully agrees with "them," considering their point of view. As to McLean, the essay stuck in his red wild Canadian hair like a burr, through the years. Indeed, in a pious orgy as late as 1919, he, in his magazine, wrote this: "Some thirty-five years ago, at Chicago, a young man read a poetical essay before a group of architects, representative of the profession in the Middle West. Few understood the metaphor, but all recognized the fervor of aspiring and inspired genius that produced Louis H. Sullivan's 'Inspiration.' He called this most remarkable blank versification a 'Spring Song,' and, though unconsciously, perhaps, it was his architectural thesis. His executions since that far-away time, with a remarkable measure of success, have been expressive of those fundamentals held by his hearers to be but abstract symbolisms."

What delicious and inspired euphemisms!

Louis regards the work as a bit sophomoric, and over-exalted, but the thought is sound. Excepting specifications he did not write again for a number of years. He was too busy thinking, working; he preferred the world of action. Still, later on, among the murals of the Auditorium Theatre, were two in reminiscence, one bearing the legend "O, soft, melodious Springtime! First-born of life and love!" and its pendant, inscribed: "A great life has passed into the tomb, and there, awaits the requiem of Winter's snows."

The drawings of the Auditorium Building were now well under way. Louis's heart went into this structure. It is old-time now, but its tower holds its head in the air, as a tower should. It was the culmination of Louis's masonry "period."

Referring again to the essay: Louis thought he would try it on the higher culture. So he sent a copy to his aged friend, Professor of Latin in the University of Michigan, who wrote in return: "The language is beautiful, but what on earth you are talking about I have not the faintest idea."

Alas, an arm chair and a class room have been known to shut out the world.

IN Chicago, the progress of the building art from 1880 onward was phenomenal. The earlier days had been given over to four-inch ashlar fronts, cylinder glass, and galvanized iron cornices, with cast iron columns and lintels below; with interior construction of wood joists, posts and girders; continuous and rule-of-thumb foundations of "dimension stone." Plate glass and mirrors came from Belgium and France; rolled iron beams—rare and precious—came from Belgium; Portland cement from England. The only available American cements were "Rosendale," "Louisville" and "Utica"—called natural or hydraulic cements. Brownstone could be had from Connecticut, marble from Vermont, granite from Maine. Interior equipments such as heating, plumbing, drainage, and elevators or lifts, were to a degree, primitive. Of timber and lumber—soft and hard woods—there was an abundance. This general statement applies mainly to the business district, although there were some solid structures to be seen. And it should be noted that before the great fire, a few attempts had been made to build "fireproof" on the assumption that bare iron would resist fire. As to the residential districts, there were increasing indications of pride and display, for rich men were already being thrust up by the mass. The vast acreage and square mileage, however, consisted of frame dwellings; for, as has been said, Chicago was the greatest lumber market "in the world." Beyond these inflammable districts were the prairies and the villages.

The Middle West at that time was dominantly agri-

PLATE 34. William P. Krause Music Store and residence, 4611 Lincoln Avenue, Chicago. 1922. Louis Henri Sullivan; William C. Presto, associate. This was Sullivan's last commission, executed two years before his death.

cultural; wheat, corn, other grains, hogs, while cattle and sheep roamed the unfenced ranges of the Far Western plains. Lumbering was a great industry with its attendant saw mills and planing mills, and there were immense lumber yards along the south branch of the Chicago River, which on occasion made gallant bonfires. And it so happened that, as Louis heard a banquet orator remark, in the spread eagle fashion of the day, Chicago had become "the center of a vast contiguous territory."

Great grain elevators gave accent to the branches of the river. There was huge slaughter at the Stock Yards, as droves of steers, hogs and sheep moved bellowing, squealing, bleating or silently anxious as they crowded the runways to their reward. The agonized look in the eyes of a steer as his nose was pulled silently down tight to the floor ring, in useless protest, the blow on the crown of the skull; an endless procession of oncoming hogs hanging single file by the heel—a pandemonium of terror—one by one reaching the man in the blood-pit; the knife pushed into a soft throat then down, a crimson gush, a turn in the trolley, an object drops into the scalding trough, thence on its way to the coterie of skilled surgeons, who manipulate with amazing celerity. Then comes the next one and the next one and the next, as they have been coming ever since, and will come.

Surely the story of the hog is not without human interest. The beginning, a cute bit of activity, tugging in competition with brothers and sisters of the litter, pushing aside the titman, while she who brought these little ones to the light lies stretched full length on her side, twitching a corkscrew tail, flapping the

one ear, grunting softly even musically as the little
ones push and paw, heaving a sigh now and again,
moving and replacing a foot, flies buzzing about thick
as the barnyard odors; other hogs of the group moving waywardly in idle curiosity, grunting conversationally, commenting on things as they are; others asleep.
The farmer comes at times, leans over the fence and
speculates on hog cholera; for these are his precious
ones; they are to transmute his corn. Mentally he
estimates their weights; he regards the sucklings with
earnest eyes; he will shave on Sunday next. To him
this is routine, not that high comedy of rural tranquillity, in peace and contentment, seen by the poet's
eye, as he hangs his harp upon the willow and works
the handle of the pump, and converses in city speech
with the farmer of fiction and of fact, in the good
old days, as the kitchen door opens suddenly and the
farm wife throws out slops and disappears as quickly.
Such were the home surroundings of the pretty white
suckling, such were to form the background of his
culture; all one family, crops and farmer, weather fair
or untoward, big barn, little house, barnyard and
fields, horses, ploughs, harrows, and their kin; cows,
chickens, turkeys, ducks, all one family, with the little
pig's cousins that romped and played—one perhaps
to dream and go to Congress, others to dream and,
when the time should come that their country needed
them, would answer their country's call, it may be to
fill little holes in the ground where poppies grow and
bloom.

Meanwhile the little white suckling grows to full
pig stature, which signifies he has become a hog, with
all a hog's background of culture. He, too, answers

his country's call, though himself not directly bent on making the world safe for democracy. He is placed by his friends in a palace car with many of his kind, equally idealistic, equally educated. The laden train moves onward. At the sidings our hero is watered to save shrinkage, and through the open spaces between the slats—the train at rest—he gazes at a new sort of human being, men doing this and that; they, too, answering their country's call, at so much per call, and he wonders at a huge black creature passing by grunting most horribly. Again the train moves on, stops, and moves on. In due time what was once the pink and white suckling, meets the man with the knife. But he is not murdered, he is merely slaughtered. Yet his earthly career is not ended; for soon he goes forth again into the work—much subdivided it is true—to seek out the tables of rich and poor alike, there to be welcomed and rejoiced in as benefactor of mankind. Thus may a hog rise to the heights of altruism. It does not pay to assume lowly origins as finalities, for it is shown that good may come out of the sty, as out of the manger. Thus the life story of the hog gains in human interest and glory, as we view his transfiguration into a higher form of life, wherein he is not dead but sleepeth. And yet, upon reflection, what about other pink and whites at the breast today? Are they to grow up within a culture which shall demand of them their immolation? or shall they not?

Inasmuch as all distinguished strangers, upon arrival in the city, at once were taken to the Stock Yards, not to be slaughtered, it is true, but to view with salutary wonder the prodigious goings on, and to be crammed with statistics and oratory concerning how Chicago feeds the world; and inasmuch as the reporter's first query would be: "How do you like Chicago?" Next, invariably: "Have you seen the Stock Yards?" and the third, possibly: "Have you viewed our beautiful system of parks and boulevards?" it may be assumed that in the cultural system prevailing in those days of long ago, the butcher stood at the peak of social eminence, while slightly below him were ranged the overlords of grain, lumber, and merchandising. Of manufacturing, ordinarily so called, there was little, and the units were scattering and small.

Then, presto, as it were, came a magic change. The city had become the center of a great radiating system of railways, the lake traffic changed from sail to steam. The population had grown to five hundred thousand by 1880, and reached a million in 1890; and this, from a pitiful 4,000 in 1837, at which time, by charter, the village became a city. Thus Chicago grew and flourished by virtue of pressure from without—the pressure of forest, field and plain, the mines of copper, iron and coal, and the human pressure of those who crowded in upon it from all sides seeking fortune. Thus the year 1880 may be set as the zero hour of an amazing expansion, for by that time the city had recovered from the shock of the panic of 1873. Manufacturing expanded with incredible rapidity, and the building industry took on an organizing definition. With the advance in land values, and a growing sense of financial stability, investors awakened to opportunity, and speculators and promoters were at high feast. The tendency in commercial buildings was toward increasing stability, durability, and height, with ever bettering equipment. The telephone appeared, and electric lighting systems. Iron columns and girders were now encased in fireproofing materials, hydraulic elevators came into established use, superseding those operated by steam or gas. Sanitary appliances kept pace with the rest.

The essential scheme of construction, however, was that of solid masonry enclosing-and-supporting walls. The "Montauk" Block had reached the height of nine stories and was regarded with wonder. Then came the Auditorium Building with its immense mass of ten stories, its tower, weighing thirty million pounds, equivalent to twenty stories—a tower of solid masonry carried on a "floating" foundation; a great raft 67 by 100 feet. Meanwhile Burnham and Root had prepared plans for a 16-story solid masonry office building to be called the "Monadnock." As this was to be a big jump from nine stories, construction was postponed until it should be seen whether or not the Auditorium Tower would go to China of its own free will. The great tower, however, politely declined to go to China, or rudely rack the main building, because it had been trained by its architects concerning the etiquette of the situation, and, like a good and gentle tower, quietly responded to a manipulation of pig iron within its base. Then the "Monadnock" went ahead; an amazing cliff of brickwork, rising sheer and stark, with a subtlety of line and surface, a direct singleness of purpose, that gave one the thrill of romance. It was the first and last word of its kind; a great word in its day, but its day vanished almost over night, leaving it to stand as a symbol, as a solitary monument, marking the high tide of masonry construction as applied to commercial structures.

The Bessemer process of making "mild" steel had for some time been in operation in the Pennsylvania mills, but the output had been limited to steel rails; structural shapes were still rolled out of iron. The Bessemer process itself was revolutionary, and the story of its early trials and tribulations, its ultimate success, form a special chapter in the bible of modern industry.

Now in the process of things we have called a flow, and which is frequently spoken of as evolution—a word fast losing its significance—the tall commercial building arose from the pressure of land values, the land values from pressure of population, the pressure of population from external pressure, as has been said. But an office building could not rise above stairway height without a means of vertical transportation. Thus pressure was brought on the brain of the mechanical engineer whose creative imagination and industry brought forth the passenger elevator, which when fairly developed as to safety, speed and control, removed the limit from the number of stories. But it was inherent in the nature of masonry construction, in its turn to fix a new limit of height, as its ever thickening walls ate up ground and floor space of ever increasing value, as the pressure of population rapidly increased.

Meanwhile the use of concrete in heavy construction was spreading, and the application of railroad iron to distribute concentrated loads on the foundations, the character of which became thereby radically changed from pyramids to flat affairs, thus liberating basement space; but this added basement space was of comparatively little value owing to deficiency in headroom due to the shallowness of the street sewers. Then joined in the flow an invention of English origin, an automatic pneumatic ejector, which rendered basement depths independent of sewer levels. But to get full value from this appliance, foundations would have to be carried much deeper, in new buildings. With heavy walls and gravity retaining walls, the operation would be hazardous and of doubtful value. It became evident that the very tall masonry office building was in its nature economically unfit as ground values steadily rose. Not only did its thick walls entail loss of space and therefore revenue, but its unavoidably small window openings could not furnish the proper and desirable ratio of glass area to rentable floor area.

Thus arose a crisis, a seeming *impasse*. What was to do? Architects made attempts at solutions by carrying the outer spans of floor loads on cast columns next to the masonry piers, but this method was of small avail, and of limited application as to height. The attempts, moreover, did not rest on any basic principle, therefore the squabblings as to priority are so much piffle. The problem of the tall office building had not been solved, because the solution had not been sought within the problem itself—within its inherent nature. And it may here be remarked after years of observation, that the truth most difficult to grasp, especially by the intellectuals, is this truth: That every problem of whatsoever name or nature, contains and suggests its own solution; and, the solution reached, it is invariably ɟound to be simple in nature, basic, and clearly allied to common sense. This is what Monsieur Clopet really meant when he said to Louis in his Paris student days: "Our demonstrations will be such as to admit of no exception." Monsieur Clopet carried the principle no further than his mathematics, but Louis saw in a flash the immensity and minuteness of its application, and what a world of research lay before him; for with the passing of the flash he saw dimly as through a veil, and it needed long years for the vision to reclarify and find its formula.

As a rule, inventions—which are truly solutions—are not arrived at quickly. They may seem to appear suddenly, but the groundwork has usually been long in preparing. It is of the essence of this philosophy that man's needs are balanced by his powers. That as the needs increase the powers increase—that is one reason why they are herein called powers.

So in this instance, the Chicago activity in erecting high buildings finally attracted the attention of the local sales managers of Eastern rolling mills; and their engineers were set at work. The mills for some time past had been rolling those structural shapes that had long been in use in bridge work. Their own ground work thus was prepared. It was a matter of vision in salesmanship based upon engineering imagination and technique. Thus the idea of a steel frame which should carry *all* the load was tentatively presented to Chicago architects.

The passion to *sell* is the impelling power in American life. Manufacturing is subsidiary and adventitious. But selling must be based on a semblance of service—the satisfaction of a need. The need was there, the capacity to satisfy was there, but contact was not there. Then came the flash of imagination which saw the single thing. The trick was turned;

and there swiftly came into being something new under the sun. For the true steel-frame structure stands unique in the flowing of man and his works; a brilliant material example of man's capacity to satisfy his needs through the exercise of his natural powers. The tall steel-frame structure may have its aspects of beneficence; but so long as a man may say: "I shall do as I please with my own," it presents opposite aspects of social menace and danger. For such is the complexity, the complication, the intricacy of modern feudal society; such is its neurasthenia, its hyperesthesia, its precarious instability, that not a move may be made in any one of its manifold activities, according to its code, without creating risk and danger in its wake; as will be, further on, elaborated.

The architects of Chicago welcomed the steel frame and did something with it. The architects of the East were appalled by it and could make no contribution to it. In fact, the tall office buildings fronting the narrow streets and lanes of lower New York were provincialisms, gross departures from the law of common sense. For the tall office building loses its validity when the surroundings are uncongenial to its nature; and when such buildings are crowded together upon narrow streets or lanes they become mutually destructive. The social significance of the tall building is in finality its most important phase. In and by itself, considered *solus* so to speak, the lofty steel frame makes a powerful appeal to the architectural imagination where there is any. Where imagination is absent and its place usurped by timid pedantry the case is hopeless. The appeal and the inspiration lie, of course, in the element of loftiness, in the suggestion of slenderness and aspiration, the soaring quality as of a thing rising from the earth as a unitary utterance, Dionysian in beauty. The failure to perceive this simple truth has resulted in a throng of monstrosities, snobbish and maudlin or brashly insolent and thick lipped in speech; in either case a defamation and denial of man's finest powers.

In Chicago the tall office building would seem to have arisen spontaneously, in response to favoring physical conditions, and the economic pressure as then sanctified, combined with the daring of promoters.

The construction and mechanical equipment soon developed into engineering triumphs. Architects, with a considerable measure of success, undertook to give a commensurate external treatment. The art of design in Chicago had begun to take on a recognizable character of its own. The future looked bright. The flag was in the breeze. Yet a small white cloud no bigger than a man's hand was soon to appear above the horizon. The name of this cloud was eighteen hundred and ninety-three. Following the little white cloud was a dark dim cloud, more like a fog. The name of the second cloud was Baring Brothers.

During this period there was well under way the formation of mergers, combinations and trusts in the industrial world. The only architect in Chicago to catch the significance of this movement was Daniel Burnham, for in its tendency toward bigness, organization, delegation, and intense commercialism, he sensed the reciprocal workings of his own mind.

In the turmoil of this immense movement railroads were scuttled and reorganized, speculation became rampant, credit was leaving terra firma, forests were

[314]

slaughtered, farmers were steadily pushing westward, and into the Dakotas; immense mineral wealth had been unearthed in Colorado, South Dakota, Northern Wisconsin, Peninsular Michigan, the Mesaba Range in Minnesota. The ambitious trader sought to corner markets. The "corner" had become an ideal, a holy grail. Monopoly was in the air. Wall Street was a seething cauldron. The populace looked on, with open-mouthed amazement and approval, at the mighty men who wrought these wonders; called them Captains of Industry, Kings of this, Barons of that, Merchant Princes, Railroad Magnates, Wizards of Finance, or, as Burnham said one day to Louis: "Think of a man like Morgan, who can take a man like Cassatt in the palm of his hand and set him on the throne of the Pennsylvania!" And thus, in its way, the populace sang hymns to its heroes.

The people rejoiced. Each individual rejoiced in envious admiration, and all rejoiced in the thought that these great men, these mighty men, had, with few and negligible exceptions, risen from the ranks of the common people: That this one began as a telegraph operator at a lonely way-station, and this one was boss of a section gang on such and such a railroad; another started in life as a brakeman; that one was clerk in a country store; this one came to our hospitable shores as a penniless immigrant; that one was a farmer boy; and their hymn arose and rang shimmering as a pæan to their mighty ones, and their cry went up to their God, even as a mighty anthem, lifting up its head to proclaim to all the world that this, their Country, was vastly more than the land of the free and the home of the brave; it was the noble land of equal opportunity for all; the true democracy for which mankind has been waiting through the centuries in blood and tears, in hope deferred. This, they cried, as one voice, is the Hospitable Land that welcomes the stranger at its gates. This is the great Democracy where all men are equal and free. All this they sang gladly as they moved up the runways.

Thus the Land was stirring and quivering in impulses, wave upon wave. The stream of immigration was enormous, spreading over vast areas, burrowing in the mines, or clinging to the cities. Chicago had passed St. Louis in population and was proud. Its system of building had become known as the "Chicago Construction." It was pushing its structures higher and higher, until the Masonic Temple by John Root had raised its head far into the air, and the word "skyscraper" came into use. Chicago was booming. It had become a powerful magnet. Its people had one dream in common: That their city should become the world's metropolis. There was great enthusiasm and public spirit. So things stood, in the years 1890, 1891 and 1892. John Root had said to Louis: "You take your art too seriously." Burnham had said to Louis: "It is not good policy to go much above the general level of intelligence." Burnham had also said: "See! Louis, how beautiful the moon is, now, overhead, how tender. Something in her beauty suggests tears to me."

And Chicago rolled on and roared by day and night except only in its stillest hours toward dawn. There seemed to reside in its dreams before the dawn during these years something not wholly material, something in the underlying thoughts of men that aspired to reach above the general level of intelligence and the raucous

[316]

hue and cry. At least Louis thought so. Then, as now, was the great Lake with its far horizon, the sweeping curve of its southern shore, its many moods, which every day he viewed from his tower windows. And there was the thought, the seeming presence of the prairies and the far-flung hinterland. In such momentary trance his childhood would return to him with its vivid dream of power, a dream which had now grown to encompass the world; from such reverie he would perchance awaken to some gossip of Adler, standing by, concerning the inside story of some of the city's great men, all of which was grist for Louis's mill, for Adler was quite literal when he told these anecdotes, and Louis listened keenly to them, and learned. The two frequently lunched together. Shop talk was taboo. But they did not talk about the coming World's Fair, as authorized by Act of Congress in 1890. It was deemed fitting by all the people that the four hundredth anniversary of the discovery of America by one Christopher Columbus, should be celebrated by a great World Exposition, which should spaciously reveal to the last word the cultural status of the peoples of the Earth; and that the setting for such display should be one of splendor, worthy of its subject.

Chicago was ripe and ready for such an undertaking. It had the required enthusiasm and the will. It won out in a contest between the cities. The prize was now in hand. It was to be the city's crowning glory. A superb site on the lake adjoined the southern section of the city. This site was so to be transformed and embellished by the magic of American prowess, particularly in its architectural aspects, as to set forth the genius of the land in that great creative art. It was to be a dream city, where one might revel in beauty. It was to be called The White City by the Lake.

Now arose above the horizon the small white cloud. It came from eastward. It came borne upon the winds of predestination. Who could fancy that a harmless white cloud might cast a white shadow? Who could forecast the shape of that shadow? It was here that one man's unbalanced mind spread a gauze-like pall of fatality. That one man's unconscious stupor in big-ness, and in the droll phantasy of hero-worship, did his best and his worst, according to his lights, which were dim except the one projector by the harsh light of which he saw all things illuminated and grown bom-bastically big in Chauvinistic outlines. Here was to be the test of American culture, and here it failed. Dreamers may dream; but of what avail the dream if it be but a dream of misinterpretation? If the dream, in such a case, rise not in vision far above the general level of intelligence, and prophesy through the medium of clear thinking, true interpretation—why dream at all? Why not rest content as children of Barnum, easy in the faith that one of "them" is born every minute. Such in effect was the method adopted in practice while the phrase-makers tossed their slogans to and fro.

At the beginning it was tentatively assumed that the firm of Burnham & Root might undertake the work in its entirety. The idea was sound in principle—one hand, one great work—a superb revelation of America's potency—an oration, a portrayal, to arouse that which was hidden, to call it forth into the light. But the work of ten years cannot be done in two. It would require two years to grasp and analyze the problem and effect a synthesis. Less than three years were available for the initiation and completion of the work entire, ready for the installation of exhibits. The idea was in consequence dismissed. As a matter of fact there was not an architect in the land equal to the undertaking. No veteran mind seasoned to the strategy and tactics involved in a wholly successful issue. Otherwise there might have arisen a gorgeous Garden City, reflex of one mind, truly interpreting the aspirations and the heart's desire of the many, every detail carefully considered, every function given its due form, with the sense of humanity at its best, a suffusing atmosphere; and within the Garden City might be built another city to remain and endure as a memorial, within the parkland by the blue waters, oriented toward the rising sun, a token of a covenant of things to be, a symbol of the city's basic significance as offspring of the prairie, the lake and the portage.

But "hustle" was the word. Make it big, make it stunning, knock 'em down! The cry was well meant as things go.

So in the fall of 1890 John Root was officially appointed consulting architect, and Daniel Burnham, Chief of Construction.

Later, with the kindly assistance of Edward T. Jefferey, Chairman of the Committee on Buildings and Grounds, Burnham selected five architects from the East and five from the West, ten in all. Burnham and Jefferey loved each other dearly. The thought of one was the thought of both, as it were—sometimes. Burnham had believed that he might best serve his country by placing all of the work exclusively with Eastern architects; solely, he averred, on account of their surpassing culture. With exquisite delicacy and tact, Jefferey, at a meeting of the Committee, persuaded Daniel, come to Judgment, to add the Western men to the list of his nominations.

A gathering of these architects took place in February, 1891. After an examination of the site, which by this time was dreary enough in its state of raw upheaval, the company retired for active conference. John Root was not there. In faith he could not come. He had made his rendezvous the month before. Graceland was now his home. Soon above him would be reared a Celtic cross. Louis missed him sadly. Who now would take up the foils he had dropped on his way, from hands that were once so strong? There was none! The shadow of the white cloud had already fallen.

The meeting came to order. Richard Hunt, acknowledged dean of his profession, in the chair, Louis Sullivan acting as secretary. Burnham arose to make his address of welcome. He was not facile on his feet, but it soon became noticeable that he was progressively and grossly apologizing to the Eastern men for the presence of their benighted brethren of the West.

Dick Hunt interrupted: "Hell, we haven't come out here on a missionary expedition. Let's get to work." Everyone agreed. Burnham came out of his somnambulistic vagary and joined in. He was keen enough to understand that "Uncle Dick" had done him a needed favor. For Burnham learned slowly but surely, within the limits of his understanding.

A layout was submitted to the Board as a basis for discussion. It was rearranged on two axes at right angles. The buildings were disposed accordingly. By an amicable arrangement each architect was given such building as he preferred, after consultation. The meeting then adjourned.

The story of the building of the Fair is foreign to the purpose of this narrative, which is to deal with its more serious aspects, implications and results. Suffice it that Burnham performed in a masterful way, displaying remarkable executive capacity. He became open-minded, just, magnanimous. He did his great share.

The work completed, the gates thrown open 1 May, 1893, the crowds flowed in from every quarter, continued to flow throughout a fair-weather summer and a serenely beautiful October. Then came the end. The gates were closed.

These crowds were astonished. They beheld what was for them an amazing revelation of the architectural art, of which previously they in comparison had known nothing. To them it was a veritable Apocalypse, a message inspired from on high. Upon it their imagination shaped new ideals. They went away, spreading again over the land, returning to their homes, each one of them carrying in the soul the shadow of the white cloud, each of them permeated by the most subtle and slow-acting of poisons; an imperceptible miasm within the white shadow of a higher culture. A vast multitude, exposed, unprepared, they had not had time nor occasion to become immune to forms of sophistication not their own, to a higher and more dexterously insidious plausibility. Thus they departed joyously, carriers of contagion, unaware that what they had beheld and believed to be truth was to prove, in historic fact, an appalling calamity. For what they saw was not at all what they believed they saw, but an imposition of the spurious upon their eyesight, a naked exhibitionism of charlatanry in the higher feudal and domineering culture, conjoined with expert salesmanship of the materials of decay. Adventitiously, to make the stage setting complete, it happened by way of apparent but unreal contrast that the structure representing the United States Government was of an incredible vulgarity, while the building at the peak of the north axis, stationed there as a symbol of "The Great State of Illinois" matched it as a lewd exhibit of drooling imbecility and political debauchery. The distribution at the northern end of the grounds of many state and foreign headquarters relieved the sense of stark immensity. South of them, and placed on the border of a small lake, stood the Palace of the Arts, the most vitriolic of them all—the most impudently thievish. The landscape work, in its genial distribution of lagoons, wooded islands, lawns, shrubbery and plantings, did much to soften an otherwise mechanical display; while far in the southeast corner, floating in a small lagoon or harbor, were replicas of the three caravels of Columbus, and on an adjacent artificial mound a representation of the Convent of La Rabida. Otherwhere there was no evidence of Columbus and his daring deed, his sufferings, and his melancholy end. No keynote, no dramatic setting forth of that deed which, recently, has aroused some discussion as to whether the discovery of America had proven to be a blessing or a curse to the world of mankind.

Following the white cloud, even as a companion in iniquity, came the gray cloud. It overwhelmed the land with a pall of desolation. It dropped its blinding

[322]

bolt. Its hurricane swept away the pyramided paper structures of speculation. Its downpour washed away fancied gains; its raindrops, loaded with a lethal toxin, fell alike upon the unjust and the just, as in retribution, demanding an atonement in human sacrifice. The thunder ceased to roll, the rain became a mist and cleared, the storm subsided, all was still. Overhead hung the gray cloud of panic from horizon to horizon. Slowly it thinned, in time it became translucent, vanished, revealing the white cloud which, in platoons, unseen, had overrun the blue. Now again shone the sun. "Prosperity" awakened from its torpor, rubbed its eyes and prepared for further follies.

It is said that history repeats itself. This is not so. What is mistaken for repetition is the recurrent feudal rhythm of exaltation and despair. Its progressive wavelike movement in action is implicit in the feudal thought, and inevitable, and so long as the feudal thought holds dominion in the minds of men, just so long and no longer will calamity follow upon the appearance of prosperity. The end is insanity, the crumbling and the passing of the race, for life is ever saying to Man: "If you wish to be destroyed I will destroy you." The white cloud is the feudal idea. The gray cloud, the nemesis contained within that idea. The feudal idea is dual, it holds to the concept of good and evil. The democratic idea is single, integral. It holds to the good alone. Its faith lies in the beneficence of its power, in its direct appeal to life. Its vision reveals an inspiring vista of accomplishment. Its common sense recognizes man as by nature sound to the core, and kindly. It as clearly sees, in the feudal scheme, a continuous warfare—as well in so-called times of peace as in sanguinary battle. It views all this as lunacy, for its own word is kindness. It bases its faith upon the heart in preference to the intellect, though knowing well the power of the latter when controlled. It knows that the intellect, alone, runs amuck, and performs unspeakable cruelties; that the heart alone is divine. For it is the heart that welcomes Life and would cherish it, would shield it against the cannibalism of the intellect.

From the height of its Columbian Ecstacy, Chicago drooped and subsided with the rest, in a common sickness, the nausea of overstimulation. This in turn passed, toward the end of the decade, and the old game began again with intensified fury, to come to a sudden halt in 1907. There are those who say this panic was artificial and deliberate, that the battle of the saber-toothed tigers and the mastodons was on.

Meanwhile the virus of the World's Fair, after a period of incubation in the architectural profession and in the population at large, especially the influential, began to show unmistakable signs of the nature of the contagion. There came a violent outbreak of the Classic and the Renaissance in the East, which slowly spread westward, contaminating all that it touched, both at its source and outward. The selling campaign of the bogus antique was remarkably well managed through skillful publicity and propaganda, by those who were first to see its commercial possibilities. The market was ripe, made so through the hebetude of the populace, big business men, and eminent educators alike. By the time the market had been saturated, all sense of reality was gone. In its place had come deep-seated illusions, hallucinations, absence of pupillary reaction to light, absence of knee-reaction—symptoms all of progressive cerebral meningitis: The blanketing of the brain. Thus Architecture died in the land of the free and the home of the brave,—in a land declaring its fervid democracy, its inventiveness, its resourcefulness, its unique daring, enterprise and progress. Thus did the virus of a culture, snobbish and alien to the land, perform its work of disintegration; and thus ever works the pallid academic mind, denying the real, exalting the fictitious and the false, incapable of adjusting itself to the flow of living things, to the reality and the pathos of man's follies, to the valiant hope that ever causes him to aspire, and again to aspire; that never lifts a hand in aid because it cannot; that turns its back upon man because that is its tradition; a culture lost in ghostly *mésalliance* with abstractions, when what the world needs is courage, common sense and human sympathy, and a moral standard that is plain, valid and livable.

The damage wrought by the World's Fair will last for half a century from its date, if not longer. It has penetrated deep into the constitution of the American mind, effecting there lesions significant of dementia.

Meanwhile the architectural generation immediately succeeding the Classic and Renaissance merchants, are seeking to secure a special immunity from the inroads of common sense, through a process of vaccination with the lymph of every known European style, period and accident, and to this all-around process, when it breaks out, is to be added the benediction of good taste. Thus we have now the abounding freedom of Eclecticism, the winning smile of taste, but no architecture. For Architecture, be it known, is dead. Let us therefore lightly dance upon its grave, strewing roses as we glide. Indeed let us gather, in procession, in the night, in the rain, and make soulful, fluent, epicene orations to the living dead we neuters eulogize.

Surely the profession has made marvelous improvements in trade methods, over the old-fashioned way. There is now a dazzling display of merchandise, all imported, excepting to be sure our own cherished colonial, which maintains our Anglo-Saxon tradition in its purity. We have Tudor for colleges and residences; Roman for banks, and railway stations and libraries,— or Greek if you like—some customers prefer the Ionic to the Doric. We have French, English and Italian Gothic, Classic and Renaissance for churches. In fact we are prepared to satisfy, in any manner of taste. Residences we offer in Italian or Louis Quinze. We make a small charge for alterations and adaptations. Our service we guarantee as exceptional and exclusive. Our importations are direct. We have our own agents abroad. We maintain also a commercial department, in which a selective taste is not so necessary. Its province is to solve engineering problems of all kinds, matters of cost, income, maintenance, taxes, renewals, depreciation, obsolescence; and as well maintenance of contact, sales pressure, sales resistance, flotations, and further matters of the sort. We maintain also an industrial department in which leading critics unite in saying we have made most significant departures in design. These structures however, are apart from our fashionable trade. Our business is founded and maintained on an ideal service, and a part of that service we believe to consist in an elevation of the public taste, a setting forth of the true standards of design, in pure form, a system of education by example, the gradual formation of a background of culture for the masses. In this endeavor we have the generous support of the architectural schools, of the colleges and universities, of men of wealth, and of those whose perspicacity has carried them to the pinnacle of eminence in finance, industry, commerce, education and statesmanship. Therefore we feel that we are in thorough accord with the spirit of our times as expressed in its activities, in its broad democratic tolerance, and its ever-youthful enthusiasms. It is this sense of solidity, solidarity and security that makes us bold, inspires us with the high courage to continue in our self-imposed task. We look for our reward solely in the conviction of duty done; our profound belief that we are preparing the way for the coming generation through the power of our example, our counsel and our teachings, to the end that they may express, better than we ourselves have done, the deep, the sincere, the wholesome aspirations of our people and of our land, as yet not fully articulated by the higher culture, in spite of our best efforts toward that end. This task we are quite aware we must eventually leave to the young who are crowding upon us, and we wish them joy in their great adventure when we relinquish our all.

In the better aspects of eclecticism and taste, that is to say, in those aspects which reveal a certain depth of artistic feeling and a physical sense of materials, rather than mere scene-painting or archæology, however clever, there is to be discovered a hope and a forecast. For it is within the range of possibilities, one may even go so far as to say probabilities, that out of the very richness and multiplicity of the architectural phenomena called "styles" there may arise within the architectural mind a perception growing slowly, perhaps suddenly, into clearness, that architecture in its material nature and in its animating essence is a *plastic art.* This truth, so long resisted because of the limited intellectual boundaries and deficient sympathy of academic training, must eventually prevail because founded upon a culture of common sense and human recognition. Its power is as gentle and as irresistible as that of the Springtime—to which it may be likened, or to sunrise following the night and its stars, and herein lies beneath the surface and even on the surface the inspiration of our High Optimism, with its unceasing faith in man as free spirit! as creator, possessed of a physical sense indistinguishable from the spiritual, and of innate plastic powers whose fecundity and beneficence surpass our present scope of imagination. Dogma and rule of the dead are passing. The Great *Modern* Inversion, for which the world of mankind has been preparing purblindly through the ages, is now under way in its world-wide awakening. The thought of the multitudes is changing, withdrawing its consent, its acquiescence; the dream of the multitudes is metamorphosing, philosophy is becoming human and immersing itself in the flow of life; science is pushing the spectres back into the invisible whence they came. The world is in travail, smeared with blood, amid the glint of bayonets; the feudal idea has reached the pitch of its insanity, yet by the way of compensation the veils are lifting rapidly, all the veils of hypocrisy and sinister intent, all the veils of plausible, insidious speech, of propaganda, of perfidy, of betrayal. It requires courage to remain steadfast in faith in the presence of

[328]

such pollution. Yet it is precisely such courage that marks man in his power as free spirit. For beneath this corruption the enlightened one perceives the everlasting aspirations of mankind, the ever-yearning heart in its search for kindness, peace and a safe anchorage within its world, and to such, the compassionate one gives out words of encouragement and prophecy, even as the gray clouds hover from horizon to horizon; a prophecy that this cloud shall melt away, and reveal aloft a shining white cloud, in the blue, announcing the new man and the new culture of faith.

It seems fitting, therefore, that this work should close with the same child-dream in which it began. The dream of a beauteous, beneficent power, which came when, winter past, the orchards burst into bloom, and the song of spring was heard in the land.

That dream has never ceased. That faith has never wearied. With the passage of the years, the dream, the faith, ever expanding in power, became all-inclusive; and with the progress of the dream and the faith, there emerged in confirmation a vague outline, growing year after year more luminous and clear. When the golden hour tolled, all mists departed, and there shone forth as in a vision, the reality of MAN, as Free Spirit, as Creator, as Container of illimitable powers, for the joy and the peace of mankind.

It was this unseen nearby presence, messenger of Life in its flowing, that sang its song of spring to the child, and the child heard what no one heard; the child saw what no one saw.

It is questionable how much of social value one who has had access to the treasures of the past, access to the best and the worst in the thought of his day, may leave behind him in his fruitage, as a quantum—an IDEA.

This narrator agrees, in such connection, that the initial instinct of the child, as set forth, is the basis of all fruitful ideas, and that the growth in power of such ideas is in itself a work of instinct; that, if it has been convincingly shown that instinct is primary and intellect secondary in all the great works of man, this portrayal is justified.

It is further the belief of this narrator, in this connection, that if he has succeeded in setting clearly forth the basic fruitful power of the IDEA permeating and dominating this narrative of a life-experience, physical and spiritual, he has done well in thus making a record in words to be pondered in the heart.

(THE END)